WOMEN'S TROUBLE

WOMEN'S TROUBLE

Natural & Medical Solutions

RUTH TRICKEY
& KAZ COOKE

ALLEN & UNWIN

First published in 1997 by
Allen & Unwin
9 Atchison Street,
St Leonards NSW 1590 Australia
Phone: (61 2) 8425 0100
Fax: (61 2) 9906 2218
E-mail: frontdesk@allen-unwin.com.au
Web: http://www.allen-unwin.com.au
Kaz's website: http://www.tantamount.com.au/kaz/

National Library of Australia
Cataloguing-in-Publication entry:

Tricky, Ruth, 1953– .
Women's trouble: natural & medical solutions.

Includes index.
ISBN 1 86448 694 5.

1. Women—Health and hygiene. 2. Gynecology—Popular works. I. Cooke, Kaz, 1962– . I. Title.

618.1

Set in 11pt Caslon 224

Some of the headings are in a font called Cooken, adapted from hand-drawn letters by Kaz Cooke. Cooken was devised and executed by the splendid Kiera Poelsma.

Printed by McPherson's Printing Group, Maryborough, Victoria

10 9 8 7 6 5 4 3 2

The information in this book is a guide: it should never be used as a substitute for consulting a qualified health practitioner.

Never prescribe yourself herbs, supplements or drugs.

The Natural Therapist's Approach and the Medical Approach sections of this book are only a guide to likely treatment, which will vary from case to case.

Always check the Self Care suggestions with your health practitioners.

CONTENTS

About the authors

Ruth Trickey has been a respected herbalist and natural therapist for many years, with a specialty in areas of women's health. She has studied both Chinese and European herbal traditions. Ruth is a qualified naturopath and has diplomas of acupuncture from both China and Australia. A former intensive care nurse and midwife, Ruth has run the Clifton Hill Natural Health Centre in Melbourne for 17 years. She regularly lectures to naturopath students and health practitioners in Australia and New Zealand. She has a professional relationship with many doctors and surgeons who refer their patients to her for complementary health care. Ruth Trickey was the Scholar in Residence at Deakin University's School of Social Inquiry in 1995 and 1996.

Also by Ruth Trickey: *Women, Hormones and the Menstrual Cycle,* a book for health practitioners, naturopaths, herbalists, students, and anybody seeking a more scholarly and expanded version of this book, published by Allen & Unwin.

Kaz Cooke is a writer, cartoonist and radio presenter. She has consulted Ruth for many years about period problems and endometriosis and has used many of her herbal concoctions, some of which taste suspiciously like eye of newt. Kaz has had period pain, PMS, feral hormones, endometriosis, ovarian cysts, herbs, drugs and gynaecological surgery (she hates the way they always make you wear that dumb shower cap and a bad frock which shows your bum). Currently she is having a good lie down.

Also by Kaz Cooke: *The Modern Girl's Guide to Safe Sex*, *Real Gorgeous: The Truth About Body and Beauty*, *The Crocodile Club* and *Get a Grip*.

Acknowledgments

Ruth gratefully acknowledges the support provided by Deakin University during her period as Scholar in Residence in 1995 and 1996. In particular, thanks to Professor Robyn Rowland, former head of Deakin University's Department of Social Inquiry and the library staff, especially Elizabeth Broadfoot and Maria Shanahan, who collected the hundreds of research papers needed for this book.

Special thanks are also due to herbalist Ross Kalla, who did much hard slog in the research department, and consulting gynaecologist Dr Claire Pettersen, who gave valuable advice and assistance on medical matters. Jo Baevski provided support and a workspace for Ruth.

Others who helped with fact-checking, providing papers and making suggestions on the manuscript include Professor Andrew Sinclair from the Department of Applied Biochemistry, Royal Melbourne Institute of Technology; breast specialist, Dr Suzanne Neal; dermatologist, Dr Barbara Breadon; herbalists Dr Wojciech Kielczynski and Kerry Bone. Thanks to gynaecologist and surgeon Bruce Downing who provided information on uterine ablation and laser surgery.

Should there be any errors in this book the authors agree that these splendid helpers are not to blame, but will prefer to accuse each other in an unseemly attempt to gain publicity from the literary equivalent of a scrag-fight behind the sheltersheds.

FOREWORD

Nobody wants some dippy doctor recommending major surgery the first time you have a period cramp. And nobody needs a whacko naturopath saying that if you have severe endometriosis you just need to drink more watermelon juice and have a good lie down. This book is about the sensible middle road, driven by the philosophy of natural therapies. It emphasises self care and prevention.

Some 'women's trouble' will require medical intervention or surgery, some will respond to a professionally prescribed mix of herbs and others can be simply fixed by some 'self-care' hints about diet and exercise. Some problems might require a mix of all three.

What we're on about is this:

- Natural ways to achieve better general health.
- Knowing how your girly bits work.
- Understanding your health problem
- Being a full partner in decisions about your treatment.
- Getting well by whatever means necessary, with an emphasis on natural therapies where possible.

Women's Trouble combines the most up-to-date research and knowledge of the ancient herbal tradition (scientific trials of herbs and nutrients are going on all the time), modern advances in natural therapies, what's available in scientific medicine today, and the growing understanding of self-care strategies to gain and maintain good health. All the medical procedures and information in this book have been checked by specialists in their field.

We've 'translated' the medical terms and explained medical conditions and procedures. There's a section explaining common screening procedures, drugs and surgery for women. And if you do need surgery, this book tells you what to expect, and how you can prepare for it and heal more quickly with the help of natural therapies.

Usually we've included the scientific name of a herb as well as its most common name. The scientific name is used because sometimes people get herbs mixed up. For example liquorice means a particular plant, not the sticky black stuff you buy at Darrell Lea while you're admiring the uniforms. And there are several kinds of ginseng.

Making herbal mixtures is a specialist area, and we cannot stress enough that you should not self-prescribe, just as you can't prescribe drugs for yourself. Herbs must be prescribed and monitored by a trained professional. (In the self-care suggestions for each problem, you'll find some simple herbal stuff you can make and take yourself, such as dandelion coffee or chamomile tea.)

The self-care suggestions in this book are never to be used *instead of* the medical or natural therapy care needed for each problem. They are extra suggestions, not alternatives. Some self-care suggestions can have dramatic results—but not for everyone, and not for everything. In some cases, putting on or taking off weight might fix the problem and using a hot-water bottle might fix period pain.

Our girly bits, however, can be rather complicated, needing a healthy approach that takes what it needs from any available discipline. That's why we need this book.

Ruth Trickey is responsible for all the brainy bits, like research and understanding what a molecule is. Kaz Cooke is responsible for 'translating' it all into everyday language, and the cartoons. It is only fair to warn you that when it says 'wind', that's because Ruth wouldn't allow 'farting'.

Now go forth, and be a bit more radiant.

Kaz Cooke and Ruth Trickey

Chapter 1

INTRODUCTION

The modern period

Menstruation, Fred, on the rag, periods, a visit from a friend, women's trouble, having the painters in—call it whatever you like. You're going to see a lot of it.

These days we start getting our periods at a younger age, eat better, use contraception and live longer—so we have heaps more periods than women in the past. The 'average' Australian woman, let's call her Sheila, can expect to get her first period at about 12 years old, and then get pregnant between 25 and 35. Then she'll have two or three pregnancies about two years apart, breastfeeding for six to nine months each time. Sheila will go on having periods until she's about 50, when she hits menopause, gets a surge of new powerful feelings and decides to take over BHP.

A modern woman will have a total of between 360 and 400 periods over about 30 years. If you add it all together, we can expect to 'bleed' for a total of three years in a lifetime, about ten times more often than our ancestors. But don't yearn for yesteryear too much. "Ere, Nell. Fank Gawd we don't 'ave to 'ave lots of periods. I've got enuff to do wot with 17 kids darn wiv Black Death and the 'usband off at the bloody Crusades again.'

In the past women got their first period at 14 or 15, started having endless pregnancies straightaway and died decades earlier than the current life expectancy of a non-Aboriginal woman in Australia. Without contraception or much in the way of independence, women were likely to be either pregnant or breastfeeding all the time, having an average of only 40 periods in their whole life.

Diet, lifestyle and stress can all easily affect the timing of your period and whether you'll have any pain. This has become less obvious since we've been able to drop a painkiller or go on the Pill as soon as there was a problem. But these days more people are interested in the delicacy of the menstrual cycle, and its dependency on nutrition and general health. Many of us would rather control or treat our period problems with commonsense and natural remedies before resorting to drugs. And most of us now want to know what's happening to our bodies.

The best way to start is by dealing quickly with any deviations from your own, normal period pattern. This book is designed to explain what's normal, what's abnormal, how to recognise warning signs and be on the way to a diagnosis, and the best ways to approach treatment for all kinds of women's problems related to periods—from PMS symptoms to urgent surgery, and from first period to menopause.

First up, it's important to recognise that periods are normal and healthy. It's only relatively recently that some people have been able to come to terms with the perfectly normal fact of periods. Others are stuck back in the Black Death era when it comes to their attitudes to the strangely named issue of 'feminine hygiene'. ('That ad for unmentionables is on the telly again, Beryl. I'm going down the shed.')

Weird ideas about periods

There are many myths, taboos, mistakes, and plain dippy carry-on about periods. The book of Leviticus in the Old Testament advises that women with their periods be isolated from the rest of the community, along with people suffering suppurating sores.

Around the second century AD, some dude called Pliny announced that a woman with her period was a spookily powerful being who could sour wine, make vines wither, fruit drop from trees, kill bees, blunt knives, discolour mirrors and make dogs rabid. Here's a gardening hint you won't find on *Burke's Backyard*: around the fourth century, Democritus wrote that 'a girl in her first menstruation should be led three times around the garden beds so that any caterpillars there would instantly fall and die . . . ' Let us go right out on a limb here and say that Democritus was a dork.

People believed that period blood was extremely toxic, to the person with the period and anybody nearby. 'Poisonous' blood was even thought to be the reason for period pain, as it harmed the tissues it touched. Having sex with a woman during her period was forbidden on pain of death, either by contact with the blood itself, or by Church decree. And a child born from such an act would be deformed, leprous, have red hair, or be a . . . *girl*.

If periods were thought necessary to purify the person, you can imagine how freaky it was when somebody didn't have their period. Popular medical texts of the Middle Ages were crammed with remedies. The unknown author of the *Medieval Woman's Guide to Health* included a rather poignant list of causes for stopped periods: ' . . . being awake too much, thinking too much, being too angry or too sad, or eating too little'.

Not having periods was believed to have frightening consequences: noxious vapours rose to the head and caused melancholia, suicidal thoughts, insanity or 'mother fits', a type of epilepsy (mother was the word for the uterus). The cure was blood-letting, a complete disaster considering the most common cause of stopped periods was anaemia or not getting enough good food. Not to mention the fact that opening a vein is just a tad confronting and dangerous.

The nonsense about periods went into overdrive when someone became menopausal. Deprived of the monthly loss of 'evil' blood, a woman was believed to become so poisonous that just by looking into the cradle, she could blind a baby. Menopausal women were often called witches and any minor deviation from normal behaviour (such as chatting to yourself) was put down to 'failure' to have periods.

Dicky theories about periods hung on through centuries. An American professor wrote in 1873 that women had the right to do anything they were physically capable of, but they shouldn't study. The female reproductive system, he said, was incapable of normal development while a woman was learning, because the female body couldn't do two things properly at the same time.

His doctor colleagues also pointed out that it was a well-known fact that if you let women into universities it would cause overstimulation of their brains, resulting in stunted growth, nervousness, headaches, neuralgia, difficult childbirth, hysteria, and insanity.

Modern weirdness

Some religions still isolate or ban women from churches during their period, and modern chefs have been known to prevent women from entering their kitchen in case they were having a period and would curdle their sauce or souffle by their very presence.

A number of unattractive books on natural therapies in the past few years have advocated the long-term use of the 'purifying' fruit-and-vegetable-only diet. One of the benefits of this diet, the authors claimed, was that women who stayed on it long enough stopped having periods—and periods are only necessary when a woman's body needs purification. Gawd. Recently an American scientist put forward the 'new' theory that periods are necessary to cleanse the body and remove sperm-borne bacteria.

Ads for tampons and pads are still so coy about the process of actually bleeding that instead they are about girls stealing each other's boyfriends, suspecting their boyfriend of having an affair, using a pad to clean up after a murder and, natch, the all-purpose blue liquid being soaked up. Blue? Hello? The ads all seem to have been written by feeble-minded dolts who come up with any outlandish idea that isn't actually about periods.

A new approach

It's time to forget this crappy old notion that women are inherently weak and unclean. Having a period once a month is no big deal as long as everything seems to be working alright and it doesn't hurt.

You wouldn't think it needed to be said since, oh, the Jurassic period, but apparently it does: periods are normal biological events, and even the very caterpillars are safe in our presence.

Luckily, some people are starting to look at the idea of celebrating the first period as a rite of passage and part of the journey to womanhood. If you have access to a computer you can find the Museum of Menstruation on the World Wide Web at http://www.mum.org. (Did you know the first name for a tampon was the fax?!) And an Aussie undies company called Bloom has produced 'Lunatics'—special undies to wear during your period. (This is the sort of company we could do with. The sizes are small, medium, large and gorgeous.) The undies have a leopard skin print and a red gusset, 'so you can howl at the moon in style'.

Chapter 2 WHEN THINGS GO RIGHT

Anatomy—your girly bits

We're going to be bandying around words like ovary and uterus, so it's best to know what we're dealing with. Front botty and back botty just isn't quite specific enough for our purposes. Here's an inventory of the relevant bits and what they're for.

The vulva

The vulva is the term for our external genitals. The word covers all the outside bits between the pubic mound (mons pubis) and the area between the vagina and the anus, which is called the perineum.

The vulva includes the vaginal 'lips' called labia minora (the smaller ones) and labia majora (the bigger ones); the opening to the vagina and to the urethra, which carries urine from the bladder; the clitoris, which serves no other purpose apart from making you feel pretty faaabulous on occasion; and the Bartholin's glands. These glands, around the entrance to the vagina within the labia minora, lubricate the area during sexual arousal. (Bet Mr Bartholin didn't usually divulge his naming claim to fame at parties.)

The labia majora are the large fleshy skin folds covered in pubic hair surrounding the vulval area. Their inner surfaces are lined with the same sort of membrane that covers the labia minora. This membrane also has glands which lubricate the area during sex.

The labia minora are joined together at the front to form the covering for the clitoris. This covering is sometimes called the clitoral hood, or the prepuce if you want to be really scientific. (It's hard to imagine using the word 'prepuce' in a conversation.) Within the folds of the labia minora are the openings to the urethra (from the bladder) and the vagina.

The uterus

The uterus is a tough, muscular organ inside the pelvis. This is where a period originates, and where a foetus will grow into a baby during pregnancy.

The uterine muscle, called myometrium, is one of the strongest muscles in the body. The uterus, also known as the womb, can stretch to hold a full-term baby and to rhythmically contract during childbirth to help it on its way through the cervix, down the vagina and into the world.

The strength of the muscle contraction affects the amount of blood loss during a period or after childbirth. This muscle contraction, which can create a 'cramping' feeling, also affects the severity of period pain.

For the relative size of your inside bits, we'll be using a fruit and nut comparison, because it's the simplest, and frankly, it amuses us no end. Normally the uterus is about the size and shape of a slightly flattened pear. This size and shape can be altered by fibroid cysts, polyps, a current pregnancy or repeated pregnancies. Variations might be first noticed during a pelvic examination and need to be investigated. (A uterus which is larger than usual is sometimes referred to by doctors as a 'bulky' uterus. Medical terms can be so tactless.)

The endometrium

The inside lining of the uterus is a thin covering of cells called the endometrium. The endometrium is shed at each period as blood and other tiny material that usually looks like blood. The endometrium grows in response to the influence of the hormones oestrogen and progesterone, which are created in the ovary and released into the body. During the first part of the cycle, just after a period, the endometrium is at its thinnest. Oestrogen then causes the lining to develop. If you ovulate (when an ovary releases an egg), progesterone is produced and the endometrium thickens and changes in structure, to be more useful if you get pregnant.

The regular shedding of the endometrium means that the hormones have affected it, but not necessarily that you have ovulated. Some people who don't ovulate still get a period.

Inside the endometrium

All the changes in the menstrual cycle are designed to prepare the uterine lining—the endometrium—in case it's needed to sustain a fertilised egg. The endometrium is made up of two layers of tissue which merge into one another and look like one layer. They are the basal layer—underneath and unchanging; and the functional layer—upper and replenishing.

The basal layer always covers the uterine muscle, it is the underfelt to the carpeting of the functional layer. (Well spotted, we have lost our fruit analogy and now we're on to home furnishings.)

The 'underfelt' basal layer stays pretty much the same all cycle long, and doesn't bleed away during a period. The 'carpet' functional layer changes with hormonal activity during the cycle, and is shed as period blood. Microscopic spiral arteries that supply this layer bleed away and are rebuilt with every menstrual cycle.

This rebuilding and shedding of the functional layer is caused by the action of the hormones oestrogen and progesterone in three phases—the proliferative (the cells madly growing to make a good endometrial covering on the uterus wall), the secretory (glands in the endometrium produce glycogen for use in case the uterus will be home to a foetus) and the menstrual phase (bleeding away in a period).

Fallopian tubes

The Fallopian tubes, otherwise known as the oviducts or egg ducts, are muscular and are lined with really tiny 'hairs' called cilia. The tubes, one each side, link the ovaries, where the eggs are made, with the uterus, where the eggs are supposed to end up. The tubes are like a very thin strand of spaghetti (okay, that's not a fruit or nut) wider at the ovary end and narrowing at the uterus end. The inside of each tube is only the width of a strand of sewing cotton (yes, well *you* try finding all these fruit metaphors).

Rhythmic contractions along the Fallopian tubes move the egg along into the uterus. These contractions also partially prevent period blood from going up instead of down, but some 'retrograde' or backward flow normally goes back along the Fallopian tubes and into the pelvis during each period.

The tiny 'hairs' in the Fallopian tubes line the entire length of each tube. Their continual wave-like motion propels any matter in one direction; in this case toward the uterus. Oestrogen hormones get the waving going—sort of like the first person to start a Mexican wave. Or not. Just trying to help.

At the ovary end, each tube ends in small finger-like projections called fimbria. They are delicate structures, usually moving, like wiggling fingertips, sweeping the egg into the Fallopian tube. Because this wiggling creates tiny waves and currents in the fluid around the ovary, the egg is drawn into the end of the tube where the muscular action and the cilia take over.

Damage to the fimbriae or adhesions from infection, surgery, or endometriosis can dramatically affect the normal workings of these bits and can cause infertility. But the body is pretty clever. It has been shown that the activity of the fimbriae is so strong that they can create a wave right over to the other side and collect an egg from a right-side ovary into a left-side tube, or vice versa, if one tube is blocked. That's some wiggle.

Fortunately, infection and adhesions are more likely to affect the wider end of the tube, but unfortunately, any change in the tiny internal diameter of the tube can affect fertility or increase the chances of an ectopic pregnancy, in which a fertilised egg gets stuck in the tube and an embryo starts to grow in the wrong place. (Yet another girly bit named after a bloke, Fallopian tubes are named after a sixteenth-century Italian one called Gabriello Fallopio.)

The ovaries

There are two ovaries, one on each side of the uterus. Each is an oval shape about the size of a small, slightly flattened hen's egg, or a large almond, if you want the nut version. Ovaries can be enlarged in cases of endometriosis, polycystic ovarian disease (PCOD), ovarian cancer or ovarian cysts.

The ovary is not attached to the end of the Fallopian tube—it is kept in place by the ovarian ligament. This is a fibromuscular cord which attaches the ovary to the uterus just below the entrance of the Fallopian tube. Each ovary has another 'guy-rope', called the suspensory ligament, which attaches it to the side wall of the pelvis and contains the ovarian blood vessels, lymphatic vessels and nerves.

Inside the ovaries

The microscopic structures of each ovary are constantly changing. At any time during the menstrual cycle, wee eggs are hanging around—some ready to be released down the tubes, some getting ready, some just starting and some disintegrating. Technically speaking, the developing egg is called a follicle and the mature egg is called an ovum. An ovum is about one-seventh the size of a full stop. The plural is ova, as in I'm completely ova all this scientific language.

The actual time when a given egg starts to mature is not known. Some believe that an egg starts to develop several cycles before the cycle in which it ovulates (goes on the journey). Others believe that eggs start to develop during obvious changes in the previous cycle.

A number of the primordial follicles (eggs-in-waiting) start to develop together, but before ovulation is due, one egg has become the dominant follicle. The others degenerate. The dominant follicle produces the egg, which is picked up by the Fallopian tubes at ovulation, usually 13 to 14 days after the last period.

The dominant follicle with the egg inside grows quickly. The ovum is released gently along with some fluid and does not 'burst' out from the follicle in a most unladylike fashion, as was once believed. It's now thought that enzymes slowly break down the follicle wall and gently help release the egg from its membrane.

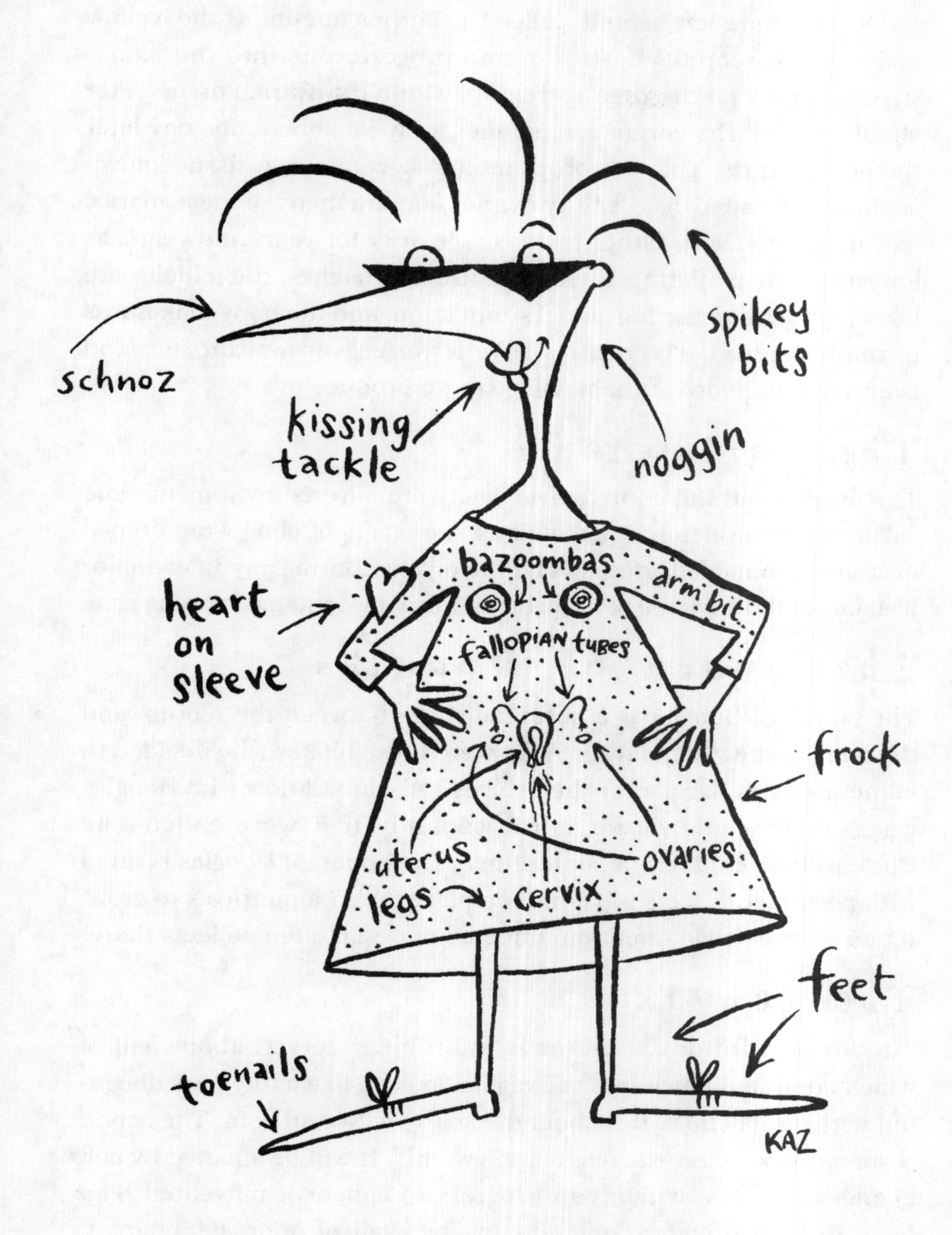

Elementary anatomy

The structure left behind, called the corpus luteum, is the 'yellow body' which secretes oestrogen and progesterone into the bloodstream. It is by far the largest structure within the ovarian tissue. After about 14 days, the corpus luteum dies away and about one day later the period starts. The old corpus luteum becomes scar tissue known as the corpus albicans. Healthy ovaries contain many of these marks.

This goes on with rather tedious regularity for years and years, as long as you're ovulating. As menopause approaches, the follicles are less responsive to the hormonal stimulation, and the body makes less of the hormones. The ovaries have fewer eggs-in-waiting left, and eventually no more of them will go on to produce ova.

The peritoneum

The ovaries and the entire pelvic cavity are covered by a membrane called the peritoneum. Imagine it as two layers of cling wrap draped over all the outside surfaces of all the organs. During any infection or bleeding in the area, the peritoneum will become irritated, causing pain.

The pouch of Douglas

The pouch of Douglas is a potential space between the rectum and the back of the vaginal wall. (Who were these blokes who decided to name women's parts after themselves? We don't know who Douglas was, but it would be far more womanly if it were called The Clutch-Purse of Mavis or something.) The pouch of Douglas is lined with peritoneum. This is a common place for endometriosis to grow. If you have a pelvic infection, infected material often collects there.

The cervix

The lower third of the uterus is the tubular cervix, about half of which continues down into the vagina, looking like a tiny pink doughnut with a small hole. It is about the size of a 20 cent coin. The cervix is sometimes called 'the neck of the womb'. It can be affected by cell changes, some of which can progress to cancer if untreated. Pap tests, explained under Screening in The Medical Approach chapter, are used to diagnose any cell changes. The cervix can also become infected or inflamed and can sometimes bleed.

The cervical opening is normally 'closed' except when it stretches during childbirth, but the opening lets period blood come out and sperm go in. If you haven't given birth your cervical opening is round, but after childbirth, it looks flattened (don't we all).

The vagina

The vagina is surrounded by the vulva. It's between the rectum (the opening from the bowel) and the urethra (from the bladder). It is the passage for the journey of period blood from the uterus to the outside. Vaginal tissue, being primarily muscular, can also stretch to many times its normal size during the birth of a baby and then return to normal.

The upper part of the vagina surrounds the cervix, and the recesses that are created between the vaginal wall and the cervix are called the fornices.

What is a period?

A period is the regular shedding of the endometrium—the lining of the uterus—once every month for most of us. It looks like blood, and we call it blood, but it's made up of other tissues and secretions as well as blood, from the inside of the uterus.

Most textbooks and doctors talk about periods in relation to pregnancy: 'Ahem. If pregnancy does not occur, menstruation will commence', with the implication that pregnancy is the usual event and a period is the second prize. Some melodramatic male authors even used to refer to periods as 'the weeping womb'. Many of us, though, don't think of a period as a missed opportunity to conceive, but rather as a relief *because* there's no pregnancy.

The menstrual cycle

Counting the days

The first bleeding day of a proper period is counted as Day One of your menstrual cycle. Premenstrual spotting, or 'false alarms' are not counted as part of a proper period. From the first day of the period to ovulation is the follicular (egg-making) phase, usually about 14 days long. (So technically, the menstrual phase is contained in the follicular phase.)

The day you ovulate the luteal phase begins, also about 14 days long and ending at the start of the next proper period, which is Day One of the next cycle.

The hormones

All the time, inside us, we produce varying levels of the sex hormones which set up a regular menstrual cycle. You seething sexual being, you. There's a lot going on, with various departments at work. The main departments are the endocrine glands found in the hypothalamus and the pituitary in the brain, and in the ovaries. These are responsible for hormone production and cycle regulation. (Sometimes this inter-departmental hormone-making action is called the 'hypothalamic-pituitary-ovarian unit' or the 'hormonal axis', or 'that thingy with the really long name'.)

The endocrine glands work together, sending messages by hormones and setting up a 'feedback loop' which means that as one hormone level falls it triggers another one to start, and when that one starts it triggers another one to fall, so the cycle continues month after month.

The feedback loop works something like this: during the cycle, the hypothalamus produces gonadotrophin releasing hormone (GnRH), which reminds the pituitary to produce luteinising hormone (LH) and follicle stimulating hormone (FSH), which signals the ovaries to release oestrogen and progesterone, which are recognised by the hypothalamus, which then produces GnRH again . . . so it all rolls around, the same sequence, over and over and over, like the plot of a Mills and Boon novel.

The follicular phase

All the hormones have special jobs to do in the loop. For example, the FSH starts the eggs growing in an ovary—at that stage the egg is called a follicle. Between 10 and 20 follicles may begin to develop, but only one of these will become dominant and mature completely to become an ovum, or egg. The others fade away and by the time of ovulation the mature follicle is the only one remaining, ready to go.

While the follicles are developing, they produce more and more oestrogen which stimulates the endometrium, the cells lining the womb, to grow like mad, known as proliferation. (The proliferative phase and the follicular phase are interchangeable terms.) When the egg is maturing, so is the uterine lining. The length of this phase is variable, but it starts immediately after a period. The cycle is counted from the first day of a period: the proliferative phase starts between about Day Three and Six of the cycle, and stops at ovulation, usually about Day Fourteen.

Stay awake! We're nearly at the ovulation bit! One of the major jobs of oestrogen is to make cells proliferate and this is given full throttle on the endometrial cells which line the uterus. After each period, the 'underfelt' base layer of endometrium is 'recarpeted' by the fast-growing endometrial cells. Within two days after a period, or by about Day Eight of a cycle, the job is complete. The endometrium thickens from about 1 millimetre at the end of the period to about 6 millimetres by ovulation.

The vaginal secretions are also changing during this phase of the cycle. The high levels of oestrogen just before ovulation convert the mucus around the cervix to 'egg-white' secretions referred to as 'fertile mucus'. (The mucus is 'clearish' like raw eggwhites, not the white colour of cooked eggs.)

Oestrogen levels continue to increase while the egg develops. Eventually, the increasing levels trigger a big effort from the feedback loop to pump out the right hormone levels which trigger the release of the egg. There's your ovulation.

The luteal phase

Ovulation is followed by the luteal phase. This stage of the cycle takes its name from the corpus luteum, the remnant of the follicle where the egg developed. The corpus luteum, influenced by the feedback loop, now starts to secrete increasing quantities of progesterone and, after an initial drop, fairly constant levels of oestrogen.

This luteal phase corresponds with the secretory phase of the endometrium. Progesterone and oestrogen act together on the endometrium causing it to become a 'secretory' tissue building up a thick glycogen-rich tissue, where a fertilised egg could embed and develop.

If the egg isn't fertilised, the corpus luteum fades away after its two-week work of producing oestrogen and progesterone, and the hormone output falls. A combination of factors including hormone levels, blood and tissue changes and prostaglandins activity causes the endometrium, which has by now reached its maximum thickness of about 8 millimetres to degenerate. Uterine contractions help it on its way down the hatch as a period. Welcome to the menstrual phase.

A 'normal' period

Right. A normal period is when a girl called Susan in a textbook has a period exactly every 28 days, for precisely five days, after which it stops like a tap going of. And it is important to note that Susan continues to ride her pony, Fluffball, throughout the entire ordeal. If your name isn't Susan and you don't have a pony, your period is probably abnormal. Or maybe we should think about it another way.

'Normal' is a strange word to use for periods, because the range of possibilities is so wide and there are so many exceptions to the rule that are just as 'normal'. It's probably easier to say what's abnormal. So let's just say we'll look at the most usual kinds of periods you can have.

Susan's is known as the 'textbook period', because it appears in every boring old textbook and if textbooks had periods it would be exactly like this: a menstrual cycle is 28 days long with a period lasting three to five days. The luteal phase (between ovulation and the start of the period) will be 14 days long to the second, and the follicular phase (from the start of the period to ovulation) will also miraculously be exactly 14 days long.

Needless to say lots of us don't have this exact pattern—so it makes more sense to talk about a normal *range* of possible times for each event.

These are the big ticket factors: how regular the cycle is; how long the whole cycle goes for; how long the period bleeding lasts; the amount of pain; and the colour and consistency of the blood.

A regular cycle

A regular cycle depends on ovulation, and on the hormone balance. Both can affect each other: not ovulating changes hormone levels, and a hormonal imbalance may interfere with the set-up for ovulation.

The most variable part of the cycle is usually the follicular phase, the time when the egg is developing, ready for ovulation. As teenagers, many of us ovulate erratically for months, when our periods first start, as our body tries to establish regular 'communication' between the hormones to get the feedback loop going. Just imagine bits of the hormonal feedback loop as a scattered gang with walkie-talkies: 'Hello ovaries, come in please.' 'This is the hypothalamus.' 'Get off the line, I'm trying to talk to the ovaries. Over.' 'Roger. Am I supposed to be doing anything?' 'What? Who's Roger?' 'Who are you?' 'Oestrogen, I think.' 'Does anybody know what time to get follicular?' and so on.

Eventually they'll all get their act together, but at this age it's also easier for stress or change to confuse the hormonal interplay and interrupt the regularity of the cycle. Erratic ovulation will make for an 'earlier' or 'later' period.

As you approach menopause you might also have an irregular cycle because there are fewer eggs being made and because the hormonal feedback loop slows down, so ovulation isn't triggered so regularly, or in the end, at all. Stress is also more likely to get in the way of a regular cycle around the time of the menopause.

Missing a period

Pregnancy is the most usual cause of a missed period, and to mutter the obvious, much more likely if you've not used contraception. Pregnancy tests which measure hormone levels in your wee are available from chemists or doctors, and will give an accurate result within days of becoming pregnant, even before the next period would be due. Blood tests can be accurate as early as ten days after fertilisation, but wait until 14 days to be absolutely sure of not getting a false negative result.

Don't worry too much if you miss a period, and you know you're not pregnant. A missed period is often just a hormonal or ovulatory 'hiccup' caused by stress (either horrible or fun) or by illness. The hormonal axis, or as we now know it, the incredibly complicated whole hormonal thingy, is very delicate and can be easily confused, temporarily. You'll usually re-establish a normal pattern once the episode is over—unless you get so stressed at missing a period you make your body do it all over again!

You may well completely stop periods when travelling and for some time after you come home. Quick weight loss due to illness, poor diet or irregular patterns of sleep and activity common amongst travellers may be the real culprits. If you're travelling or otherwise stressed, try to maintain a regular lifestyle and diet pattern and you'll avoid associated problems like loss of bone density.

And don't assume that if you have irregular periods you can't get pregnant and don't need contraception. Missing a period or even a series of periods does not necessarily imply infertility. Ovulation can spontaneously sneak up on you at any time. Of course, not expecting a period, you mightn't realise you're pregnant for a few months. It might be then too late to safely have a pregnancy termination; or those few too many drinks and cigarettes might have harmed the developing embryo.

Contraception options can be explored at a Family Planning Clinic or local doctor. May we put in a good word for the humble and particularly splendid condom—because when used properly (i.e. 'No, Darryl I don't think it goes on your ear. Read the instructions, pie-face.') it's the only contraception to protect against sexually transmitted diseases. (And, just to make it all a bit more eeky, many sexually transmitted diseases have female infertility as a possible side effect.)

Missing a period for more than six months is a recognised condition needing investigation, and we'll get on to that later.

The length of the cycle

Most menstrual cycles are between 21 and 35 days long. You might have cycles that are regularly longer or shorter than this pattern but if you're physically well, eating properly, full of beans and raring to party, at a reasonable weight for your height; and have a problem-free period, your cycle is normal for you.

While doctors often show no interest in cycle lengths that fall outside the 21 to 35-day range if you have no evidence of disease, herbalists may view this as a sign that the body is not functioning as well as it might and will look for other signs of ill health. If there aren't any, there's no need for treatment.

Very short cycles can be caused by erratic ovulation. (They can be mistaken for mid-cycle bleeding.) And very long cycles can be a problem if you're trying to get pregnant. You might even have regularly irregular cycles. This is usually a sign of erratic ovulatory patterns, which, although not 'normal', isn't a serious health problem.

You should see a health care practitioner if you have very short or very long cycles and you also have signs of ill health, or if you start having deviations from your own usual cycle length.

The length of the period

Between three and five days of bleeding is the accepted length of a normal period. Periods that last for fewer days may be related to a number of conditions including thyroid disorders, anaemia and low body weight.

Longer periods may be an indication of hormonal imbalance, in particular that you're not ovulating, a process dependent upon normal hormone interactions. Very long periods can also be a sign of disorders and some serious gynaecological conditions.

The length of a period does not include any days you have pre- or post-period spotting. Spotting near the time of a period can be an indication of serious problems and may need to be investigated; and any spotting between periods must be reported to a doctor as soon as possible.

The amount of blood

A normal period 'loss' is said to be 50 millilitres and a heavy period is anything over 80 millilitres, but this is pretty useless. Who sits on a measuring cup for five days? (No, really, don't write in.) It is far easier to talk in terms of a *need* to change pads or tampons.

A number of large studies show that women who were worried about bleeding too much or were diagnosed with heavy periods actually had huge differences in the amount of period blood. Some women who only bled about 10 millilitres thought that they were bleeding heavily, while other women who bled 300 millilitres thought their periods were normal!

Basically, if you need to change a pad or tampon more often than after two hours because it is totally soaked with blood (not just because you like to change that often), and you need to do this all day or for longer during your period, that's heavy bleeding. If your pad has just a line of blood down the middle or your tampon has less than the top third absorbed with blood, and you only 'bleed' for a day, that's a very light period.

Even if your pad or tampon doesn't get fully 'used' they should be changed at least every four hours or so. You can keep a little guide yourself to check by marking on a menstrual calendar, or in your diary.

Period pain

Unless you move in long-distance swimming circles, any mysterious mention of 'the cramps' is always assumed to be about period pain. So many of us get period pain that it could be called usual—but that doesn't make it normal. The pain response is a survival mechanism indicating that something has gone wrong. Here's the basic rule of judging period pain: is it bad enough that you want to do something about it?

Period pain usually only happens in a cycle that you have ovulated in, and period pain often only starts in earnest about two years after the first-ever period, when ovulation has become regular. That's why an occasional period can be surprisingly pain-free—maybe you didn't ovulate in that cycle.

Symptoms of pelvic discomfort, heaviness or mild pain during a period are often fixed by eating well, exercising regularly and stress reduction. Stronger, crampy pain can also be helped by specific diet and lifestyle changes, and although it seems more serious, this type of pain is not necessarily caused by a gynaecological disease. Period pain is often related to abnormal cramping of the uterine muscle caused by a prostaglandins imbalance.

Get on to a doctor to investigate any strong pain before a period, pain which is only on one side of the body or pelvic pain that doesn't seem related to your period. But *any* pain which is worrying or interfering with your life needs investigation and treatment. There's a whole section on period pain in the When Things Go Wrong chapter.

Colour and consistency of blood

Don't think it's weird if a natural therapist asks what colour your period blood is, or whether it seems thin or thick. For natural therapists, it's often used to diagnose and suggest the right herbal treatment. (There's more detail on herbs in the Natural Therapies chapter.)

Medical practitioners are less interested because there's not much scientific history of using this kind of information. This does not make one or the other system better or more thorough; they just require different sorts of information to assist with prescriptions.

The following is simply a list of associations. These signs would need to be accompanied by at least two other symptoms of disease before they could be even suspected to relate to a disorder or disease.

Bright red blood

Generally bright or dark red blood indicates that the period is normal. Very bright red blood may mean a prescription for 'Cooling' herbs or for astringent herbs.

Dark, brown or thick blood

Dark blood which is thick, looks too old or is brown is usually caused by sluggishness of the period flow. Very sluggish, dark blood may indicate a need for herbs which regulate uterine muscular activity; increase the expulsive ability of the uterus or help the uterine muscle relax.

Watery, thin or pale blood

Very thin, pale pink blood can mean poor blood quality and usually indicates a need for blood-enriching herbs, or hormone regulation. Pale blood can be a sign of hormone imbalance, especially if you're weak, tired, exercising too much or not eating well. Watery period blood is common after surgical procedures in the uterus, such as terminations and curettes (D&C—explained in the Surgery section), because the endometrium has been removed. (It grows back.)

Clots

Clots generally indicate excessive flow and are formed when the anti-clotting factors normally in period blood can't keep the blood in a fluid state. Clots could indicate the need for herbs to improve uterine tone and reduce the flow.

An odd period

Most of us will have at least one 'odd' period in our lives; some will have lots. The cycle may be unusual, the flow different from normal; pain may be new or different; or the colour and consistency of the blood might change.

Here's what you need to ask about a strange period:

- Is it possible you're pregnant?
- Are there other signs of ill health?
- Has there been a stressful episode (either fun or difficult)?

If the answer to either of the first two questions is yes, get thee to a doctor. If the third option is a possibility, have a cup of tea and a good lie down; in other words, relax, wait for another cycle and see what happens.

Period regularity diary

Here's a menstrual diary you can photocopy and use to chart your period's regularity and any other symptoms associated with it, like pain, or type of blood loss. It may be useful to your health practitioner in diagnosis. (Look out for leap years.)

Period regularity diary

Circle each day of your period throughout the year and watch your pattern emerge.

Jan 1	29	26	26	23	21	18	16	13	10	8	5	3	*31*
2	30	27	27	24	22	19	17	14	11	9	6	4	**Jan** *1*
3	31	28	28	25	23	20	18	15	12	10	7	5	*2*
4	**Feb** 1	**Mar** 1	29	26	24	21	19	16	13	11	8	6	*3*
5	2	2	30	27	25	22	20	17	14	12	9	7	*4*
6	3	3	31	28	26	23	21	18	15	13	10	8	*5*
7	4	4	**Apr** 1	29	27	24	22	19	16	14	11	9	*6*
8	5	5	2	30	28	25	23	20	17	15	12	10	*7*
9	6	6	3	**May** 1	29	26	24	21	18	16	13	11	*8*
10	7	7	4	2	30	27	25	22	19	17	14	12	*9*
11	8	8	5	3	31	28	26	23	20	18	15	13	*10*
12	9	9	6	4	**Jun** 1	29	27	24	21	19	16	14	*11*
13	10	10	7	5	2	30	28	25	22	20	17	15	*12*
14	11	11	8	6	3	**Jul** 1	29	26	23	21	18	16	*13*
15	12	12	9	7	4	2	30	27	24	22	19	17	*14*
16	13	13	10	8	5	3	31	28	25	23	20	18	*15*
17	14	14	11	9	6	4	**Aug** 1	29	26	24	21	19	*16*
18	15	15	12	10	7	5	2	30	27	25	22	20	*17*
19	16	16	13	11	8	6	3	31	28	26	23	21	*18*
20	17	17	14	12	9	7	4	**Sep** 1	29	27	24	22	*19*
21	18	18	15	13	10	8	5	2	30	28	25	23	*20*
22	19	19	16	14	11	9	6	3	**Oct** 1	29	26	24	*21*
23	20	20	17	15	12	10	7	4	2	30	27	25	*22*
24	21	21	18	16	13	11	8	5	3	31	28	26	*23*
25	22	22	19	17	14	12	9	6	4	**Nov** 1	29	27	*24*
26	23	23	20	18	15	13	10	7	5	2	30	28	*25*
27	24	24	21	19	16	14	11	8	6	3	**Dec** 1	29	*26*
28	25	25	22	20	17	15	12	9	7	4	2	30	*27*

This menstrual calendar is in lines of 28 days, the 'average' time between periods.

PERIOD SYMPTOMS DIARY: Record the relevant coded number to describe your bleeding and symptoms.

Name:______________________ Age:________ Height:________ Weight:________

BLEEDING: 0–none 1–slight 2–moderate 3–heavy 4–heavy and clots

SYMPTOMS: 0–none 1–mild; does not interfere with activities 2–moderate; interferes with activities 3–severe; disabling; unable to function

Day of cycle	1	2	3	4	5	6	7	8	9	10	11	12	13	14	15	16	17	18	19	20	21	22	23	24	25	26	27	28	29	30	31	32	33	34	35	36
DATE																																				
BLEEDING																																				
PMS-A SYMPTOMS:																																				
Nervous tension																																				
Mood swings																																				
Irritability																																				
Anxiety																																				
PMS-H SYMPTOMS																																				
Weight gain																																				
Swelling of extremities																																				
Breast tenderness																																				
Abdominal bloating																																				
PMS-C SYMPTOMS																																				
Headache																																				
Craving for sweets																																				
Increased appetite																																				
Heart pounding																																				
Fatigue																																				
Dizziness or faintness																																				
PMS-D SYMPTOMS																																				
Depression																																				
Forgetfulness																																				
Crying																																				
Confusion																																				
Insomnia																																				
PSM-P SYMPTOMS																																				
Pain																																				
Cramps																																				
Backache																																				
General aches/pain																																				

Period symptoms diary

This much more detailed menstrual symptom diary (left), once photocopied, will give you a much clearer picture of all the symptoms which go with your period. It will help you work out if you have PMS, and what type of PMS, for example. (There is more on PMS and its sub-categories in the When Things Go Wrong chapter.) It will be indispensable in helping your health practitioner to diagnose a problem. Keep a photocopy for yourself.

Pads or tampons?

It's up to you. Both tampons and pads have been around for thousands of years, made of wool, linen or, in ancient Egypt, rolled papyrus for tampons. Each method has advantages and disadvantages.

Pads

Pads are thin, absorbent and easy to wear because they have an adhesive strip to stick them on a gusset (just had to use the word gusset). In the old days, there were huge pads ten times the size and far less absorbent, attached with a complicated system of belts, suspender pulleys and safety pins, and it felt like sitting on a double futon. Pads now come in a blinding array that invites experimenting to find the one you like best. There are several sizes and shapes for heavy days, night-time use, light days and the rest.

Don't worry too much that people might be able to see your pad through your clothes or smell your period blood. (Period blood changes in odour when it comes in contact with air.) You're much more conscious of it than anybody else will be. Smells can be avoided by changing the pad often. And the thinner pads can't be seen through clothing, unless you're wearing a G-string and some kind of weirdo is lying underneath the bus-stop with a pair of binoculars.

Tampons

Tampons make swimming possible during a period—which is great for women who find that swimming relieves period pain. A tampon cannot get lost somewhere inside your body (it's impossible for a tampon to pass through the opening in the cervix). It can happen, on rare occasions, that the string comes off, or the tampon gets pushed too high for your fingers to get a grip on it. Don't worry—a doctor can fish it out easily. (Make sure you insist on a same-day appointment.)

Tampons can't make anybody lose her virginity. The hymen (the membrane which partially covers the vaginal opening, usually until you first have penetrative sex) has already been perforated by the time you have your first period—otherwise the period blood wouldn't be able to come out. The hymen is elastic and stretches to allow a tampon to be inserted. Virginity relates to sex, not tampons.

The biggest problem experienced with tampons is not inserting them high enough inside where the vagina is less sensitive. When the tampon is put up high enough, you won't even be aware that it's there. If you're constantly distracted by being able to feel the tampon, you'll be walking around with a very quizzical look on your face, so go and give the tampon another shove.

Sponges

Some people put sea sponges up their vaginas during their periods. Apart from the obvious difficulty in washing, changing and storing them (especially in a public toilet!) sea sponges may harbour bacteria, sand and grit—no matter how much they're washed. If you're really worried about the environment, leave the sea sponges alone and join the Australian Conservation Foundation.

Toxic shock syndrome

Toxic shock syndrome is a very rare condition, but it can have fatal effects which are caused by the release of a toxin from the *Staphylococcus aureus* bacteria ('golden staph'). The toxin attacks various organs in the body and causes symptoms including a rash and a high fever. 'Toxic shock' can affect anyone who is infected by golden staph, but is much more likely to be linked to periods and tampons in particular. None of its symptoms should be taken as part of a 'normal' period.

Signs and symptoms

- Headaches, sore throat and aches in the joints and limbs, and 'flu-like' symptoms are usually the first signs of toxic shock. These usually come on a few days into the period.
- This is followed by a sudden onset of fever (temperature usually more than 39 degrees Celsius) with vomiting and diarrhoea.
- After about 48 hours, there may be a dramatic drop in blood pressure which causes the symptoms of shock. These are sweating, paleness, dizziness, collapse and sometimes disorientation or loss of consciousness.
- A skin rash often accompanies these symptoms. The skin becomes red and then peels as though it is sunburned.
- Sometimes the kidneys are affected and stop producing urine.

Prevention

- Not using tampons will dramatically reduce the chances of developing toxic shock syndrome, but bear in mind that it is a very rare condition.
- Change tampons regularly—at least every four hours. This may help to reduce the incidence.
- 'Super-absorbent' tampons are associated with the highest risk, possibly because of their composition. (Use the smallest size of tampon that will last you for four hours, to encourage frequent changes.)
- Don't leave tampons in overnight. Women who alternate tampons and pads have a lower incidence of toxic shock.
- Toxic shock syndrome may even be related to synthetic fibres used in tampons and so there is a possibility that natural fibres, such as cotton, may reduce risk. Tampons made from organic and untreated fibres are now sold, but there is no proof that they are any better.

Treatment

Toxic shock syndrome is an acute medical emergency. If you develop its symptoms, immediately remove the tampon and go straight to a hospital for evaluation. This is *not* a condition to be treated by natural medicine. Toxic shock syndrome is treated with antibiotics and is likely to require admission to hospital.

Do keep in mind that although toxic shock syndrome is very rare, its symptoms can be those of other medical emergencies. In other words, any violent fever accompanied by a skin rash, etcetera, needs to be checked out immediately, even if you don't use tampons.

Chapter 3

IT'S YOUR HORMONES, DEAR

Feel free to skip this whole chapter if you don't want to get down into the nitty gritty of your complicated little critters like hormones and prostaglandins. Don't mind us. We've just spent months researching it and trying to make it as simple as possible. And none of your girly bits would do their thing without the hormones. But you don't really *need* to read it, unless you *really* want to know how your body works, or you have a hormone problem. On the other hand, it will help you better understand a whole lot of problems—ranging from period cramps caused by prostaglandins imbalance, to stopped periods that can be kick-started again by fiddling with hormone levels.

Meet your hormones

All month long, a whole bunch of hormones get together and do a funky hormone dance to make the menstrual cycle work. Alright, forget the dance metaphor. This is complicated enough already—let's get scientific. The hormones that are the main players are all 'steroid hormones'. The steroids are all made by the body using the chemical building block of cholesterol. They are the androgens (pronounced and-roe-jens), oestrogens (east-roe-jens) and progesterones (pr-oh-jest-er-owns).

Some hormones start off as one kind, and are then made into a series of other hormones so they can perform the right tasks to make the whole menstrual cycle pump along.

For example, one hormone starts out called pregnenolone, is then changed by the body into progesterone, then to testosterone and finally into one of the oestrogens, called oestradiol. At each step, the hormone will have a special job to do. At the end of the line each hormone is changed into a different form, into another type of hormone, or broken down to be excreted from the body.

Before its life is finished, each hormone will have an intricate part to play in the 'feedback loop' which runs the menstrual cycle month after month. But the really big players are progesterone and oestrogen.

For everything to go smoothly, the hormones must remain in some sort of balance with each other, and like actors they all must make their entrance and exit at the right time. (Great, now we've got a theatre metaphor.) We're going to briefly look at how each hormone is involved. You wouldn't believe all the stuff your body gets up to when you're not looking.

The Stage Manager Hormones

The hypothalamus, a gland at the base of the brain, produces a number of stage manager hormones which send messages to tell other hormones when to do their stuff in the cycle. Or, these stage manager hormones block the other hormones until their cue to come on.

Gonadotrophin releasing hormone (GnRH)

The hypothalamus sends messages to the nearby pituitary gland in the form of intermittent pulses of GnRH every 60 to 90 minutes. The pulsing of GnRH increases mid-cycle and around the period, and reminds the pituitary when it's time to pump out extra follicle stimulating hormone (FSH) and luteinising hormone (LH).

Dopamine

If you are not breastfeeding, the hypothalamus also releases sufficient quantities of a hormone called dopamine to control the production of prolactin, the hormone responsible for producing breast milk.

The Director Hormones

The pituitary gland produces gonadotrophins, bossy hormones which tell ovaries what to do. In other words, these are the director hormones who tell the other hormones when to play their roles.

Luteinising hormone (LH)

Low levels of oestrogen trigger the slow rise of LH levels during the follicular, egg-making phase of the cycle. Just before mid-cycle, a dramatic surge in oestrogen, LH, and FSH causes ovulation. The LH stimulates the ovaries to make more oestrogen and progesterone. In the luteal, post-ovulation phase, the increasing progesterone levels signal the pituitary gland to hold back on the LH. Further push-me pull-you stuff between the hormones finally triggers the period.

Follicle stimulating hormone (FSH)

Follicle stimulating hormone (FSH) does exactly what its name suggests—stimulates the growth and development of the ovarian follicle—the bit which houses an egg. Levels of FSH increase in the follicular, egg-making phase of the cycle, which reminds the follicle cells to pump out some more oestrogen. This is all part of the feedback loop—the initial rise in oestrogen triggers the release of GnRH and a surge of FSH. A few hours later, when oestrogen levels are even higher, FSH production is turned off. Just before a period, oestrogen levels fall, which reminds the hypothalamus to send out a hormonal message of GnRH to the pituitary and get it to start releasing FSH again.

Prolactin

Prolactin, produced by the pituitary gland, is the hormone responsible for breast milk, and for making your breasts bigger during pregnancy. Non-pregnant women have low levels of prolactin which normally increase slightly at night, with stress, and during the luteal phase of the menstrual cycle.

The Star Actor Hormones

The ovaries and the adrenal glands above the kidneys make the steroid hormones oestrogen, androgen and progesterone. These 'actor' hormones do most of the heavy work. As girly hormones go, they are the stars.

Oestrogen

Oestrogen is the big-time player—in fact there are three main oestrogens—oestradiol (pronounced east-rar-dye-al), oestrone (east-rone) and oestriol (east-ree-ol). When people talk about oestrogen or oestrogen levels, they usually mean the cumulative effect of these three in the body, even though it sounds like there's one oestrogen diva going at it all alone.

Some of the effects of oestrogen are most obvious during puberty. Oestrogen gives you a proper girly stomach and hips and breasts. It stimulates the growth of the uterine muscle and endometrium. All through life, oestrogen helps to maintain skin structure, blood vessels, and bone strength.

One of the most important functions of oestrogen is to stimulate an increase in the number of cells (proliferation) where there are oestrogen receptors, for example, in the endometrium.

The lifespan of the oestrogens

Every month after the period, the ovaries start to secrete active oestrogen called oestradiol. Some of the oestradiol is converted into a weaker oestrogen called oestrone, and then both oestradiol and oestrone go on a trip together in the bloodstream, travelling to exotic lands . . . sorry. They travel to oestrogen-sensitive cells to stimulate cell growth. The ovaries pump out the most oestrogen after ovulation, and cut back just before the period.

Meanwhile, the body makes a second source of oestrone from androgen hormones. This process, using an enzyme, is referred to as 'peripheral conversion' or 'aromatisation'. Aromatisation happens in the hair follicles, the skin, the brain, bone and bone marrow, muscle and fatty tissue. About 25 per cent of the conversion goes on in the muscle and 10–15 per cent in the fat. (After the menopause, we make almost all our oestrogen from aromatisation, as our ovaries 'retire'.)

The rest of us manufacture most of our oestrogen, in the form of oestradiol, in the ovaries. We also make some oestrone from androgens, mostly by the aromatisation in our fatty tissues. If you're thinner than your body should be, you mightn't get enough of this important secondary source of oestrogen and could develop menopausal symptoms like hot flushes and vaginal dryness; or may stop ovulating and having periods. If you're obese, you may be making too much oestrogen and be at risk of conditions linked to too much oestrogen, including breast cancer and endometrial cancer.

Eventually, all the different oestrogens are carried to the liver. There they change into different forms which are less active, and are sent to the intestine. Once in the intestine, some of the oestrogen will be excreted from the bowel and some will be recycled back into the bloodstream.

All of the oestrogen circulating in the blood will eventually pass through the kidneys where it is excreted in the urine as the very weak oestrogen called oestriol. This forms the basis of some pregnancy tests and can be used to determine the health of the placenta during pregnancy. Although it contributes to the oestrogen pool, oestriol is about 80 times less potent than oestradiol.

The 'oestrogen pool'

Sounds like a rather good name for a sexy nightclub, but it refers to the range of oestrogens available for use by the body. There are many factors that cause oestrogenic effects which can come from outside the body. These include the phyto-oestrogens produced in plants, which are good for you; and the much more dangerous 'environmental oestrogens', which are consumed as hormones added to foods or as contaminants of foods, such as pesticides. All of these different types of 'oestrogens' can have oestrogen-like activities in the body.

An oestrogenic effect is caused by any substance which has the ability to connect to an oestrogen receptor site. It has to be said, quite frankly, that oestrogen receptor sites are pretty stupid, and will often accept any substance which has a molecular similarity to the oestrogen produced in the body, even if it's a chemical pesticide.

The receptor sites can be monopolised by oestrogen-like substances from plants which don't have a very strong oestrogenic effect. The substances have, in a way, taken most of the oestrogen parking spaces. The stronger oestrogens, made in the body, can't get as many parks, so they can't go to work and do their stuff.

In this way the body can be exposed to a weaker combination of oestrogens. Before menopause, this can help protect against the disorders linked to having too much oestrogen.

After menopause, when you're not making so much oestrogen in your own body because your ovaries have 'retired', plant oestrogens or oestrogenic herbs can help fill all the empty parking spaces and help boost your depleted 'oestrogen pool'.

The available information on the nastier 'environmental oestrogens' is less clear. There are a whole heap of chemicals which may work in combination to cause strong oestrogenic effects. These incude the pesticides such as endosulphan, toxaphene, dieldrin, chlordecone, DDT and DDE; the polychlorinated biphenols (PCBs) found in a range of products such as hydraulic fluid, neon tubes and plastics such as nonylphenol released from modified polystyrene; bisphenol-A, a plastic found in the 'lacquer' used to coat food cans; and other plastics used as a substitute for mercury-based amalgam fillings.

The real health implications of these chemicals are unknown. Research is continuing to see if there is a link between exposure to insecticides and cancer development. High levels of DDT have, however, been found in fibroid tissue, and there are concerns that these chemicals may affect male fertility and sexual development, and increase cancer risk.

Exposure to chemicals will have varying effects on different people depending on how long they were exposed, which chemicals, and their body's elimination systems. And even though some of these products have only a weak oestrogenic effect, they must be suspected of some harm because many are poisons designed to kill plant or insect life. Suffice to say it's probably safer to stay away from DDT sandwiches and try to minimise the use of chemicals in your body, your home and your local area.

Progesterone

Progesterone, the other big star of girly hormones, is the building block starter for many of the other steroid hormones. So it plays an important role not only in periods and reproduction, but also in a number of other jobs in the body.

It stimulates changes in organs with progesterone-sensitive tissue. In the uterus, progesterone stimulates the endometrium so that it can support a developing embryo. If the egg is not fertilised, the level of progesterone falls, the endometrial tissue disintegrates and is shed as a period.

Progesterone initiates glandular changes in breast tissue so that the breast is capable of giving milk. It also keeps the normal female levels of androgen (blokey) hormones in check. Once progesterone production slows or stops, like after menopause, androgen levels increase. This may account for hair falling out of the head but mysteriously turning up on the chin when some of us get older.

Progesterone has other actions that include improved fat metabolism, an increase in bone density, good moods, and a natural diuretic (fluid loss) effect. It also helps to prevent both cancerous and benign breast changes by counter-balancing the effects of oestrogen in the breast, and has the same protective and counter-balancing effect on the endometrium.

Progesterone is also the building block of the hormones called corticosteroids which maintain stable blood sugar levels, reduce inflammation and help the body fight the effects of stress.

The lifespan of a progesterone

Progesterone is produced by the corpus luteum—the remnant egg sac—in the ovaries. Small amounts are also secreted by the adrenal glands. The body changes cholesterol into pregnenolone and then to progesterone. The progesterone might then be converted into any one of the other steroid hormones including oestradiol, oestrone, testosterone or cortisone.

Progesterone circulates in the blood and interacts with cell receptors, but eventually it will pass through the liver where it is 'turned off' and excreted into the bile and urine.

Androgens

Androgens are blokey hormones, found naturally in both men and women. When androgen levels are too high, such as in polycystic ovarian disease (PCOD), it can interfere with the menstrual cycle and gynaecological functions. It can also cause more hairiness, a deeper voice, and a more 'male' body shape, with smaller breasts and a larger waist.

The star of the blokey hormones is testosterone. You might be surprised to know that we've got some too. Testosterone is the strongest and most abundant androgen found in the blood of normal women. A quarter of it is made in the ovaries, a quarter in the adrenal glands and half is made in the body by converting other hormones. In muscle, testosterone acts directly on the androgen receptors to produce growth-promoting ('anabolic') effects.

The carrier proteins

Most of the steroid hormones circulate in the blood transported by proteins (albumins and globulins). Each hormone appears to have a specific binding globulin or carrier protein which is responsible for its transport. When hormones are bound to the globulins, they can't interact as easily with target tissues as when they are floating 'free' in the plasma. For example, if a blokey androgen hormone isn't bound to carrier proteins it's more likely to be surging around in your blood giving you a hairy chin and other problems. So it's important to keep a good balance of carrier proteins.

Balancing the hormones

Balancing the hormones

Any hormone imbalance will have an effect on health. These changes range from the virtual absence of a hormone when you become menopausal to a case where the hormone level is lower than it ought to be, or relatively lower in relation to other hormones. If you have PMS, for example, you may have low levels of progesterone in relation to your levels of oestrogen.

Hormone levels can also be too high, be around for too long, or they can reach levels that are too high in relation to other hormones. Women with endometriosis and fibroids, for example, are thought to have too much oestrogen for too long.

Too much oestrogen

Many of us are relatively overexposed to the stimulatory effects of oestrogen simply because we have about ten times more periods than our ancestors. Oestrogen excess does not happen just because the ovaries make too much oestrogen. The modern lifestyle (you party animal) also seems to slow down the usual process of getting rid of excess oestrogen through the liver and bowel, and to favour higher circulating levels of available oestrogen. Levels of oestrogen that stay too high seem to be significant risks for diseases. The environmental oestrogens are introduced into the body from outside, mostly through food and water, and can stimulate cells in much the same way as the oestrogens made in the body.

Symptoms

Heavier than usual periods, longer than usual periods, and PMS. Oestrogen excess is linked to endometriosis, fibroids, fibrocystic breast disease, breast and endometrial cancer.

Diagnosis

Excessively high levels of oestrogen are comparative to the levels of other hormones and so excess oestrogen cannot be detected on a single blood test for the oestrogen level. It's usually diagnosed by the symptoms.

Possible causes

- Women who eat more fat have significantly higher blood levels of oestrogen. Reducing fat intake leads to lower oestrogen levels. A high fat intake has been linked with benign breast disease, breast cancer, heavy periods, endometriosis and fibroids.
- Obesity can cause high oestrogen levels and interfere with ovulation. The fatter you are, the more fat cells the body has to convert androgens into oestrogens. This can lead to a higher risk of breast cancer, fibroids, and endometriosis. Obesity is not just being overweight or carrying a few extra kilos. Women at increased risk are substantially overweight and are in the highest range of the Body Mass Index. To find out how to calculate your Body Mass Index, read the Being Obese section in the When Things Go Wrong chapter.
- The ingestion of introduced chemicals, pesticides, hormones, plastics and preservatives in the food chain can have an oestrogenic effect.

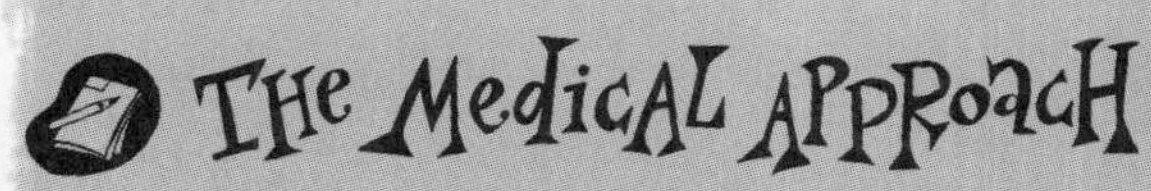

Doctors acknowledge that oestrogen can be 'proliferative', and if they perceive a problem with this, will probably prescribe oestrogen-blocking drugs such as GnRH agonists and Tamoxifen. (For more info on these, look under Drugs in The Medical Approach chapter and under The Usual Suspects in the When Things Go Wrong chapter.)

Natural Therapies & Self Care

- Eat less fat and refined carbohydrate.
- Eat more fibre. Natural fibre as part of whole food is recommended, rather than fibre-only breakfast cereals which provide no other wondrous nutrients. See the 20 Diet Hints in the Self Care chapter for more info on fibre.
- Eat more cultured milk products and real yoghurt. Researchers found that eating these foods is associated with a lower incidence

of breast cancer which they attributed either to the reduced reabsorption of oestrogen or to other immune-enhancing effects of the lactobacillus bacteria.

- Eat more plant oestrogens, like soya products, ground linseeds and sprouted alfalfa. A whole section on these plant oestrogens is in the Self Care chapter.
- Eat up the cabbage family. It helps break down oestrogens in the body. This includes green, purple and white cabbages, broccoli, brussels sprouts and radicchio.
- Look at your protein intake. Higher intakes of protein improve metabolism of oestrogen in the liver. Careful you don't overdo it—many other complaints are caused by excess protein. Try to get most of your protein from grains, legumes and low-fat meat and keep it down to 60 grams a day. See the 20 Diet Hints in the Self Care chapter for more info on protein.
- Take vitamin B6. In vitamin B6 deficiency, tissues in the uterus and breast are more susceptible to the stimulating effects of oestrogen, and sadly, B6-deficient women with breast cancer have a poorer survival rate.
- Cut down on alcohol. Moderate alcohol consumption (one glass of beer, one glass of wine or one shot of spirits daily) has been linked to a lower incidence of uterine cancer (particularly in overweight women); but an *increased* risk of breast cancer. If you have other risk factors for breast cancer it's probably best to cut right down on alcohol. Other women, including anyone with an increased risk of heart disease, can safely drink one to two standard glasses every second or third day.
- Moderate exercise helps to reduce the production of oestrogen and increase its clearance from the body.
- Foods which will help the liver break down oestrogen include beans, legumes, onions, and garlic.
- Bitter green leafy vegetables and bitter herbs prescribed by a herbalist will help liver function, which may help clear excess oestrogen.

- Reduce pesticide use in your home and garden and campaign for the same in your local area.
- Buy fresh, non-packaged food. (Fatty foods like cheeses, wrapped in cling wrap, can absorb oestrogen-like components from the plastics.)
- Buy foods packaged in glass rather than in plastic or polystyrene.
- Buy organic foods if you can, especially organically grown or range-fed meats.

Not enough oestrogen

A *relative* oestrogen deficiency happens when:

- too much oestrogen is cleared by the body
- too little is recycled for use by the body
- and/or the fat cells aren't making enough oestrogen from the androgen hormones.

An *actual* oestrogen deficiency happens after menopause, when your ovaries stop making it.

Symptoms

Low bone density, poor fertility, low sex drive, irregular periods, and premature ageing or excessive dryness and brittleness of tissues including vagina, bones and skin.

Possible causes

- Body weight 15–20 per cent below the recommended range of the Body Mass Index (BMI) can often stop periods and cause oestrogen levels to fall below normal. The cycle can also become erratic, and fertility and bone density are also reduced. (See Being Underweight in the When Things Go Wrong chapter for how to calculate your BMI.)
- Too much fibre lowers oestrogen levels and may increase your chances of developing osteoporosis. Avoid eating lots of wheat-bran only cereals. Fibre taken as part of whole food isn't a problem.

- Vitamin A deficiency causes low oestrogen. You can get levels up by eating more betacarotene in orange, yellow and green vegetables or fruits. (Taking vitamin A supplements is not safe during pregnancy.)
- Antibiotics reduce substantial numbers of the gut bacteria needed to convert oestrogen into a more active form for use in the body. Yoghurt and cultured milks can eventually improve bowel colonies, but it's better to avoid antibiotics, except in severe infection.
- Overexercising reduces the levels of circulating oestrogens, and can cause stopped periods and low bone density.
- Smoking alters the metabolism of oestrogen so that more of the inactive oestrogen is produced. If you smoke, you'll be relatively oestrogen deficient, and have an earlier menopause and an increased risk of bone fractures.

The Medical Approach

If a doctor perceives there is a problem, the Pill or hormone replacement therapy (HRT) will probably be prescribed. The Pill is fully explored under Drugs in The Medical Approach chapter. HRT is given full throttle under Menopause in the Finishing Up chapter.

Natural Therapies & Self Care

- Follow the obvious path suggested by possible causes listed above, like not overexercising or getting too thin, eating a moderate fibre intake, avoiding cigarettes and antibiotics, and making sure you don't have a vitamin A deficiency.
- Eat food from plants which contain oestrogens. There's a whole section on plant oestrogens in the Self Care chapter.
- Eat foods containing steroidal saponins. Substances called saponins in foods and herbs seem to improve mineral uptake, and can lower blood cholesterol levels. Foods with saponins include soya products, all legumes and potatoes with their skins on.

- You may be prescribed herbs containing high levels of steroidal saponins, including *Chamaelirium luteum, Trillium erectum, Dioscorea villosa* and *Aletris farinosa*. Some of these seem to have definite oestrogenic and hormone balancing effects. Herbs are explored in the Natural Therapies chapter.

Not enough progesterone

Changes in progesterone levels seem to be the baddies in a number of common gynaecological complaints, but exactly why and how is really hard to work out. By far the most common problem is too little rather than too much. Progesterone is produced by the corpus luteum, the remnant of the egg sac after it has released the egg at ovulation. So the first obvious suspicion is that if you don't have enough progesterone, you probably haven't been up to speed in the egg dispatch department.

Symptoms

Related conditions include PMS, dysfunctional bleeding patterns, lumpy or painful breasts and some types of infertility.

Possible causes

No ovulation. Ovulation fails and no progesterone is produced by the body in the second half of the cycle, the luteal phase. This is a normal, temporary state after childbirth, miscarriage, a pregnancy termination, after stopping the Pill, and while breastfeeding. It is also seen in dysfunctional bleeding patterns, after stress, and around the menopause and the first period.

Luteal phase defects. After ovulation, the remnant egg sac, called the corpus luteum, is supposed to secrete progesterone during the luteal phase of the cycle, which is ended by the period.

A luteal phase defect is believed to contribute to some cases of premenstrual tension, fibrocystic breast disease and infertility. Types of luteal phase defect include:

- Corpus luteum insufficiency. For unknown reasons, the corpus luteum may not produce enough progesterone, or produce it for long enough.
- Luteinised unruptured follicle syndrome. This condition is thought to cause infertility, and may particularly affect women with endometriosis. The follicle develops, but the egg is not expelled, and although progesterone is produced, levels are often lower than normal.
- Abnormal hypothalamic-pituitary function. Sometimes the organ or tissue being told what to do by the hypothalamic-pituitary unit just goes on strike. This failed response can happen in the developing follicle, the endometrium, or other progesterone-sensitive tissues including the breast. It can lead to low or no progesterone and cause delayed development of the endometrium or sore breasts before the period. Prolactin seems to increase when progesterone levels are low, and may be implicated in this abnormal tissue response to progesterone.

  Infertility, premenstrual syndrome and benign breast disease are believed to be linked to this kind of progesterone problem.

Diagnosis

Progesterone deficiency can be diagnosed in a number of ways.

- A period symptoms diary (there's one under A Normal Period on page 24 that you can photocopy) can be filled out daily for one or more months to ascertain the type, severity and timing of symptoms.
- Symptoms related to a progesterone deficiency or lack of availability come on only during the luteal phase of the cycle and include tension, irritability, anxiety or other mood changes.
- Basal body temperature (taken by mouth thermometer) can be used to determine the availability of progesterone in the luteal phase. The temperature is taken first thing every morning before any activity at all (including talking or rolling over in bed—you may simply reach languidly for the thermometer). A normal, old-fashioned thermometer gives the most accurate reading. The

slight, but detectable rise in the temperature in the luteal phase, which indicates progesterone is present, is reliable about three times in four.

- The length of the luteal phase can be measured to find out whether progesterone is produced for long enough. The exact date of ovulation is needed and fewer than 11 days from ovulation to the period means you probably have luteal phase defects. Ovulation can be detected using the basal body temperature, a mid-cycle blood or urine test to check for the mid-cycle surge in luteinising hormone (LH), or an ultrasound scan to view the developing follicle. A scan is the most accurate way of detecting the ovulation date—the least effective way is to subtract 14 days from Day One of the period.
- Blood levels of progesterone are usually taken between seven and nine days after ovulation. But blood tests to determine progesterone levels can get results which fluctuate widely and can range from normal to very low within a short time-span.
- If you are having trouble conceiving and don't know why, a doctor may suggest an endometrial biopsy to evaluate endometrial development, usually performed during a hysteroscopy (explained under Surgery in The Medical Approach chapter). Luteal phase defects are associated with slow maturing of the endometrium, but some doctors don't believe that luteal phase defects are relevant to infertility.

The Medical Approach

Many doctors won't perceive progesterone levels as a problem unless ovulation has stopped, and it causes bleeding or infertility. Doctors will often prescribe progestogen drugs, such as Provera, Primulut N and Micronor for dysfunctional uterine bleeding (DUB) caused by not ovulating and low progesterone. Progesterone vaginal suppositories may be prescribed for women who have had several miscarriages, although this is controversial because some miscarriages are a natural way of dealing with a pregnancy which isn't developing normally. More info on progestogens is under Drugs in The Medical Approach chapter.

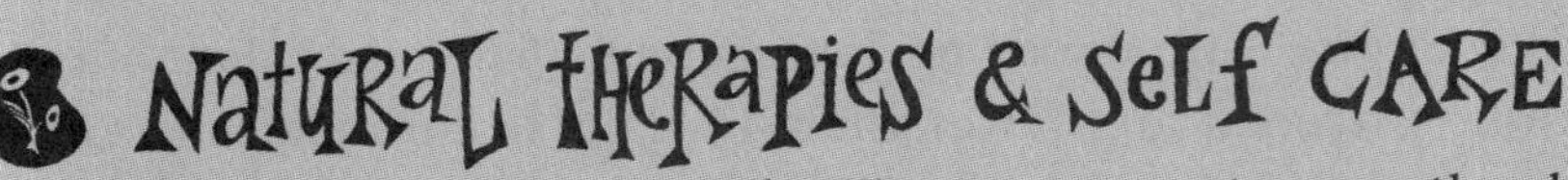

Natural Therapies & Self Care

- A herbalist may prescribe *Vitex agnus castus*, or other herbs which contain steroidal saponins and which seem to normalise ovulation.
- Treatment for symptoms like mood changes is under PMS in the When Things Go Wrong chapter.

Wild yam creams

Many natural therapists have begun prescribing a product called wild yam cream which they claim your body will convert into natural progesterone. Well, it won't. We recommend you steer clear of wild yam creams and their ilk until more research is to hand about its effects. Here's why.

The progesterone molecule is a unique substance made by your body from cholesterol. Unhelpfully, some manufacturers and practitioners refer to both the body-made progesterone and the wild yam creams as 'natural progesterone'. They are not the same thing.

Many people like the sound of a commercially available 'natural progesterone' in pills and creams made from plants, because it sounds less heavy than 'progestogens', the chemical drugs sold under brand names like Provera, Primulut N and Micronor, which can have side effects.

Confusion arises from the suggestion that herbal creams 'contain natural progesterone' or 'contain plant-based progesterone'. Hang on a minute. Some people claim that plants such as wild yam and mistletoe contain progesterone, but there is no scientific evidence to confirm that 'naturally-occurring progesterone' exists in plants at levels which would be effective in a human body.

Further confusion arises when people equate the effects of wild yam creams with the effects of body-made progesterone. In the case of wild yam, some people assume that the steroidal saponin found in the yam, dioscin, will be converted by the body into progesterone. This does not happen.

When the body makes progesterone, it starts with the building block of cholesterol. When your body is making hormones deep inside your cellular bits, it couldn't give a toss what you're rubbing into your skin. In fact, because cholesterol is the real building block for progesterone, it makes just as much sense (i.e. none) to rub butter into your skin instead of wild yam.

Dioscin, from yams and other plant sources, has been used for many years as a starting material for the commercial production of a number of steroidal drugs, including cortisone and progesterone. But for dioscin to become progesterone, a carefully controlled series of chemical steps are performed in a laboratory or factory—the same process can't happen in the body when dioscin-containing substances like wild yam are applied to the skin or swallowed.

A study on wild yam creams showed that they did not produce a boost of progesterone levels. All sorts of claims are being made about these creams but so far no independent or peer review studies have been done to support any of them. The bottom line is that there is only one 'natural progesterone'—the one made in your body.

Wild yam creams have been found to have an effect in improving hot flushes, and reducing PMS complaints. But this is not because they create more progesterone. It's much more likely that the dioscin behaves like a weak plant oestrogen.

Traditionally, herbalists have always used wild yam as an oral preparation for bilious colic, colitis, period pain, diverticulitis and appendicitis. It has been used for pregnancy nausea in small but controlled doses under the strictest supervision of a herbal specialist. Wild yam also has additional hormone regulating effects, as do all the dioscin-containing herbs.

So why is it being flogged specifically as a cream? (If you want the effects of dioscin, it's easily absorbed in a pill or oral herbal extract.) Let's just say that marketing this cream is big business, and the cream is more expensive than a pill.

Meet your prostaglandins

To work properly, ovulation, periods and childbirth all depend on the hormones to behave themselves. It is not so well known that they also rely on some complicated, hormone-like substances called prostaglandins to behave themselves as well.

Prostaglandins are made by the body to control heaps of different functions, for example, bleeding, clotting, anti-inflammatory action and muscle spasms. This makes them big players in the menstrual cycle, what with all that experience in stopping and starting bleeding and controlling crampy things.

Some prostaglandins might become too dominant in cases of infection, inflammation, allergy, hormone variations or poor diet. These imbalances may be temporary, or continue indefinitely, and are believed to be causes of period pain, heavy periods, PMS and endometriosis. (All of these problems have their own sections in this book.)

It may help to think of prostaglandins as a large family of hormone-like substances which perform many functions throughout the body.

The prostaglandin family is really a sub-group of an extended family of microscopic substances found in most tissues called the eicosanoids (I-ko-san-oids). In the eicosanoid extended family, there are two clans—the large and well-known family called the prostaglandins, and a smaller branch of rellies called the leukotrienes.

The prostaglandin family is itself made up of even smaller families, like nuclear families in an extended clan. These families include the prostacyclins and the thromboxanes as well as a group of individual prostaglandins. Each of the members of the extended family has a broad role to play: the prostaglandins influence blood clotting, the activity of muscles and the inflammatory responses throughout the body; the thromboxanes are involved with blood clotting and blood vessel activity; and the leukotrienes are regulators of inflammatory and allergic reactions.

Whenever you bleed, get a scab, throw up or have a muscle spasm, there's a prostaglandin working overtime.

Within each of the thromboxane, prostaglandins and leukotriene families, each of the members has its own more detailed role. As with all families, some of the members tend to be nuisances, others are more useful. Just as some rellies are liable to go off the deep-end at any given time (especially Christmas), some of the rellies in the prostaglandin family can go a bit feral from time to time. And then there are the distant rellies—some of whom can be unreliable. For example, one of the leukotrienes will start some of the processes of inflammation, and another one, either a close or distant clan relative, will have the role of calming everything down.

The prostaglandins do various conflicting jobs in the menstrual cycle, so they need to be in balance. One type of prostaglandin stops platelets from clumping together and dilates blood vessels, which causes heavier period bleeding. Another prostaglandin strongly increases muscle contraction, but in the Fallopian tube, it causes relaxation. Another one is always complaining that the young people of today get it too good. Sorry, that's one of *my* relatives.

Rogue prostaglandins can be responsible for the crampy type of period pain, because some prostaglandins cause blood vessels in the endometrium to constrict and cause muscle spasm. When some are too dominant, it can cause period pain from the cramping muscle.

And in general, leukotrienes stimulate uterus contractions, so when some of these leukotrienes go into overdrive, the contractions cause crampy period pain. One type of leukotriene attracts white cells to inflamed tissues and is found in high levels when women have endometriosis. It may also be involved in breast cancer.

Balancing the prostaglandins

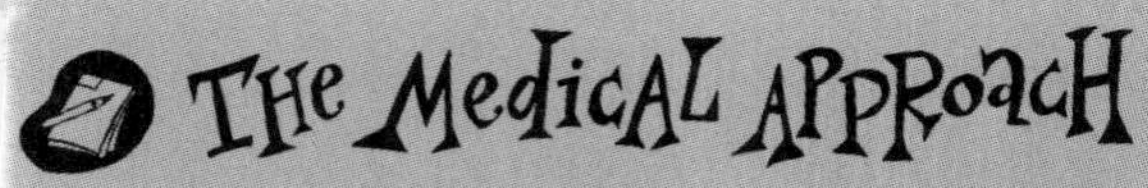

In some cases of period pain, prostaglandins-inhibiting drugs will be prescribed. These are fully explained under Drugs in The Medical Approach chapter.

Natural Therapies & Self Care

The body uses Omega-3 fatty acids to make leukotrienes and thromboxanes, and Omega-6 fatty acids to make prostaglandins.

The fatty acids that can treat conditions caused by an imbalance of prostaglandins are found in certain foods and should be regularly included in the diet. For the best healthy effects, you need to eat more essential fatty acids and less of the 'bad oils' which interfere with them. (Essential fatty acids, and what foods they're in, are explained under Bad Fats and Good Fats, number 8 of the 20 Diet Hints in the Self Care chapter.)

If you want to have balanced prostaglandins, it's essential that you read and follow it.

Chapter 4

STARTING OUT

Adolescence

Right at the time you get your first period, all this other stuff happens as well, including amazing body changes and mad crushes on people. All your hormones seem to explode at once, transforming your body *and* your mind.

Some girls just shrug their shoulders and go for a 47 trillion kilometre bushwalk, but some suffer a range of symptoms from inexplicable sobbing to a pimple extravaganza. These symptoms are most often caused by hormones affecting mood swings and physical changes, not the period itself.

Quite often the period is used as an excuse. 'I'm really depressed.' 'It's probably your period, dear.' 'I feel tired a lot.' 'That'd be your women's business.' 'Large corporations are conspiring with world governments to oppress the poor and maximise their profits.' 'It's probably because you're premenstrual.'

Most adolescent changes are normal and truly 'just a stage'. Some of the more horrible side effects of growing up can be overcome with treatment or changes in lifestyle (yes, you may have to stop trying to exist solely on Tim Tams and fried lettuce and learn to occasionally worship at the Sacred Shrine of Tofu). Of course, other problems may need help from a health practitioner. The following will help you to tell the difference between a foul mood and an alarm going off in The Ovary Department.

The changes

The first period

The first period usually arrives between 12 and 13 years old, but anywhere between 9 and 16 is considered normal. This onset of menstruation is called menarche. (Why is it called menarche? Because it is Latin and doctors simply adore Latin almost as much as lawyers and herbalists do.) Anyway, the time you start menstruating is decided by a grab-bag of factors, including genes. A good diet, plenty of rest and moderate exercise are also necessary to begin periods.

Maintaining a normal body weight is essential (and this is the reason that the normal menarche is artificially delayed for many gymnasts, ballet dancers and training athletes who overexercise). Periods start after a weight of about 47.5 kilograms has been attained, and that body weight is made up of between 26 and 28 per cent fat. For periods to continue, the weight must stay higher than the level it was at the first period. Obviously, you wouldn't drop below the weight you were in your young teens unless you got really sick.

If you haven't had a period by the time you turn 17, check out the section called No Periods in the When Things Go Wrong chapter, and see a doctor.

Stage one: between 9 and 11

Physical changes usually start around 9 to 11 years old (but if it doesn't happen until 14 or 15, it's still perfectly normal, so no peeking and panicking). These changes usually include:

- Sudden increase in height and weight. It can take a while to get used to a new size and shape—so don't be surprised by elbows-and-knees-in-the-wrong-place clumsiness and alternating bouts of energy and exhaustion. These extremely rapid changes can seem awkward and embarrassing, especially if relatives or friends bang on about it. Tell them to shut up or ignore them. This sudden, mega-growing phase can lead to temporarily being over- or underweight (not because of eating disorders—which are discussed later).

- Changes in body shape. During this early stage the nipples enlarge, but there is no increase in the size of the breasts; the waist becomes more defined and the hips rounder, as natural fat is added.
- Pubic hair debut. A few pubic hairs appear, often a paler colour than they will eventually be. After the first signs of pubic hair it's usually about two years to go to the first period. Usually the pubic hair is darker than the hair on your head.
- Mood changes. Sudden changes in mood are common—feeling hysterically happy one minute, and then sad or grumpy as anything the next (adults sometimes have these feelings too, but have had more practice in disguising them and giving them more serious-sounding names like 'executive stress').

Stage two: about 12 to 14

- Changes in body shape. The hips and waist continue their journeys to whatever size they're meant to be for you, and the breasts start to develop. The nipples get bigger again and stick out more (this is obviously some sort of conspiracy created by bra manufacturers).

  The increasing levels of the oestrogen hormone cause the labia to enlarge, and the production of mucus-like vaginal secretions which are slightly white, or clear. (These vaginal secretions continue throughout grown-up life. Although they never say so, this is what all those wussy ads for 'panty-liners' are all about, but really it's no big deal if you change your undies every day.)
- Body hair. The pubic hair thickens, becomes darker and less fluffy. Underarm hair usually grows about two years after the first pubic hairs appear. These changes are related to the normal production of weak androgens (male hormones) by the adrenal glands and the ovaries.
- Skin changes. The skin becomes much oilier, particularly over the chin, nose and forehead, and this sometimes causes pimples.

Suddenly you seem to blush a lot. We know it seems like this will go on forever (and the more you blush, the more you can't stop it), but in fact wild blushing is only a phase. (Honestly. Look at all those adults lying, cheating, starting wars, running around in the nuddy on film and not a blush among them.)

- Changes in moods. Most girls get really moody about the time of their first period.
- Periods. On average, periods start at the age of twelve-and-a-half. Ovulation and periods gradually become more regular during the first 40 cycles. For most of us, ovulation doesn't happen for the first year after the first period. Even after four or five years of periods, up to one-fifth of girls still might not have started ovulating.

Stage three: about 15 to 18 years

- Establishing a regular cycle. Usually the period settles down to become more regular and predictable—predictable for you, that is. There is a wide range of variation in the regularity, heaviness and frequency of periods at this age. You might have light periods which last for a few days and you can carry on like those giddy girls in tampon ads who can't decide between swimming and climbing Mount Everest, or you might have a really heavy period that goes on for more than a week and you lie down on the couch looking like a vampire victim because you're anaemic. (In which case go straight to the heavy periods section to find out what you can do about it.)

First periods: what's normal?

Read the previous chapter's bit on normal periods to find out—and to help you decide whether to use pads or tampons. There's also a checklist of warning signs which mean you should be checked out by a doctor.

The period diary

Keeping a menstrual diary can be useful to help get to know your own cycle. (A menstrual diary is included on page 23 in the When

Puberty

Things Go Right chapter, but an ordinary calendar will do just as well.)

If you keep a menstrual chart you'll be able to more accurately predict when you'll usually want to rip somebody's head off, or burst into tears, or need tampons or pads. But the menstrual cycle will often be quite erratic. If you're trying supplements (like evening primrose oil) for PMS or painkillers for period pain, keeping good records will tell you when to take them, and whether or not they worked for you.

Don't forget to chart how long your period lasts, especially when it goes for more than a week. Doctors and natural therapists can use your records to make a more accurate diagnosis or prescription.

Exercise

There are some old-fashioned ideas about how young girlies who have their periods shouldn't play sport, have a bath or wash their hair. This advice originated in the Middle Ages when people knew so much about women they used to burn them as witches and thought that periods were caused by sickness or injury. It's time we chucked the advice of some mangy old dead monks and decided ourselves what to do during our periods.

There are, however, two cautions. (Three if you count 'Never trust a man with a polyester moustache'.) Firstly, getting cold can aggravate period pain because it slows circulation, and so swimmers (or hair-washers!) may need to be careful about the temperature of the water and of changing rooms. Secondly, some women have a lot more pain if they go in for vigorous rather than gentle exercise during their periods.

Common teenage period problems

Heavy bleeding and erratic cycles

Very heavy periods (called menorrhagia) each month for many months, can lead to anaemia. You need to find out what's causing the problem before any treatment is decided on. In most cases your 'history' (the signs and symptoms you've experienced) is enough to work out the cause, and you won't need a physical examination.

Doctors often prescribe the Pill for young women who are troubled by heavy periods, but you don't have to automatically agree. Both heavy bleeding and erratic cycles are usually caused by hormonal fluctuations and erratic ovulation, things that many teenagers have in common. The hormones should settle down by themselves in a few months. If you think you have a continuing problem, see the sections on Bleeding Too Much or Too Often and on Erratic Bleeding in the next chapter.

It is rarely necessary to interfere with ovulation—either to make it more regular with herbs, or to stop it altogether with the Pill. Because stress can delay ovulation, you might want to consider stress management techniques (see under Stress in the Usual Suspects section of the When Things Go Wrong chapter).

The sorts of natural remedies recommended for 'functional menorrhagia' under the heading Bleeding Too Much in the When Things Go Wrong chapter can be used to control symptoms of heavy bleeding. Herbalists shouldn't prescribe you the commonly used herb *Vitex agnus castus* for adolescent heavy bleeding, except in a very limited number of cases.

Period pain

See the next chapter for the whole shebang on period pain.

Diet

Right at the time when the big growth spurt needs good nutrition and increased calories to do the job, some girls want to 'go on a diet' because they think they're too fat, other girls do end up with too much fat because they eat lots of sugary and fatty foods and do no exercise. Maintaining normal weight and getting enough of the vital nutrients can only be achieved by regular exercise and a balanced diet. (Not stupid short-term weight loss diets like the ones you see in the magazines where you can only eat pineapple for three days, or the ones with not enough food so you're tired and hungry and grumpy all the time. You know the sort.) There's a zillion more hints on diet in the Self Care chapter.

And may we just say that the normal weight is not to be judged by any of the following:

(a) what size your mother is or used to be
(b) ditto sisters
(c) ditto prepubescent models
(d) ditto any other models
(e) looking at the entrails of a chicken.

Minerals

The rapid growth rate during this time means teenagers need a lot more minerals than grown-ups. Zinc, iron, magnesium and calcium are in especially high demand. You need to read the info page on each one in the Minerals section in the Self Care chapter.

Vegetarians

If you're a vegetarian you have to be careful that you're getting enough iron. If you decide to be a vegetarian, particularly if you decide to become one as a teenager, you'll have to learn how to eat pulses, beans, nuts and all sorts of other things. If you just stop eating chops and only eat milkshakes and apples you are going to damage your health, skin, hair—the works. See the diet hints in the Self Care chapter.

Exhaustion

The physical changes of adolescence can be very taxing on the body and result in episodes of exhaustion. It is enough to make one fall onto a chaise longue, press one's hand delicately to one's forehead and demand that the servants fetch one one's slippers and a large chocolate cake. Unfortunately, the servants are probably imaginary.

When you get tired, it is a good idea to get more rest by going to bed by ten o'clock. You can make energy drinks after school (see the Self Care chapter for recipes), eat plenty of vegetables, including vegie snacks throughout the day and, of course, cutting back on fatty, greasy, salty, crappy, expensive, vile, disgusting junk food will also help (obvious enough yet?). Follow the 20 Diet Hints in the Self Care chapter for a balanced eating regime. (Actually I think we should dispense with the word regime. It sounds rather military and depressing. Let's just call it a Wild Balanced Eating Romp.)

Moodiness

Hormonal Imbalance

The types of feelings you can experience when you're premenstrual (before the period) are very similar to anxiety or depression. In fact you'd probably need a microscope to tell the difference. These symptoms are known to be part of premenstrual syndrome (PMS)—there's a whole section on it in the next chapter.

Hypoglycaemia

Hypoglycaemia, or wild fluctuations in the blood sugar can lead to feelings of depression and anxiety, as well as tiredness. This syndrome is discussed under The Usual Suspects in the When Things Go Wrong chapter.

Depression

Depression (at the very least a visitation of heavy sighing) and anxiety (low-level terror) are the most common mood changes experienced by teenagers. The menstrual cycle and hormones are becoming established and regular, and the tear ducts might be getting a good workout as well.

This can be related to the hormonal fluctuations—it's somewhat like being premenstrual all the time. It's a wonder more young girls aren't arrested for biting people in the street. There may be other factors, such as problems at school or home which become harder to deal with because of the additional stresses of puberty.

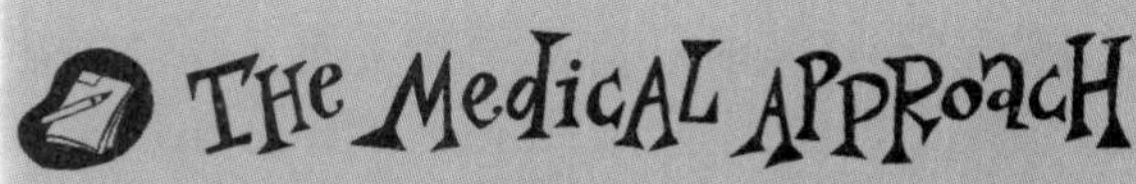

Unless there is a serious mental health problem, doctors will be reluctant to prescribe drugs, and will probably suggest some of the following more gentle approaches. Drugs for depression or other mental problems should be prescribed only by a psychiatrist specialising in adolescents.

Natural therapies & Self Care

- LSD, in this instance, is not the hallucinogenic drug, but a very useful technique for improving the response to stress: Long Slow Distance exercise. This includes walking at a moderately fast rate for about 45 minutes and swimming.
- Eat well. Eliminate most junk food, any foods or drinks which contain caffeine (like colas, coffees and normal tea) because they aggravate anxiety symptoms and depression. Eat smaller meals often, have healthy snacks and follow the 20 Diet Hints in the Self Care chapter. You'll have less sugar cravings.
- The section on stress (under The Usual Suspects) at the start of the When Things Go Wrong chapter explains how to reduce tension, improve concentration and get better quality sleep.
- Talking with friends and family about problems is usually a good idea. While feeling miserable might be new for you, most people go through down stages. If you feel you can't talk to friends and family, the school counsellor, a trusted teacher, or your doctor may either be able to help or suggest someone who can. The law makes doctors keep your conversations private.

Pimples

About half of girls between the ages of 14 and 17 (and about three-quarters of young guys) develop pimples. Usually by the time you turn 20 the problem has cleared up and you just get the occasional one.

Acne is not caused by 'dirty' skin, poor hygiene, chocolate eclairs, the approach of a big date or oily hair on the face. There are real causes of acne—all related to the surge of androgens (blokey hormones) around puberty. Some people have hormonal imbalances, but don't get any pimples. (Which is outrageous behaviour on their part.) Some people's skin just seems more likely to respond badly to androgens.

Another reason that androgens may cause pimples is that increased levels of the hormone in the skin can cause thickening around pores, and an increase in sebum (oil). The bacteria which grows on the surface of the skin can infect the pores and cause inflammation. This seems to be genetic, so when in doubt, blame your parents. They should be used to it by now.

The Medical Approach

Doctors often prescribe lotions which include retinoic (tretinoin or Retin A) for non-inflamed pimples; or which contain antibiotics such as clindamycin, for inflamed pimples. An older preparation, benzoyl peroxide, which comes as a cream, gel or wash, is still suggested by some doctors. Newer preparations which contain glycolic acid (often called fruit acid) are gentle skin 'peels' to remove dead skin and keep the pores open. If any lotions make you develop a skin reaction, stop using them and get advice from the prescribing doctor.

Pills for acne include isotretinoin (Roaccutane) and, more commonly, antibiotics such as tetracycline (Mysteclin, Tetrex, Vibra-Tabs, Minomycin). Occasionally erythromycin is used if pregnancy is a possibility or you're allergic to tetracycline. To be effective, antibiotics need to be taken strictly to quite complicated instructions about when and how.

Isotretinoin (Roaccutane) can only be prescribed by a specialist dermatologist and no wonder: it has a number of common side effects including cracked lips, facial dermatitis, severely irritated eyes and eyelids, nose-bleeds from dry and sore nasal passages, high cholesterol levels, and certain forms of eczema. Some people also develop photosensitivity, and sun block must always be used. Muscle and joint pains can sometimes happen and more rarely, bony outgrowths can develop throughout the skeleton. Occasionally the liver enzymes are also affected, but they return to normal after you stop the drug.

Doctors usually insist that if you take Roaccutane, or a similar drug, you must also be on the Pill because if you get pregnant, the drug will cause abnormalities in a foetus.

Natural therapies

Natural therapists use an approach which combines diet, vitamin and mineral supplements, hygiene, hormone regulation, skin healing and bacterial control. Different combinations of treatments seem to be effective for some people, but not others, and so getting it right can be complicated.

Herbs

Herbalists have a few routine prescriptions for acne. These include *Echinacea angustifolia*, *Calendula officinalus* and *Arctium lappa*. *Vitex agnus castus* is also useful when there is severe acne caused by hormonal irregularities. More on these herbs under Herbs in the Natural Therapies chapter.

Self care

Diet

Giving up one supposedly pimple-causing 'food', like chocolate or sugar, never works. Comprehensive diet changes are more successful, but it's complex.

You need to eat plenty of fresh fruit, vegetables and fibre, and very little fat and refined sugar. Foods which have high levels of betacarotene, such as yellow and orange fruit and vegetables and dark green leafy vegetables; and zinc supplements will reduce inflammation, and help with healing and regulating hormone levels.

Chromium, found in brewers' yeast improves acne. And no, that doesn't mean you can go out and drink a slab of beer. Brewers' yeast comes in powder. Yeast products can cause problems with vaginal candida (thrush) and gut disturbance, especially if antibiotics or the Pill are taken at the same time. But taking brewers' yeast with yoghurt usually prevents these problems.

- Acne that gets worse just before a period is often helped by vitamin B6, either alone, or better still with B complex or zinc. It may help to take 25–50 milligrams of vitamin B6 and one teaspoon of brewers' yeast each day, in the week or ten days before your period.
- Antibacterial face washes containing tea tree oil are useful, not to stop pimples, but to stop pimples from getting infected—unless you develop a skin reaction and have to stop. A good, home-made 'face pack' can be made from one dessertspoon of yoghurt, one teaspoon of honey and one of lemon or orange juice. For skin that is very dry, add a dribble of olive oil. Apply to the face for half an hour, and then wash off with warm water. Or if you get bored you can always eat it for morning tea.
- Stress can aggravate acne, maybe because stress increases the production of androgens from the adrenal glands—or maybe because stress can disrupt the normal hormonal balance. Whatever the reason, reducing stress (ideas under The Usual Suspects in the When Things Go Wrong chapter) might be the best pimple cure for some people.

Chapter 5

WHEN THINGS GO WRONG

How will you know if something is abnormal? Well, if your horoscope says you are going to be eaten alive by a giant squid on Thursday, the dog really *does* eat your homework or you get to work and find that you've been replaced by a robot run on beetroot juice and Hollywood actually casts a leading actress who weighs more than a Mintie, there'll be an inkling that things are a wee bit strange.

On the subject of periods and related problems, if anything on the following list applies to you, then skedaddle off to a doctor for diagnosis. When you have a diagnosis, you can read the relevant bits in this book, and get treatment from a doctor and/or natural therapist.

When to see a doctor

- There's no sign of the first period by 17 years old.
- Your period has stopped for more than a couple of months.
- There's any sudden change or series of changes in your menstrual cycle. For example you used to be regular as clockwork and now it's all over the shop, or you used to have a really light period and now you're wondering if you should buy tampons in bulk (an abnormally heavy period means suddenly needing to change pads

or tampons every two hours) or any new and unusual pain related to the period.

- There's excessive pain during or before each period. (Excessive pain means the level of the pain interferes with or restricts your life—for example, you have to lie down with a hot-water bottle calling for Milo instead of going dancing.)
- If you're having abnormally long periods—which means longer than seven days if you don't usually bleed for that long.
- You bleed between each period (usually called 'spotting') even if it is very light.
- You have a yellowish or smelly vaginal discharge, or any vaginal itch or soreness.

All the major things that can go wrong with periods are covered in this book. Read the section on anything you think you might have, or have been diagnosed with.

The usual suspects

Heaps of different things can affect your period and other functions of the hormonal cycle: being stressed, being underweight, dieting, fasting, mineral deficiencies and various drugs of the prescribed and not-so prescribed sort.

If things are going wrong you might like to investigate the obvious possibilities first. These 'usual suspects' can be a lot easier to fix than the other diseases and disorders of the reproductive bits that can cause similar symptoms with your period.

Stress

'Stress' is any event or series of events, physical or emotional, in a person's life that leads to physiological and biochemical changes. These events or feelings, either happy or horrible, can include exams, travelling, moving away from home, relationship problems, getting married, getting unmarried, serious illnesses or extreme physical exercise.

Effects on the period

Stress can interfere with normal hormone levels. This can cause periods to stop temporarily; heavier than usual periods; erratic cycles; dysfunctional uterine bleeding (DUB); and increased period pain. Stress can affect fertility by causing ovulation to stop temporarily, or by disrupting the cycle.

PMS can become worse with stress—some researchers even think that most women have some premenstrual symptoms, but stressed and anxious women develop worse PMS because they are unusually sensitive to hormone fluctuations and find it harder to cope.

Stress increases the perception of pain and blunts your coping skills. It may cause changes in the hypothalamic-pituitary hormones which regulate the menstrual cycle. Some people get worse period pain when they're stressed. Period pain in some teenagers has been linked to stress caused by family tension, guilt feelings about sex, or being encouraged to think of periods as unclean and a problem.

The good news is that the stressful time usually ends and the periods return to normal.

Symptoms

The body's first reaction to stress is an 'alarm' response. Messages from the hypothalamus stimulate the nervous system which in turn stimulates the adrenal glands to produce adrenalin. This leads to a faster heart rate; increased production of sweat; contraction of the spleen to return blood to the circulation; dilation of the pupils, and of the bronchioles in the lungs; and release of stored sugars. Digestion and the production of urine slows down.

This response is the 'fight or flight mechanism' and was much more in demand when it was regularly necessary to go four rounds with a woolly mammoth. A rapid heart rate and contraction of the spleen means that more blood is available for muscles, a sudden burst of glycogen sugar gives instant energy, you can see better, breathe faster and be more alert.

These days, when we get stressed about relationships, work, or money, we can't run away screaming or try to bash up a prehistoric elephant. So the excess adrenalin remains circulating in your system, leaving you edgy, or 'wired'. In times of prolonged stress including chronic illness, pain, or emotional trauma, the 'alarm' response changes into the 'resistance' response. Many organs become distracted from their usual jobs by special functions to deal with stress.

The body increases the excretion of potassium, right at the time you need extra help with the normal function of the heart, other muscles, and the nervous system.

The body comes under enormous physical strain and needs a lot more nutrients than usual but the stress makes you lose your appetite, get indigestion and not assimilate nutrients properly. The combination of hormone production and fluctuating blood sugar levels creates a sense of irritability and sometimes, anxiety attacks. There's often disturbed sleep and night sweats. (Not to be mistaken for menopause!)

Some stresses are just too extreme or go on too long. This leads to the 'exhaustion' phase of the stress response. Many of the organs go into decline, minerals are excreted in the urine, the immune response weakens, sleep is unrefreshing and often disturbed by weird dreams about octopus wrestling (or that kind of thing) and you feel exhausted and daunted all the time. Other symptoms include being depressed, moody, anxious and unable to remember anything. Utterly repressible.

The Medical Approach

Few modern doctors are still keen to prescribe some dubious tranquillisers. These drugs are not appropriate for temporary, stress-related changes to your period. Stress management techniques are favoured by most doctors and natural therapists.

Natural Therapies

All the following herbs must be prescribed by a herbalist specialising in menstrual problems. You can't go ferreting around with them on your own. (There's more info on them under Herbs in the Natural Therapies chapter.)

- A group of herbs called the adaptogens helps the body adapt to stress. This group of herbs includes the ginsengs, especially *Eleuthrococcus senticosus*.
- Nervine herbs are also useful when sleep is disrupted, along with B vitamins, and magnesium supplements taken in the mornings. Some herbalists prescribe an oral extract of the green oat seed (to be taken in a liquid herbal mixture) or *Hypericum perforatum* for depression.
- Herbs which regulate periods after stressful episodes are *Vitex agnus castus* for erratic periods and PMS; *Cimicifuga racemosa* (especially if you're approaching menopause); *Leonurus cardiaca* and *Verbena officinalis* for period irregularities linked with anxiety and palpitations; and *Chamaelirium luteum* if ovulation has stopped.
- When bleeding is heavy you might be prescribed astringent herbs. One herb with a specific effect on both the uterus and hormones is *Trillium erectum* for heavy, erratic periods like those seen in dysfunctional uterine bleeding (DUB); another is *Alchemilla vulgaris* for heavy bleeding in teenagers.

Self Care

- Try the hypoglycaemic diet in the Self Care chapter which will improve many of your symptoms, and your ability to cope with long-term stress.
- Avoid stimulants such as coffee, alcohol, cigarettes, and wild affairs in the Bahamas.
- Adopt stress management techniques such as yoga, 'long slow distance' exercise, relaxation tapes or meditation. (If you're bored with the idea of meditation, anything that makes you have fun or feel relaxed will do, which is where a wild affair in the Bahamas might come in handy.)
- If your budget doesn't quite stretch to lust in the tropics, try herbal teas such as chamomile and lime flowers, which can be mixed together. Lemon balm tea is useful for stomach upsets

caused by anxiety, especially when combined with chamomile tea.
- Eat oats or porridge, it's good for the nervous system.
- Rub a little oil of ylang ylang or lavender on your temples to reduce anxiety. Some people find these oils useful for tension headaches. You can also use a few drops in an atmospheric oil burner floating on water, or in the bath. (Whatever you do, don't swallow essential oils.)
- Rescue Remedy, a Bach flower essence available from health food shops and most natural therapists, is useful to relieve anxiety caused by one-off worrying events like exams or public speaking. It can also be used for sleeplessness caused by worry.

Improving sleep

This is a three-parter: dealing with the ease with which you get to sleep, the quality of the sleep and the time you wake up. Waking up too early, such as five o'clock every morning, can be a sign of depression and indicate a need for professional help.

- Cut out stimulating activities such as strenuous exercise or watching Alfred Hitchcock movies just before bed.
- Cut down or give up stimulants such as caffeine and sugar.
- Set up a relaxing bed-time routine such as having a lavender-scented bath and a warm drink like soya or cow's milk with honey.
- Establish a regular routine by going to bed at the same time.
- Go early. Many of the eastern traditions suggest that the two hours before midnight are the two most valuable hours of sleep to have.
- Avoid chemical sleeping tablets. Try over-the-counter herbal sleeping tablets, such as Nutricare's Kalms, which contain small amounts of valerian and other herbs that improve relaxation and shorten the length of time it takes to get to sleep. Because these tablets contain so little of the herb valerian, they do not cause drowsiness or fogginess in the head the next day.
- Too much vitamin B, especially B6, can cause wild dreams or nightmares. If you take vitamin B, take it in the mornings.
- If nothing works, get professional help.

Being underweight

Being underweight is a very common cause of period disruptions. It's defined as having a body-fat composition of less than 22 per cent. One of the ways to tell if body weight is within the normal range for your height is to calculate your Body Mass Index (BMI). You need to divide your weight in kilograms by your height in centimetres squared.

For example, if you weigh 52 kilos and your height is 1.7 metres, you divide the weight (52) by the square of your height (1.7 times 1.7 is 2.89). The answer to the calculation is 17.99. Rounded up to the nearest full number, your BMI is 18, and that puts you in the underweight category.

Roughly speaking, on the BMI scale:

- Less than 20 is considered to be underweight.
- 20–25 is normal.
- 26–30 is overweight.
- Over 30 is considered to be obese.

The BMI is only a guide, and if your body frame is very slight or very large, give yourself a bit of latitude. (You know the phrase, 'Big-boned girl'? This is where it comes in handy.) And don't forget that calculating your BMI means nothing at all until you've gained full height—that is after 18 or 20 years old.

Effects on the period

We each need fat to make up about 17 per cent of our total body weight, or we won't be able to have a period at all. We need about 22 per cent body fat to have periods regularly. On average, we stop having periods once our body-fat composition is below 20 per cent of our total body weight. Many underweight girls and women stop having periods, including sportswomen, gymnasts, ballet dancers and dieters.

When you're underweight, hormone levels drop, and ovulation stops as well as the period. Bones and other tissues which depend on oestrogens begin to weaken and may eventually fracture or crumble quite early in life, and menopausal symptoms may develop, including hot flushes and vaginal dryness.

Causes

Extreme weight loss can be caused by serious illnesses such as cancer, malabsorption syndromes and severe dysentery. The most common cause, though, is overexercising without eating enough good food. Young women who suddenly become vegetarian or vegan can sometimes lose too much weight if they don't know how to manage these diets properly. ('I'm a vegetarian—so I'll just have a packet of Twisties, some gummy bears and a milk shake.')

Some people believe that they should be very thin to be attractive, or healthy—both of these ideas are untrue. Sometimes they find it hard to believe that they are 'too thin' instead of needing to lose more weight. We need to understand that we are all meant to be different healthy, gorgeous shapes and sizes. And if you have stopped having periods and then when you put on some healthy weight your periods come back, it means you were too thin for you.

The Medical Approach, Natural Therapies & Self Care

- You'll be encouraged to understand what is a healthy weight range for you, individually and never mind what Cindy Crawford looks like—the woman has different genes entirely. (We pause here for a short plug for Kaz's book about how to feel good about your natural size and shape, *Real Gorgeous: The Truth About Body and Beauty,* published by Allen & Unwin.)
- Read the info on food and diet in the Self Care chapter of this book, and follow the advice. Don't let yourself go hungry.
- Don't go on short-term weight-loss or so-called 'purifying' diets! (More on this below.)

Eating disorders

These conditions can be very difficult to recognise because people with eating disorders often deny they have a problem, or have lost sight of reality for the moment, and try to hide their behaviour. If family or friends have noticed that the person is behaving in a worrying way, they may need to be quite persistent to get the person to seek help.

The symptoms which might indicate a problem include:

- Extreme weight loss and denial that weight gain is necessary.
- Going to the bathroom after eating, or long stays in the bathroom. Running the tap or flushing the toilet to disguise vomiting.
- An overwhelming fear of gaining weight.
- Constant 'weight-loss' dieting.
- An obsession with food—thinking and talking about food all the time.
- An unrealistic body image—feeling fat all the time and not being able to see your body weight is normal for you.
- Avoiding social situations which involve eating or saying 'I've just eaten' all the time.
- Overexercising.
- Checking weight on scales once a day or more often.
- Inability to concentrate or think clearly; depression.

For more information on treatment, support and advice, contact your local hospital or the anorexia and bulimia support group in your area (contact numbers are at the back of this book).

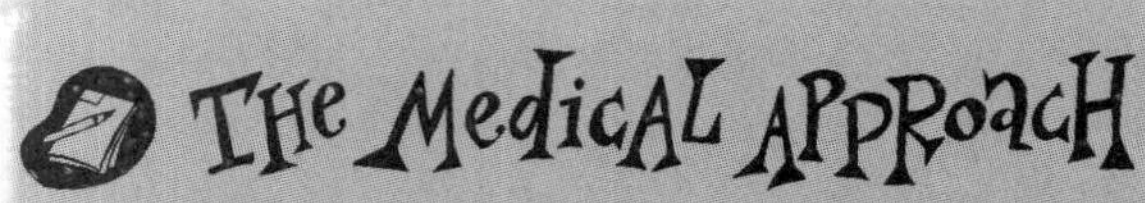

Anorexia and bulimia nervosa require some form of specialised counselling or therapy to help somebody change their perception of themselves and their relationship to food. This might be family therapy, individual counselling or group counselling. Very occasionally drug therapy is used for severe depression. Hospitalisation can become necessary in cases of life-threatening low weight. In the case of a well-advanced disorder, treatment can be very complex and long term. It is always best to start tackling the problem as soon as it's noticed.

GPs and general psychiatrists should refer patients to a specialist in eating disorders. Doctors can also refer patients to a dietitian to explain a balanced diet and the importance of the food groups. Sometimes a special diet will be needed to boost particular nutrient deficiencies.

Natural therapies

Natural therapies such as herbs, homoeopathics or diets can't fix eating disorders. People with these conditions need specialist counselling to help them recover, although natural remedies may help with some of the physical problems.

Zinc deficiency seems to play a major role in anorexia nervosa, and some research suggests that correcting zinc levels may help with stress in eating disorders.

Herbal groups such as the bitters and the nervines may be prescribed to assist with digestion, assimilation and stress. Hormone regulating herbs such as *Vitex agnus castus* may be given to regulate the period once you're back to a healthy weight. You may be given a general tonic and nutritive herbs such as *Eleuthrococcus senticosus* (Siberian ginseng) and *Medicago sativa* (alfalfa). All these herb categories are explored in the Natural Therapies chapter.

Eating plant oestrogens can help temporarily with low oestrogen symptoms, but they can never replace the effects of body-made oestrogens. There's more info under Plant Oestrogens in the Self Care chapter.

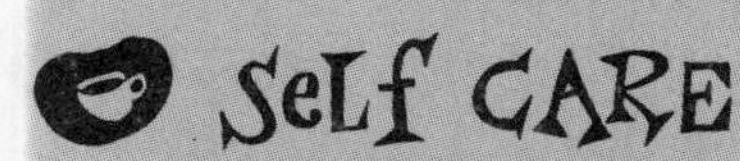

Don't expect to get over an eating disorder on your own—lots of people can help, including former sufferers who have made it through. There is an anorexia and bulimia support group in your

State or Territory, ready to help. There's a list of contacts, to help find them, at the back of the book.

Try to remember that while you think you're 'in control', actually your illness has taken over, and you need to accept help and get in control of your recovery.

There are many books that might help. One is called *Mary Jane* by Sancia Robinson, who regained her health after 15 years of anorexia and bulimia nervosa. For anyone over 13, it's published by Random House Australia and is good for friends and family, as well as people with an eating disorder.

Dieting and fasting

Effects on the period

Beware of fasting, raw food diets, 'elimination' diets and other types of purification promoted by the more feral fringe of the 'natural health' movement. Some people believe that being healthy is a mysterious, tortuous process which involves a restricted diet, if not a complete fast.

Some natural therapists are very fond of these strategies to 'improve' health and a number of books bang on about the virtues of a 'clean' diet and correct way to eliminate 'toxins' from the system. Some natural therapists assume everyone is 'toxic' (a rather rubbery term) which causes all illness (an even more dubious concept).

This can be music to the ears of those who believe that periods are somehow impure. The argument—usually implied—is that if you have difficult periods, or bleed heavily, or even have periods at all, you're in some way 'toxic' and in need of a purifying regime. Someone ought to tell them the Middle Ages is, like, over.

The proponents of this dotty theory quite happily tell their patients to fast or use extreme elimination diets to reduce or stop period flow. Restricted diets *do* reduce or stop periods, not because the body is cleansed or purified—but because the body weight is too low to ovulate and get a period. Too much fibre in the diet can cause light periods and damage bone density because it reduces the availability of oestrogen.

Sometimes a long deficiency of iron and vitamin B12 can cause anaemia and heavy periods. This can also be caused by diets that result in a deficiency in bioflavonoids and vitamin A.

Self Care

- Avoid short-term diets of any kind unless they are for a special, therapeutic reason such as treating irritable bowel syndrome. They should always be used with professional supervision.
- Steer clear of food-fad theories which don't include food from all food groups, whether they're in magazines, 'natural health' literature or advice from practitioners. Be especially scornful of 'one food'-type diets, like all fruit and vegetable or all cheese or all banana daiquiris.
- Remember that short-term diets to reduce weight are unsuccessful: the weight always comes back. A long-term change in eating habits is needed, with the aim of gradual change.
- As a general rule, don't even think about fasting.
- Any weight-loss program must include sensible exercise.

Being obese

This is nothing to do with 'feeling too fat'. And it is a different category to overweight. 'Obese' is a medical definition that is probably best diagnosed by applying the Body Mass Index (BMI) calculations. Here they are again: you need to divide your weight in kilograms by your height squared.

For example, if you weigh 92 kilos and your height is 1.7 metres, you divide the weight (92) by the square of your height (1.7 times 1.7 is 2.89). The answer to the calculation is 31.83. Rounded up to the nearest full number, your BMI is 32, and that puts you in the obese category. (As a rough guide, a BMI less than 20 is underweight; 20–25 is normal; 26–30 is overweight; and over 30 is obese.)

Remember that the BMI is not gospel, and doesn't take into account how big your frame is. And the BMI can't be done until you've gained full height—usually after age 20. It means nothing on a teenager.

Effects on the period

Obesity can cause heavier periods, and alter the menstrual cycle in unpredictable ways. It also gives you an increased risk of breast and endometrial cancer, because more oestrogen is made in the fat cells and those cancers are linked to high oestrogen levels. Usually, obesity will also mean a low level of sex hormone binding globulins in the blood, and this can mean that androgen hormones are freed up to cause symptoms like excess hairiness.

The Medical Approach

Some doctors prescribe diet pills, but most doctors are coming to realise the dangerous side effects of diet pills including liver damage, drug dependence and wild mood swings. Doctors will usually recommend long-term adjustment of eating habits and a program of exercise. Short-term weight-loss diets are notoriously unsuccessful, and there is evidence that they actually encourage extra weight gain because of changes to the body's metabolism.

Natural Therapies

Natural therapists should also focus on long-term diet changes and exercise. Herbs are not a weight-loss method in themselves, despite what some people claim, and shouldn't be prescribed as such.

Self Care

- Don't go on short-term diets.
- Beware of all the 'quick fix' methods advertised such as so-called 'slimming teas' and 'meal replacements'. There is no magic potion.

- A nutritionist can help set you up with a long-term eating plan and exercise program. Your doctor can refer you to somebody local.
- If there is an underlying psychological problem you'd like to tackle, seek professional help from a specialist counsellor.

Not exercising at all

Effects on the period

Not exercising at all isn't much good for anything. Exercise can reduce or fix period pain, improve PMS symptoms and even reduce period flow.

Regular exercise cuts the incidence of other gynaecological problems too, and may lower the risk of endometriosis because it probably slows down oestrogen production. The incidence of endometriosis increases among women who lead bum-sitting lives and among younger women who stop exercising earlier than their peers. Premenstrual sore breasts and cystic disease of the breast are also less likely if you exercise moderately and regularly.

Self Care

We pause for a short disclaimer: in case you already have a medical condition, check with your health professional before suddenly hurling yourself about in a frenzy of exercising. Now: the 'moderate exercise' needed to get benefits in the menstrual department might be as little as half an hour a few times a week; period pain and PMS can even improve if you exercise only during the week leading up to the period.

- Exercise which increases the heart rate (aerobic exercise) like walking, swimming, cycling, jogging, team sports or aerobics deliver the most all-round benefits, but anything will do.
- Specific yoga exercises which improve pelvic blood flow can be a great help with period pain. Yoga often includes relaxation skills,

useful to help cope with pain and PMS. These exercises can be taught by a yoga teacher or learned from a book with specific exercises for the pelvic region.

- The best de-stressing exercise is long, slow, distance exercise (called LSD, apparently, if you can believe it). This is when rhythmic and repetitive exercise, usually walking, bike-riding or swimming, is sustained at a moderate pace for between 45 minutes and an hour. This calms the nerves, shuts off the inappropriate adrenal response and improves stamina.
- Any weight-bearing exercise, but particularly types which stress the large muscles, has the potential to improve bone mass. The best types are walking, running or playing sport. Swimming and cycling are still important even though they are not classically included in the weight-bearing group. For maximum benefit, exercise should be daily or every second day for about an hour.
- Staying fit and active is important for older women too. Muscle strength and physical fitness increases bone mineral density, improves agility, and cardiovascular health, and reduces your chances of falling and serious injury.
- For beginners, quick walking for half to one hour every second day and then every day as stamina improves is an easy way to start. *Instant Vitality*, an exercise program written by Debbie Flintoff-King (published by Anne O'Donovan), is a good book with advice for a varied fitness program.

Too much exercise

Effects on the period

Overexercising can cause many problems with the menstrual cycle throughout life. In teenagers it can delay the period and puberty, including growing to normal height. Infertility is also common because ovulation is either erratic or stops. Another big worry is the possibility of irreversible changes to bone density. This can lead to a failure to reach peak bone mass, reduced bone density, spinal curvature and stress fractures in the bones.

Women who engage in strenuous physical activity *during* the period have an increased risk of endometriosis, thought to be related to the increased amount of blood going back up the Fallopian tubes.

If you do prolonged, over-rigorous or endurance exercise, a reversible oestrogen deficiency can develop, which stops ovulation and periods. This could be the body's way of avoiding pregnancy in times of stress and physical endurance.

This stopping of the period by overexercising can be influenced by other factors:

- Young women who start to overexercise before their first period or before their cycle is properly established are inclined to delay their first period. And if the heavy training starts about the same time as the first period, a history of missed periods is more likely to develop.
- If you already have irregular menstrual cycles, light periods or missed periods, overexercising will continue the problem.
- If you're underweight or you lose heaps of weight during training you'll be more likely to get period irregularities.
- Not getting enough kilojoules or minerals to replace what exercising uses up will increase the chances of period disorders.
- The further you run, the more likely you are to get problems with your period. Women who run more than 80 kilometres per week are more likely to have no periods.
- Runners, gymnasts and ballet dancers are more likely to have no periods than swimmers.

The Medical Approach

If you are 'addicted' to exercise or do too much, you may need to be referred for specialist counselling. If you have prolonged period irregularities or absent periods, consider the Pill if your bone density is also low.

Natural Therapies & Self Care

- Don't overdo it.
- Athletes need to eat a balanced diet and enough of it to maintain enough body fat, still get their period and protect bone density. This is often in conflict with coaching advice and sometimes a decision must be made between continuing wellbeing and sporting goals. The Self Care chapter has 20 Diet Hints to help.
- During exercise you have an increased need for most minerals, especially calcium, iron, zinc, magnesium and potassium. A deficiency may contribute to the delayed physical development and period problems. Take calcium supplements in the range of 1–1.5 grams a day—the higher range is necessary when periods are erratic or stopped. Info pages on calcium, zinc, iron and magnesium are under Minerals in the Self Care chapter.
- Endurance training will need to be balanced by additional complex carbohydrates to meet the kilojoule requirements.
- See the dietary advice under Not Enough Oestrogen in the Hormones chapter.
- Including plant oestrogens in the diet may also be a help. There's a whole section on these plant oestrogens in the Self Care chapter.

Prescribed drugs

Effects on the period

Some drugs increase period flow, others reduce it; some influence the regularity of the cycle; and some can even stop periods temporarily. Not all drug influences are negative—some drugs are deliberately prescribed to re-establish period flow and regularity; and to reduce pain or heavy flow. There is more info on them, including possible side effects, under Drugs in The Medical Approach chapter.

Oral contraceptives (the Pill). The Pill is used for many gynaecological conditions, not just as a contraceptive. It reduces period flow and period pain, and establishes more regular cycles.

Progestogens. These drugs are commonly prescribed for endometriosis and abnormal bleeding. They can often cause bloating, fluid retention, weight gain and mood changes (not generally known as a real *party* drug, your progestogens).

Gonadotrophin releasing hormone agonists (GnRH agonists). These drugs cause a temporary menopausal state which causes stopped periods, menopausal symptoms and a loss of bone density. They are used for fibroids and endometriosis, and their use for PMS and benign breast disease is under review.

Corticosteroids. The corticosteroids, used most often in cases of severe asthma or auto-immune disease, can cause period irregularities or no periods, and androgenising (male hormone-like) effects. Loss of bone density is a common and serious side effect from long-term corticosteroid therapy. The common types of corticosteroids are prednisolone (Solone), hydrocortisone (Hysone), betamethasone (Celestone) and dexamethasone (Decadron).

Prostaglandins-inhibiting drugs. The prostaglandins synthetase inhibitors, like Ponstan and Naprogesic, are used for period pain and occasionally for heavy periods as well. Sometimes they can delay the onset of the period and their use is linked to an increased risk of gastrointestinal ulcers.

Anti-coagulant drugs. Drugs which affect clotting time can occasionally increase period flow. These include Calciparine, Dindevan, heparin and warfarin.

Cytotoxic drugs. The cytotoxic drugs which are used in the treatment of cancer, such as cyclophosphamide, chlorambucil, mechlorethamine and vincristine, can lead to infertility, irregular periods, no periods and premature menopause.

Tamoxifen. Tamoxifen is an anti-oestrogen in the treatment of breast cancer, and sometimes for benign breast disease. It can cause menopause-like symptoms, and sometimes, abnormal vaginal bleeding and irregular periods.

Drugs which affect prolactin levels. The drugs which affect prolactin levels can interfere with the menstrual cycle. They are discussed under hyperprolactinaemia, in the Stopped Periods section of this chapter.

Self Care

- Make yourself aware of any effects on your cycle likely to be caused by drugs you have been prescribed. Change drugs if you can.
- Ask your doctor or natural therapist to help you offset any annoying or avoidable side effects.

Other drugs

Effects on the period

All 'social' and illegal drugs can affect hormones. These effects can translate into more serious problems such as osteoporosis and infertility.

Coffee is linked to infertility. It can increase period pain especially if you drink it while you have your period. If you have endometriosis, too much alcohol can stop ovulation and cause infertility, and grog increases the risk of developing endometriosis by about 50 per cent. Alcoholism increases the chance of early menopause, and can also increase prolactin production. These complaints can be related to erratic cycles, heavy or stopped periods.

Cigarette smoking lowers oestrogen levels, and is related to an increased incidence of irregular periods, infertility and earlier menopause.

Cocaine can elevate prolactin levels and cause abnormal menstrual cycles.

Methadone (and possibly other opiates) increases prolactin levels, but doesn't seem to have long-term effects on ovulation.

Self Care

- Knock it off.
- Okay, it's not that easy. But you might be surprised at how much help is available, including support groups of other people who've been through it. Many counselling and other services are available. You can start with the Drug and Alcohol Foundation in your area or your local hospital or doctor.

Functional hypoglycaemia

When things go right, you eat a well-balanced meal which causes your blood sugar levels to become pleasantly elevated. Then there is a gently undulating decline of the blood sugar levels until the next well-balanced meal, so the levels are always pretty stable.

But if you eat too much sugar or easily metabolised food, the blood sugar levels go way up really quickly—you know, that buzzy feeling. So the body overcompensates, dropping the blood sugar levels too low—and suddenly you feel exhausted and crabby and hungry even though you had a Mars Bar just a while ago.

Then when you eat again, the whole pattern is repeated, and you're on the roller-coaster called functional hypoglycaemia. Hypoglycaemia just means low blood sugar levels. Functional hypoglycaemia refers to the up and down effect. (Functional hypoglycaemia often comes with other complaints, caused by long periods of stress or anxiety. These include chronic fatigue syndrome and post-viral fatigue syndrome.)

Heaps of different symptoms can be caused by hypoglycaemia. True hypoglycaemia should start to respond to the suggested diet within a week. If it doesn't, other reasons for the symptoms should be sought. For example, if you are snapping at your boyfriend, do you need a new boyfriend?

Symptoms

- Tiredness, vagueness or shakiness which goes away when you eat.

- Tiredness or irritability first thing in the morning if meals are late.
- Sugar cravings.
- Being hungry all the time or soon after eating.
- Headaches when meals are delayed.
- Inappropriate feelings of anxiety or inadequacy which disappear after eating.
- Waking up in the night feeling really hungry.

Effects on the period

Functional hypoglycaemia can be wrongly assumed to be PMS, because it, too, causes tiredness and mood swings.

Causes

Many things can bring on functional hypoglycaemia including prolonged periods of stress, a number of dietary factors affecting blood sugar levels including too much refined carbohydrates and sugars, hitting the grog without eating at the same time, or drinking alcohol with sugar-based mixers. In other words, a glass of wine at dinner is probably fine, but go easier on ordering the Fluffy Poindexter Cointreau and cream pineapple daiquiri rocket fuel cocktail in a coconut shell with three paper umbrellas. Especially if you want to eat the paper umbrellas.

People who go on short-term diets often get hypoglycaemia because their diets are badly designed and don't provide enough energy. Starving, they 'break out' and eat large amounts of starchy or sugary foods. The rapid drop in blood sugar starts a pattern of sugar craving, hypoglycaemic symptoms, and weight gain. The hypoglycaemic diet is a successful way to lose weight slowly and progressively because it breaks the cycle of 'fast and feast'.

Diagnosis

Health practitioners will usually exclude other possibilities as the cause of your symptoms, and see how you respond to treatment for hypoglycaemia.

- The most effective treatment for functional hypoglycaemia is changing what and how you eat. Follow the hypoglycaemic diet, in the Self Care chapter, very strictly for about three weeks and then you can be a bit more relaxed with it, depending on the severity of the problem and how your body responds to the new diet.
- Chromium, niacinamide, and magnesium supplements improve functional hypoglycaemia. Some commercially available formulas are specially designed to treat blood sugar problems, and may contain a combination of minerals and vitamins. Follow the instructions on the bottle.

PMS: The premenstrual syndrome

Aarrrgghhhhhhh!!! Ah yes, the rallying cry of premenstrual women everywhere and here's the rallying cry of the people who have to live with them: 'Get out of the house! Save yourselves!' There are some women who sail through the time before their period being unbelievably jolly and robust, and for the purposes of this chapter we shall ignore them entirely.

Usually in the week or two before their period, premenstrual women can become grumpy, tearful, have a bloated stomach and breasts, get ravenous cravings for Tim Tams, any other sort of food and maybe when that runs out, the furniture, come over all fainty or clumsy or self-hating and generally feel like the world is ending and it's probably not such a bad idea come to think of it. There are many families, housemates and partners who mark red-letter days in their calendar or hang a red scarf from the kitchen light fitting to warn everyone of the vile horrors to be expected.

The good news is that most premenstrual symptoms can be treated—once the right treatment for the individual symptoms is worked out.

PMS (premenstrual syndrome) and PMT (premenstrual tension) are really interchangeable terms, but some people use the term PMT to describe only the emotional symptoms—like tension, irritability and tearfulness. To avoid this confusion, we'll go with PMS to describe both the emotional and physical symptoms known to the vast scary army of the premenstrual.

Originally, premenstrual symptoms were thought to have bizarre origins. One of the more outrageous ones, believed by doctors in medieval times, was the theory of the wandering womb. That's right, the uterus was believed to just potter around the body looking for a baby. While on its amblings, it might cause symptoms of 'hysteria' (*hystera* is Greek for uterus) and suffocation if it was hanging around the chest, or a choking sensation if it lodged in the throat. Of course when it tootled back to its rightful spot each month, the symptoms would resolve and a period would begin.

While it was a pretty weird idea, this explanation at least gave the women who developed PMS some credibility for their symptoms. Not so between about 1900 and the 1970s when conventional medical wisdom decided that PMS was a problem of 'nerves', not coping, or even—you guessed it, hysteria. Women were often prescribed tranquillisers.

Today we are no closer to a definitive answer, but we know the symptoms exist and we know how to alleviate them. We know that symptoms only happen during those cycles when you've ovulated, they go away when the period starts, and stop altogether after menopause. Hormonal factors have been suggested as the cause but tests have not been developed to identify which group of hormones create the symptoms. Many explanations remain guesses, educated or otherwise.

Symptoms

We mightn't know exactly what causes it, but we know how it makes us feel. A rather ostentatious 150 different symptoms have been recorded in association with PMS. Luckily, no-one gets all of them at once. Most women have their own little collection of regular PMS symptoms, with the occasional extra one. Symptoms might also change after a major biological event—such as childbirth or illness—and you tend to develop different types of symptoms as you approach menopause. Premenstrual headaches, for example, can become more common.

But it is the timing that tells whether you have PMS. There should be no symptoms in the week after the period, but symptoms appearing at any time in the two weeks before a period, and then declining when the period starts.

Most common physical symptoms

- abdominal distension, bloating and discomfort
- breast swelling, pain, discomfort and/or painful, benign breast lumps
- headaches
- abnormal appetite, craving for sweet foods, alcohol and/or fatty foods
- fatigue and weakness
- weight gain of more than 2 kilos
- fluid retention
- premenstrual acne
- joint pains and/or backache
- pelvic discomfort or pain
- increased incidence of upper respiratory tract infections, including sinusitis and recurrent colds
- premenstrual genital herpes outbreaks, recurrent vaginal thrush and/or other infections
- change in bowel habit
- palpitations
- dizziness or fainting
- altered libido.

Most common emotional and mental symptoms

- nervous tension
- irritability
- depression
- confusion
- lack of concentration
- insomnia
- mood swings
- anxiety
- tearfulness
- aggression
- forgetfulness

PMS sub-groups

To try and break it down a bit, PMS has been divided into five sub-groups by a research doctor, each based on a different hormonal, biochemical and/or nutritional cause. They are:

- PMS A (A for anxiety) associated with nervousness and irritability;
- PMS C (C for cravings) related to premenstrual sugar cravings and hypoglycaemic symptoms;
- PMS D (D for depression) associated with depression and withdrawal;
- PMS H (H for hyperhydration) where fluid retention is the main symptom; and
- PMS P (P pain).

Some women with PMS may recognise themselves in more than one of the sub-groups. Treatment for each one is set out below.

Theories about the causes

There is no definitive answer about why PMS happens. Theories we've got. Theories about abnormal hormone levels, ranging from oestrogen to progesterone ratios, faulty progesterone receptors, too many adrenal hormones, too much prolactin. There are theories about misbehaving prostaglandins. One wackier theory says it's all caused by candida (thrush).

There's theories about biochemical pathways, theories about nutrient deficiencies or inappropriate diet. A whole lot of nutrient deficiencies have been given a guernsey, including vitamin B6, vitamin E, and vitamin A, although studies haven't always agreed.

Research has shown that magnesium and vitamin E are the most useful, although B6 is most often prescribed. (Doses of vitamin B6 should be kept to safe levels—between 2 and 6 grams a day for more than a year can cause reversible nerve damage.)

We've got theories that PMS is caused by mixed-up brain chemistry, or psychological problems and there's even a 'multi-factorial model'. This sounds like a model who can pose and fit hub-caps at the same time, but actually means a theory which incorporates hormonal, dietary, lifestyle and emotional factors. There's even a theory that premenstrual aliens came to earth and . . . well, okay, we made that one up.

Diagnosis

There are no blood tests that can diagnose PMS. The best diagnostic method is to photocopy and fill in the menstrual symptom diary which outlines the classical symptoms: it's on page 24 in the When Things Go Right chapter. The diary should reveal the timing which suggests PMS—no symptoms after the period; and an increase in symptoms in the two weeks before the period. It may help you find your category of PMS, or rule out PMS.

Mistaken identity

Functional hypoglycaemia

Functional hypoglycaemia can be easily confused with PMS because of the similarity of the symptoms. If functional hypoglycaemia is the problem, the symptoms will not vary dramatically during the month. You can read all about it under The Usual Suspects.

Depression and anxiety

Some women seeking treatment for PMS, genuinely believing that their mood swings are 'hormonal' find instead they have 'menstrual distress syndrome' or 'menstrual magnification'. Their symptoms are present all month, but get worse before a period. A really useful treatment must tackle the anxiety or depressive state.

The Medical Approach

The medical treatment of PMS concentrates on relieving symptoms with diuretics for retained fluid (they can make you wee what seems about a million times so don't take them at night), prostaglandins-inhibiting drugs or anti-depressants. The other medical focus is on the manipulation of the hormones with drugs that disrupt ovulation (the Pill, Danazol, GnRH agonists) because if you don't ovulate you don't get PMS, or selectively target one of the abnormal hormones (Bromocriptine). These drugs are explained in the section on drugs in The Medical Approach chapter.

Just treating the symptoms is not acceptable for many women and hormonal manipulation can have risks and side effects, so many doctors lean towards the natural therapy approach, and suggest drug therapy only if you don't respond.

Natural Therapies

Treatments for PMS are based on the five different sub-categories of PMS and are composed of a mixture of supplements and dietary advice, herbal remedies and lifestyle changes. Herbs are more fully explored in the Natural Therapies chapter.

PMS A (A for anxiety)

This type of PMS is thought to be related to a relative oestrogen/progesterone imbalance, with a relative excess of oestrogen and a relative deficiency of progesterone, possibly related to poor liver clearance of oestrogens, abnormal progesterone production or faulty progesterone receptors.

Symptoms

- nervous tension
- irritability
- mood swings
- anxiety

Treatment

- You may be prescribed a herbal extract of *Vitex agnus castus*

That time of the month

berries starting on the first day of the cycle and continuing for between three and six months.

- Vitamin B6: 100–200 milligrams, or vitamin B complex containing 50 milligrams of vitamin B6 for ten to 14 days before the period.
- Magnesium: 200–800 milligrams daily of elemental magnesium in the form of magnesium phosphate, aspartate, orotate or chelate.
- Nervines such as *Valeriana officinalis* (valerian), *Scutellaria laterifolia* (skullcap), *Matricaria recutita* (chamomile) for anxiety.
- *Withania somnifera* for anxiety with exhaustion.
- *Anemone pulsatilla* tincture is especially useful for tension headache with nervousness, especially when combined with *Passiflora incarnata* (passionflower).
- *Betonica officinalis* (wood betony) is used for headache and extreme anxiety, especially in combination with *Scutellaria laterifolia* (skullcap).
- *Bupleurum falcatum*, *Paeonia lactiflora* and *Angelica sinensis* is a common combination used in Chinese medicine for irregular periods with premenstrual anxiety and irritability.
- Plant oestrogens in foods and herbs (more info on plant oestrogens is in the Self Care chapter).
- Herbal and dietary bitters to aid liver clearance of oestrogens.
- Restriction of dairy products and sugar.
- 'Natural' progesterone creams, claimed to be made from plants such as *Dioscorea villosa* (wild yam) are sometimes advocated for the treatment of PMS, but the jury is still out on whether they help. For more info on this, see Not Enough Progesterone in the Hormones chapter.

PMS C (C for cravings)

PMS C rarely exists as a form of PMS in isolation and often comes with PMS A. It's linked to functional hypoglycaemia which may be caused by a magnesium deficiency, a sugar-induced sensitivity to insulin, or an imbalance in prostaglandins.

Symptoms

- headache
- increased appetite
- fatigue
- craving for sweets
- palpitations
- dizziness or fainting

Treatment

Blood sugar:

- Magnesium: 200–800 milligrams daily of elemental magnesium in the form of magnesium phosphate, aspartate, orotate or chelate.
- Small meals often.
- Restricted sugar and salt intake.
- Dietary and herbal bitters to regulate blood sugar metabolism.

Balancing prostaglandins:

- Essential fatty acid supplements, such as evening primrose oil or star flower oil. Doses of 3 grams of evening primrose oil containing 216 milligrams of linoleic acid and 27 milligrams of gamma linoleic acid (GLA) or the equivalent taken daily from mid-cycle until the period may be useful in regulating prostaglandins.You'll need vitamin B6 and zinc to make it work. Diet can also be altered to take in more essential fatty acids. (See Bad Fats and Good Fats, number 8 of 20 Diet Hints in the Self Care chapter.)
- Vitamin E: between 100 and 600 International Units (IU) daily can also help balance prostaglandins.

PMS D (D for depression)

This form of PMS is accompanied by depression and withdrawal and is thought to be related to relative oestrogen deficiency. The causes might include lower oestrogen production around the menopause; a depleted oestrogen pool caused by being too thin or eating too much fibre; blocked oestrogen receptors caused by high lead levels; or a progesterone level which is relatively too high.

Symptoms

- depression
- crying
- insomnia
- forgetfulness
- confusion

Treatment

- Magnesium: 200–800 milligrams daily of elemental magnesium in the form of magnesium phosphate, aspartate, orotate or chelate, to decrease lead absorption and retention.
- Eat plant oestrogens (see the plant oestrogen section of the Self Care chapter for more info).
- The 'oestrogenic herbs' which contain steroidal saponins such as *Chamaelirium luteum* (helonias), *Aletris farinosa* (true unicorn root), *Dioscorea villosa* (wild yam), as well as *Angelica sinensis* (Dang Gui) and *Paeonia lactiflora* (white peony).
- *Cimicifuga racemosa*, especially if you get premenstrual headaches.
- *Hypericum perforatum* and *Withania somnifera* for symptomatic treatment of depression.

PMS H (H for hyperhydration)

PMS H is related to fluid retention thought to be brought about by an increase in the adrenal hormone, aldosterone, which is responsible for salt and water retention. This may be a response to lower progesterone secretion, too much oestrogen, magnesium deficiency, other hormone irregularities, or stress. Prolactin may be implicated when breast soreness is a big symptom.

Symptoms

- breast tenderness
- weight gain
- bloating
- swelling in lower body and eyelids

Treatment

- All treatments for PMS A and those for prostaglandins in PMS C,

especially vitamin E: 100–600 IU daily, if breast tenderness is a problem.
- *Taraxacum officinale* leaf (dandelion leaf) as a tea is a mild diuretic and reduces fluid retention. Herbal diuretic tablets are also available.

PMS P (P for pain)

In this category of PMS, the major problem is an increased sensitivity to pain which is believed to be caused by a prostaglandins imbalance. Causes are thought to be elevated oestrogen levels, or eating too much animal fat.

Symptoms

- aches and pains
- reduced pain threshold
- period pain

Treatment

- Magnesium reduces sensitivity to pain in doses of 200–800 milligrams a day.
- Essential fatty acids such as evening primrose oil, 3 grams a day, with vitamin B6 and zinc, in doses prescribed by a practitioner. Diet can also be altered to take in more essential fatty acids. (See Bad Fats and Good Fats, number 8 of 20 Diet Hints in the Self Care chapter.)
- The herb *Tanacetum parthenium* (feverfew) is a prostaglandins-inhibitor and may help period pain and migraine headaches if taken long term.

Diet

All types of PMS seem to improve with dietary changes:

- Increase the intake of complex carbohydrates (there's more info on this in the 20 Diet Hints in the Self Care chapter).

- Eat more often—a 'grazing' or hypoglycaemic diet (see the hypoglycaemic diet in the Self Care chapter). Little meals more often is the go. The positive effects may be related to stabilisation of blood sugars as well as to indirect influences on progesterone.
- When fluid retention, bloating and weight gain are problems, cut down on salt—most processed foods, including cheese, are high in salt. Also eat vegetables, grapefruit juice and bananas for potassium.
- If you have breast soreness, muscle or joint pains or period pain you'll probably respond well to reducing animal fats, processed vegetable oils, coconut, and increasing essential fatty acids and vitamin E. (Essential fatty acids are explained under Bad Fats and Good Fats, number 8 of the 20 Diet Hints in the Self Care chapter.)
- Coffee, alcohol, and chocolate aggravate feelings of depression, irritability and anxiety, as well as worsening many breast symptoms. Leave them alone during the premenstrual phase.
- Many of the symptoms of PMS have been attributed to magnesium deficiency (there's a magnesium info page in the Minerals section of the Self Care chapter). If that sounds like you, eat more magnesium-containing foods and restrict dairy products.
- PMS related to high oestrogen levels relative to other hormones means you need to eat more plant oestrogens. Plant oestrogens also improve symptoms of a rapid decline of oestrogens just before the period such as headaches, migraines and depression. (There's a whole section on plant oestrogens in the Self Care chapter.)

Exercise and stress management

Women with PMS who use long slow distance exercise or yoga seem better at handling their physical PMS symptoms. There are some suggestions on managing stress in The Usual Suspects section at the start of this chapter.

Period pain

There are legions of washed-out looking women clutching hot-water bottles to their stomachs, dragging around the joint in dressing-gowns and making sure they never run out of painkillers—the ones with 'cramps', or period pain. 'It's that time of the month', they mutter, and everyone nods sympathetically, without even suggesting that a filthy old dressing-gown is not a good look at 4 pm. Is this something we have to put up with? (The pain, not the dressing-gown.)

Nope. The bottom line here is that pain is, well, a pain. Pain makes people tired and crabby and more likely to go see their health practitioner than any other symptom—maybe it's caused by a disease, maybe by a disorder, maybe by just a slight hormone imbalance that's easy to fix.

Lots of people, some of them doctors and natural therapists, think that a bit of period pain is normal. Patients get used to hearing stuff like, 'Grin and bear it', that hoary old chestnut 'It will be better once you have a baby', and even 'It's just part of being a woman'. Bollocks. It's not something you should put up with, or expect as part of your womanly life. (You're a woman now, and you will have period pain and an automatic instinct for the correct hat for every occasion? Not very scientific.)

The thing is, a bit of period pain is *usual*, but just because it's common, doesn't mean that it's normal or nothing to worry about. The most important thing about persistent period pain is to find out what's causing it. If your treatments for the pain aren't working, get investigative—it could be a warning from your body about something serious.

The two questions to ask about period pain are: 'Does it bother you enough to want/need to do something about it?' If not, you are excused. Go and sit in the corner and try on some hats until the end of this section. If your period pain is enough to make you do something about it, here's another question: 'Are you happy with the treatments you are using?' If not, read on. It may be well worth your while: after all, on average you have 12 or 13 periods a year, and if you get pain for two or three days, that adds up to a month of pain each year: yikes.

Doctors often call period pain dysmenorrhoea. It sounds rather disgusting, but is basically just ancient Greek for painful periods—*dys* meaning difficulty with, and *menorrhoea* meaning to do with menstruation. It's pronounced Dis-men-oh-rear. Dysmenorrhoea is a symptom, not a disease—so the first aspect of any successful treatment is to find out why you're getting pain.

Period pain falls into two major categories:

- The uterine muscle is behaving abnormally and causing cramps, but is otherwise healthy. This is called naughty uterus. No, it's actually called primary dysmenorrhoea. (Primary dysmenorrhoea is sometimes also called functional dysmenorrhoea. Are they just deliberately trying to confuse us or just SHOWING OFF?)
- A disease of an organ or organs which has pain as one of its symptoms. This is called secondary dysmenorrhoea. Common causes of secondary dysmenorrhoea include endometriosis and pelvic inflammatory disease (PID).

But sometimes primary dysmenorrhoea can cause really bad pain and secondary dysmenorrhoea is not so bad—that is, really bad pain doesn't automatically mean you have a disease—in fact in some cases disease doesn't cause pain—PID is often called a 'silent' disease because in many cases you don't even know you've got it until you're being tested for infertility.

Before treating your period pain, make sure you get a diagnosis of primary or secondary dysmenorrhoea from your health practitioner. The way doctors diagnose this is explained below. If you have secondary dysmenorrhoea, you can get some helpful information from this section, and also check out the section more relevant to your particular problem, for example, endometriosis, or adenomyosis. (Make sure your doctor rules out pelvic inflammatory disease.)

Causes of 'ordinary' period pain

By this, we mean primary dysmenorrhoea, the period pain which is caused by a naughty uterus, not by an underlying 'nasty', like a disease.

A problem with uterine tone

First, a word about where 'cramps' come from. When you have a period, the uterus helps to get the blood out through the cervix and down the vagina by having small contractions.

These muscle contractions continue all the time, even when the uterus is apparently at rest. You just can't feel it. During a period, or childbirth, the uterine activity is amplified many times, but if the period contractions are normal, the pain is not a problem.

The 'resting phase' or 'resting tone' between contractions is important. Normally, the blood flowing through the uterine muscle carries oxygen and other nutrients. When the muscle doesn't rest, the lack of oxygen supply leads to muscle spasm: in other words, cramps. Some women compare this kind of period pain to labour pains. Sometimes the cramping can get so bad it causes severe pain before the period. This usually gets better once the period starts.

Many women also develop diarrhoea, needing to wee all the time, or vomiting—all this is because of the reflex spasm in nearby organs.

The opposite problem can be caused by poor muscle tone in the uterus, accompanied by heavy bleeding or 'flooding' during the period. There may be a sense of heaviness or pelvic congestion, often described as dull, dragging heaviness. Lack of tone can be caused by many pregnancies, recent childbirth and conditions which prevent adequate contraction of the uterus, for example, fibroids, polyps and adenomyosis.

A prostaglandins imbalance

The cause of cramping is usually an imbalance in the prostaglandins levels. Oh, don't get us started on prostaglandins, they are hideously complicated critters (for the whole shebang, check out the Prostaglandins section in the Hormones chapter). Suffice to say that prostaglandins are hormone-like substances which are found in most body tissues. Lots of different prostaglandins control several bodily functions by working together as an integrated team. When the prostaglandins are all in balance, the period runs smoothly. But if there are too many of the kind of prostaglandins which increase muscle spasm, then you'll get period cramps.

Symptoms

You name it. Period pain can vary dramatically from person to person, and even from period to period. Some have severe pain that feels sharp, or maybe dull. Others have pain that comes in fits and starts. The most common description of period pain is a continual, dull, 'background' ache or sense of heaviness (someone came over all Greek and called it congestive dysmenorrhoea), also accompanied by episodes of cramping pain (spasmodic dysmenorrhoea).

The pain is usually central and under the navel. Sometimes a heavy aching pain extends to the groin, the back, and down the thighs. Most often, the pain that starts before you see the first blood of the period is congestive and aching. Sometimes this sort of pain is accompanied by a heavy dull sense of dragging in the vagina or a sense of fullness in the bowel. This is the feeling often described as though 'everything will fall out'. (You'll be relieved to know it never does.)

Most often, though, the pain starts with the first blood of the period and intensifies as the flow becomes heavier, or when clots are in the period blood. Usually the spasmodic, crampy-type pain is the shortest part of the pain but it feels the worst.

All that contracting can annoy the neighbours—and the bowel is just next door to the uterus. The bowel tends to be affected by hormone changes too. Many women become constipated before their period and this can exacerbate the sense of fullness and heaviness felt with congestive period pain. Irritable bowel syndrome aggravates period pain and is aggravated *by* it. The bowel and uterus share a similar nerve supply and when either organ is in spasm, the other will spasm in sympathy.

Diagnosis

Diagnosing primary dysmenorrhoea is about exclusion—ruling out other complaints as the origin of the pain. To do this, a health practitioner needs to consider the individual features of your medical, menstrual and obstetric history; your age; and your level and manner of sexual activity. For example, if you've had sex without a condom you have a higher risk of pelvic inflammatory disease, and older women are more likely to have adenomyosis than younger women.

The history of the pain gives other important hints. Relevant clues include: where it is; how long it lasts; which other symptoms accompany the pain; whether it radiates; what treatments have already failed; and whether the pain happens mostly before, during or after bleeding. If you keep a diary which keeps track of these symptoms you will help the diagnosis.

Pelvic examinations

A doctor may suggest an internal examination of the pelvic organs. This usually involves looking at the cervix to see whether it looks normal and healthy, and examining the pelvic organs by inserting a gloved hand into the vagina to feel the size, state and position of the organs. The doctor will be looking for secondary causes of period pain such as an enlarged ovary or uterus, which suggests a problem. Pelvic exams and the reasons they are performed are described in the Screening section of The Medical Approach chapter.

Laparoscopy

Sometimes surgery is needed to make a diagnosis—the operation is usually a laparoscopy (a description of a laparoscopy is in the Surgery section of The Medical Approach chapter). It is often recommended if the history is suggestive of secondary causes of pain, or if the pain fails to respond to the medication used for straightforward period pain.

When to see the doctor

- Your period pain changes in some way or you get period pain for the first time.
- The pain is interfering with your lifestyle.
- Pain is on one side and/or radiating (spreading to the thigh or another area).
- You have pain at the time of your period that is not like your usual period pain, and there's a possibility you might be pregnant.
- Your usual ways of controlling the pain don't seem to work any more.

- New symptoms accompany the pain, for example, vomiting, diarrhoea, or feeling faint.
- The pain gets worse towards the end of the period.
- Pain is aggravated by pressure, bowel motions or sex.
- A fever or discharge accompanies the pain.

The Medical Approach

Prostaglandins-inhibiting drugs like Ponstan are the most likely first suggestion for ordinary period pain, but also common are the Pill and some painkillers. Sometimes, if the pain is severe and fails to respond to the usual treatments, very strong hormone drugs like Duphaston are used. (There's more info on all these under Drugs in The Medical Approach chapter.)

When period pain is really bad and all other treatments have been unsuccessful, the uterosacral nerve is sometimes cut to destroy the perception of pain in the uterus. This is a drastic last step and is rarely used. If it is recommended to you, we hesitate to say run for the hills, but at the very least get a second opinion.

Natural Therapies

Everyone experiences period pain differently and has their own combination of symptoms. Herbal formulas which are individually prescribed should try to deal with as many of these symptoms as possible. Over-the-counter herbal remedies for period pain can't have exactly the right combination of herbs for everyone.

It can be quite complicated to design a remedy for period pain. You'll need a specialist herbalist to prescribe your individual formula. You're likely to be prescribed a 'cocktail' of the following herbs, tailored to your individual diagnosis. For more information, check out the Herbs section in the Natural Therapies chapter.

- The uterine tonics including *Chamaelirium luteum*, *Aletris farinosa*, *Caulophyllum thalictroides*, *Angelica sinensis* and *Rubus idaeus*.

- The anti-spasmodic herbs including *Viburnum opulus* and *V. prunifolium*, *Caulophyllum thalictroides*, *Dioscorea villosa* and *Paeonia lactiflora*. *Paeonia lactiflora* is usually combined with *Glycyrrhiza glabra* (liquorice) to obtain the best effect. *Caulophyllum thalictroides* is used when the spasm seems to be localised in the cervix, resulting in acute crampy pain with very little flow. Once the flow gets going there should be pain relief.
- Emmenagogue, or expulsive herbs. This category of herbs especially should only be used by a properly trained herbalist: as Aunty Myrtle always said, never let an amateur near your uterus, dear.
- Warming herbs: especially two specific for the pelvic region: *Zingiber officinale* (ginger) and *Cinnamomum zeylanicum* (cinnamon). Both can be added to a herbal mix in the form of a tincture, or taken as a tea, either alone, with other therapeutic herbs or in an ordinary cuppa.
- Nervine (relaxing) herbs are useful to help the action of the anti-spasmodic and pain-killing herbs, and also if anxiety or tension accompany the pain. Some nervine herbs are also anti-spasmodics, the best being *Valeriana officinalis*, *Paeonia lactiflora*, *Piscidia erythrina*, *Corydalis ambigua*, *Verbena officinalis* and *Matricaria recutita* (chamomile).
- Anodyne, or pain-reducing herbs. *Corydalis ambigua* from the Chinese Materia Medica is the most potent of these, and can be used for pain anywhere in the body. It also reduces heavy period flow. Other important anodynes for period pain are *Piscidia erythrina*, *Lactuca virosa* and *Anemone pulsatilla*.
- Prostaglandins-inhibiting herbs include *Zingiber officinale* (ginger), *Tanacetum parthenium* (feverfew) and *Curcuma longa*. There are probably others, but there is little research in this area.
- Herbs which regulate the hormone levels. The most valuable of the herbal hormone regulators is *Vitex agnus castus,* which is very useful for congestive period pain, especially if PMS is also a problem. Vitex is a very difficult herb to prescribe successfully and should be prescribed by a specialist practitioner.

- Other herbs include *Paeonia lactiflora* and *P. suffruticosa* and *Cimicifuga racemosa* which are anti-spasmodics and may also competitively inhibit the activity oestrogen; and *Verbena officinalis* which is a sedative and has been traditionally used for hormonal period disorders.
- Congestive period pain, the heavy, dull, dragging type of pain experienced by many women before their period, is often improved by taking liver herbs or bitters such as *Berberis vulgaris* which is also an emmenagogue. Other liver herbs include *Taraxacum officinale* (dandelion), *Silybum marianum* (St Mary's thistle).
- Herbs for spasmodic or congestive period pain accompanied by constipation and irritable bowel syndrome. The 'aperient' (laxative) herbs such as *Cassia senna* (senna pods), *Rhamnus purshiana* (cascara) and *Aloe barbadensis* (aloe) can be used but will often aggravate spasm in the uterus if taken during the period. Beware of laxatives bought from the chemist with these elements, as the effects can be rather, ahem, violent.

By far the best method to treat constipation is to increase the level of fibre and fluids in the diet. (A sensible high-fibre diet is included in the Self Care chapter.)

Irritable bowel syndrome often becomes worse around the period and can aggravate period pain—sometimes it is even mistaken for period pain. (An irritable bowel syndrome diet is also in the Self Care chapter.)

Acupuncture

Acupuncture can help some period pain. It involves the insertion of needles into the skin which sounds scary, but if you breathe in really quickly as each needle goes in you don't feel a thing. Obviously what you'll need is an experienced acupuncturist, not some mad pal with an old school compass—the placing of the needles is very precise. The treatments are usually given twice a week.

Chiropractic and osteopathy

Some chiropractors and osteopaths believe that period pain can be aggravated by pressure on the spinal nerves that supply the uterus. They treat this problem by manipulating the lower back. Any likely positive response should be obvious within one or two treatments.

Self Care

- Cut down on animal fats (especially meat, egg yolk and prawns/shrimps) and increase essential fatty acids in foods. The oil of evening primrose and especially fish oils can improve period pain. Usually a dose of 3 grams a day of either in capsule form is necessary to achieve good results. For the first few months, taking the supplements daily is a good idea. This can be expensive, but the dose can be reduced once pain control is achieved. Try fish oils first. Essential fatty acids are explained under Bad Fats and Good Fats, number 8 of the 20 Diet Hints in the Self Care chapter.
- Calcium and magnesium supplements will sometimes relieve period cramps. Follow the recommended dose on the label. Usually, a combination of calcium and magnesium together is best. (An info page on both is in the Minerals section of the Self Care chapter.)
- Relax: it helps you cope with pain. Guided imagery and meditation can be useful as well, if you're into that sort of thing. Guided imagery is when you imagine yourself to be free of pain—if that works, try imagining you've won the lottery.
- Make ginger tea: grate 2–4 centimetres of fresh root ginger, place in a stainless steel saucepan with one to two cups of water, cover and bring slowly to the boil. Keep covered and simmer for about ten minutes. Strain, add honey to taste and sip while still hot. If possible, also have a warm bath. Other herbs can be taken at the same time. Ginger also eases nausea and is useful for period pain accompanied by nausea and vomiting. Commercial tablets such

as Travel Calm (Blackmores), are quite useful for mild period pain.

- A therapeutic massage just before or during the period can help. Some specific massage techniques like shiatsu, acupressure, and foot reflexology can be used to relieve pain, pelvic congestion and symptoms of hormone imbalance.
- Try aromatherapy. Clary sage, lavender, and chamomile oil are all useful for period pain because of their anti-spasmodic and relaxing properties. They can be used regularly in the bath, as a component of massage oil or as a warm compress, but should not be swallowed. These oils are not applied to the skin 'neat', and should be diluted with a base oil such as olive oil, or water.
- To make a massage oil, add between 1 and 3 millilitres, or 20 and 60 drops of each essential oil to 100 millilitres of a base oil (olive, almond or apricot kernel oil are good). Massage into the lower abdomen and back when pain is a problem. It may be useful to have a hot bath first, then use the massage oil. You may also find it useful to have the massage done by a large muscly fireman called Sven, who then slowly . . . I beg your pardon.
- You can make a hot compress by adding about 5 drops of each essential oil to a bowl of very hot water, soaking a cloth and then applying it to the painful area of the stomach after wringing out the excess water. The cloth can be repeatedly dipped in the water each time it cools. Alternatively, a hot-water bottle can be placed over the compress to keep it warm.
- An aromatherapy bath is easy. Usually only about 5–10 drops are needed in a full bath tub. Valerian oil can be very useful if the period pain prevents sleep, or when it is useful to 'sleep the pain off'. It can make some people quite drowsy, so don't expect to be the life of the party afterwards. (Although we do know of a determined girly who used to take her hot-water bottle with her to nightclubs and fill it up at the urn.)
- Heat of any sort will help to relieve muscle spasm. A hot-water bottle or a hot bath is cheap and easy. It is also possible to buy

small hot packs that can be worn close to the skin—some manufacturers even sell them with specially made undies with a little pouch to hold the pack in place. ('Warmease' is the name of one product, but try a chemist before the sexy lingerie department.)

- Try a warm ginger pack on the lower abdomen. (It's kind of messy.) Place grated root ginger between several layers of cloth and place a hot-water bottle over the top. A little oil on the skin first will prevent burns from the ginger juice. Remove the pack if the skin starts to burn or sting.

While warmth is helpful, getting cold can increase pain. Swimming in cold water can be a problem. The swimming itself can relieve pain, so go for a heated pool.

- If your period pain gets worse with exposure to cold, or better with heat, avoid iced drinks, ice cream or food straight from the fridge. Raw foods, like salads, can also be a problem, and raw vegies can bring on irritable bowel syndrome because the stomach has to work harder to digest them. Try warm food at room temperature or hotter; and add warming spices to food, like ginger, cardamom, coriander, turmeric and cinnamon.
- Having sex or an orgasm can sometimes help to reduce period pain by reducing muscle spasm and pelvic congestion. Hotsy totsy!
- There is an ointment you can buy at pharmacies which is made of wild yam cream and other herbal extracts, marketed under brand names such as ProBalance. We recommend that you give this a miss until further research on its effects is available. The creams may work because they contain spasmolytic herbs, but there's no reason to rub it in rather than the easier and cheaper method of swallowing a herbal mixture or tablet. Last time we looked, the ointment price was about $45 for two months, and you're supposed to rub it into different parts of your body two to three times a day! For more info on wild yam creams see under Not Enough Progesterone in the Hormone chapter.

Pelvic congestion syndrome

The most common symptoms are a dragging or heavy lower abdominal pain, congestive period pain, low back ache and pain during penetrative sex. There may also be a vaginal discharge. The pain can come on around and during the period, or become worse towards the end of the day when the blood pools in the veins. Often anxiety, fatigue, headache and insomnia—in other words PMS—accompany the pelvic symptoms. The syndrome mostly affects women over 35 who have had several pregnancies.

In many cases, when a pelvic examination or laparoscopy is performed, the pelvic blood vessels are engorged, and the uterus is enlarged and tender. Even so, no consistent relationship has been seen between pelvic blood vessel engorgement and pain—you can have swollen blood vessels without pain.

The causes of pelvic congestion syndrome are still a matter of theory. It may be related to tension and stress; or chronic pelvic inflammatory disease.

The Medical Approach

Some doctors treat pelvic congestion with progesterone drugs (say, Provera or Primulut) because they believe that it has a hormonal origin; or sometimes a hysterectomy is suggested. (Needless to say, always get at least one other opinion of your own choice if a doctor wants to take out all your bits.) Other doctors think it is a psychosomatic condition. ('It's all in yer mind.') Others believe that the problem can be alleviated by making sure you have an orgasm each time you become sexually aroused. This is, quite frankly, the best medical approach suggestion in the entire book and we suggest that you regularly tell somebody cute that you simply *must* have an orgasm immediately as it's good for your health.

Natural Therapies

In natural medicine, pelvic congestion is believed to be related to constitutional weakness, hormonal imbalance, lack of exercise, constipation, or stress and tension. All these should be targeted.

Herbs

Hamamelis virginiana (witch hazel), *Aesculus hippocastanum* (horse chestnut) and *Ruscus aculeatus* (butcher's broom) are used to treat any condition related to venous congestion or blood vessel inflammation. These herbs have anti-inflammatory, anti-haemorrhagic, and astringent effects and are useful when pelvic congestion is accompanied by heavy periods, or when other blood vessels are affected and aching haemorrhoids or varicose veins are also a problem.

Older women or women who have had repeated pregnancies often develop symptoms similar to pelvic congestion syndrome which are caused by pelvic floor or uterine prolapses. The specific herb in this case is *Aletris farinosa* (true unicorn root). This herb also contains bitters and is a general tonic. It is ideal for women who are tired and who have heavy, dragging pain, prolapses or low back pain.

Diet and supplements

The bioflavonoids are a group of natural compounds often found in vitamin C-rich foods which improve the integrity of blood vessels. The bioflavonoids are unlikely to have a really direct effect on the pain.

Rutin and hesperidin are often added to vitamin C supplements and are found in citrus fruits, capsicum and buckwheat leaf tea. Bioflavonoids are found in many berries, fruit, seeds and barks with a red or purplish colour, blueberries, and the herb *Vaccinium myrtillus*. The most potent bioflavonoids of all, pycnogenols from grape seed extract, are available in pills as a supplement. The dose is usually between 150 and 300 milligrams per day.

Self Care

Exercise will get the blood moving again, and helps to prevent it from pooling in the pelvic blood vessels. When symptoms are severe, try non-weight bearing exercise, such as swimming or cycling. Other exercise should be taken in the morning before the veins become too engorged, for example, a bit of a brisk stroll or a roll in the hay. Sometimes sleeping with the foot of the bed elevated on a brick helps relieve the symptoms of pelvic congestion.

A high fibre intake will also help to prevent constipation, which aggravates the symptoms of pelvic congestion. More info on fibre is in the 20 Diet Hints in the Self Care chapter.

Bleeding too much or too often

Heavy periods can drive some of us mad: carrying around industrial-strength tampons by the carton load, rushing to the loo every hour or so to check whether there's a 'leak', and knowing, deep in the heart, that popping on a pair of white trousers is about as likely as having Elvis pop in for afternoon tea. And for others, a heavy period might arrive unexpectedly, giving us a bit of a fright.

Sometimes women who have nothing to compare themselves to think they have heavy periods when they're actually quite normal. One heavy period, unless the bleeding is startlingly heavy, isn't enough reason to get toey. Uncharacteristic periods every now and then are not unusual, especially after stress or overseas travel.

There are lots of reasons why a couple of periods might be heavier than normal and each of these should be investigated.

Most often, the cause is 'functional' where nothing terribly dangerous is happening, but something is not doing its job properly. Treatment of the functional causes can be relatively simple. The other most common cause is the presence of fibroid tumours, usually just called fibroids. (There are a few types of fibroids and most of them are not dangerous. We'll get on to the full info further down.)

Other more complicated causes include malfunctions of the hypothalamic-pituitary glands or the ovary; too much oestrogen overstimulating the endometrium; an imbalance of prostaglandins; hypothyroidism, low iron levels; clotting abnormalities; lack of uterine tone, intra-uterine devices (contraceptive IUDs), and uterine infections. Again, these conditions are treatable.

Diagnosis

So what is the definition of 'too heavy' and 'too often'? Doctors call heavy periods which come at the usual intervals menorrhagia—pronounced men-o-rah-jia. (If you think that's an over the top word, try the one for heavy but infrequent periods, oligohypermenorrhoea.)

Most medical books and some doctors suggest you've got a menorrhagia problem if your period:

- continues for more than seven days;
- happens more often than every 21 days; and/or
- exceeds 80 millilitres in volume (about half a cup).

Quite frankly this is not a great help unless you're the sort of person who wants to sit on a measuring cup for the length of your period. If you want to work it out for yourself, it makes much more sense to define too much period bleeding as a change in your usual pattern. Using this definition, the period:

- lasts for, say, three days longer than expected;
- requires two or more pads or tampons per day than is usual; and/or
- arrives five days or more earlier than usual.

This method is simple and practical. It identifies deviations from your own normal, natural pattern, and it's much more likely to help you keep alert to any changes.

Don't let *anybody* treat your abnormal period bleeding without knowing its cause. An accurate diagnosis is vital. Sometimes a diagnosis can be made using only the history of your period patterns, and routine examinations; sometimes you'll need simple surgery, such as dilatation and curettage (D&C), laparoscopy or hysteroscopy. (These procedures are explained in the Surgery section of The Medical Approach chapter.)

The diagnostic techniques used by natural therapists such as iris, tongue or pulse diagnosis, are much less invasive (and therefore much more fun), but they're often not good enough for what we're dealing with here. They should never be used as an alternative to the appropriate medical examinations.

Common causes of heavy periods

Functional menorrhagia

The word menorrhagia is used by doctors to describe heavy periods as a usual pattern as well as any functional disorder which causes heavy periods. So functional menorrhagia means abnormally heavy periods within a usual cycle length. No disease or problem is revealed from tests on the uterus or blood.

Uterine fibroids

These are non-cancerous, fibrous tumours of the uterus, usually in the myometrium (muscle wall) and diagnosed by ultrasound.

Endometriosis

This is caused by the endometrium (normal cells lining the uterus) growing elsewhere—on the ovaries, tubes, pelvic ligaments, bowel or bladder. These cells still bleed during periods, often causing cysts, and heavy periods are common.

Adenomyosis

Adenomyosis is like endometriosis but the displaced cells grow in the uterine wall. Their monthly bleeding into the muscle layer causes pain and sometimes heavy periods.

Pelvic inflammatory disease (PID)

PID is caused by infection, which may or may not be sexually transmitted. The symptoms can include abnormal bleeding and heavy periods in about 30 per cent of cases, but more typically cause fever, malaise and pelvic pain, and it can also show no apparent symptoms and cause infertility. A bloody or yukky discharge is common if the PID is caused by gonorrhoea, a sexually transmitted disease.

Contraceptives

The IUD or 'loop' can cause heavier and more painful periods. Some women experience bleeding between periods, especially in the first three months after IUD insertion. Severe pain and/or bleeding may indicate that the IUD has dislodged or an infection has developed and requires immediate assessment. Tubal ligation ('having your tubes tied') has been linked to heavy periods. This may be caused because the Pill is stopped after the operation.

Non-gynaecological causes

Disturbance in hormone levels, blood clotting or deficiencies of certain nutrients may result in heavier periods. The more common causes are related to the following systems:

The blood

Disorders of blood production or blood clotting can be related to heavy periods. Causes range from anaemia, lack of nutrients (especially iron), blood clotting abnormalities and rare blood disorders.

The endocrine system

Heavy bleeding can be caused by imbalances of the adrenal hormones, from a disorder of the thyroid gland or hypothalamic-pituitary unit or as a side effect of drugs on those parts of the body.

The liver

The liver metabolises hormones and has a role in blood clotting. Poor liver function can lead to heavy periods.

Pregnancy

Pregnancy-related conditions are the most common causes of abnormal bleeding, sometimes with pain, among women between 20 and 40.

Miscarriage

A late and/or painful, heavy period may be an early miscarriage or a case of the foetus failing to develop normally. Bleeding later in an established pregnancy, and before the fourteenth week, might also be a miscarriage. About one in five pregnancies ends in a miscarriage.

Heavy periods (functional menorrhagia)

If you're going to have heavy bleeding, this is the best kind to have. Even though being told you have functional menorrhagia sounds scary, it actually implies that you *don't* have any reproductive diseases. Feral hormones and prostaglandins imbalance might be the cause of the heavy bleeding. 'Functional' means that your uterus is healthy but it has a rather disordered function when it comes to bleeding. If you've got functional menorrhagia you have heavy periods, but your menstrual cycle is otherwise normal.

Cause

Heavy periods are almost always related to a prostaglandins imbalance. Prostaglandins are hormone-like substances made by the body to control a whole range of bodily functions—including the relevant ones, in this case, of blood clotting, and dilating blood vessels. If prostaglandins get out of whack and you have too much of one called prostacyclin 2, you will get heavy periods.

The Medical Approach

A doctor will eliminate all diseases and 'organic' complaints as the reason for the heavy period. Tests and interviews may focus on past and present period history, Pap test results, an internal examination and blood tests.

If there are no obvious causes of the heavy period, a diagnosis of functional menorrhagia is made. The medical practitioner might suggest the following treatments, usually starting at the top of the list and progressing though until the problem is fixed.

Prescriptions

The following drugs are more fully explored under Drugs in The Medical Approach chapter.

Heavy periods

- The Pill. The Pill is a common treatment and is often the most efficient way to establish a regular cycle and a lighter period.
- Prostaglandins-inhibiting drugs such as Naprogesic, and Ponstan. The drugs work best if you are ovulating, or in combination with the Pill or progesterone tablets.
- Progestogen tablets to be taken in the second half of the month or continually (often Provera or Primulut). Progestogens are used even though many women who have heavy periods don't have irregularities in either progesterone production or hormone balance. When the drug is stopped after 10–20 days, the period often goes back to normal. Progestogens can also be given continuously, which causes shrinkage of the endometrium, the lining of the uterus which comes away during a period, so there's less to come out each time.
- Drugs which induce a temporary menopause, the gonadotrophin releasing hormone agonists—called GnRH agonists for short, such as Zoladex and Synarel. They are used only rarely when nothing else has worked.

Surgery

All these procedures are explained more fully under Surgery in The Medical Approach chapter, where there's also advice on preparing and recovering from an operation.

- A hysteroscopy (a surgical examination of the uterus) or diagnostic dilatation and curettage (D&C) in which any diseased parts of the endometrium are removed, may be suggested for older women, if there is a probability of a pre-cancerous or cancerous endometrial condition, or if there is a suspicion of an intrauterine lesion such as a polyp or fibroid. These ops are done for diagnosis rather than treatment, although heavy periods often stop after a D&C—nobody is sure exactly why.
- Uterine endometrial ablation. A big old phrase for an operation under general anaesthetic in which the endometrium is destroyed, usually by laser. It can be a complicated procedure and should be performed by an experienced surgeon.

- Hysterectomy surgery under general anaesthetic. This is the removal of the uterus, which may also involve the removal of the ovaries. This should always be the last resort.

Natural therapies

Many women visit natural therapists for abnormal bleeding because 'nothing else has worked'. Often they have been examined by a doctor and told that they just have heavy periods, and that nothing is wrong. If a physical examination has not been performed, your natural therapist should refer you to a doctor for the official look-see and diagnosis.

A complete gynaecological check-up is recommended first for anyone over 40 with heavy periods and anyone who has symptoms which may indicate other conditions (we're talking internal examination, we're talking breast examination, and we're talking Pap test, all explained under Screening in The Medical Approach chapter).

Once underlying conditions are ruled out, the first step in a natural therapist's diagnosis is to determine whether the excessive bleeding is caused by a hormonal imbalance. This is more likely if you have symptoms like PMS, an irregular cycle, and spotting or bleeding between periods.

The therapist may ask you to take your basal body temperature reading by a thermometer in the mouth first thing each morning to assess whether you're ovulating. Without wishing to be screamingly obvious, if there's no evidence of a hormonal irregularity, you won't need remedies to regulate hormones.

Natural therapists can use a variety of clinical assessments to evaluate the causes and the type of treatment for heavy periods caused by functional menorrhagia. Problems might be confined to the uterus, or be part of a complaint related to your whole 'constitutional state'.

You may be diagnosed with a uterine problem caused by any of: an abnormal uterine tone; a prostaglandins imbalance; or an excess of Heat, Cold, Dryness or Moistness in the uterus. (These are traditional natural therapy concepts used to describe a person's general constitution.)

You may be diagnosed as having heavy periods because of an imbalance in your entire system that is caused by one of the following: nutritional deficiencies; weakness and lack of vitality leading to a systemic imbalance and (usually) a tendency to become Cold; liver congestion characterised by irritability and headaches, and a tendency to become Hot.

Your natural therapist may make a diagnosis and form a treatment based on an overlap of these conditions. For example, uterine tissue tone problems can happen when there are nutritional deficiencies, especially of iron, and when there's a general lack of vitality. Herbs like *Angelica sinensis,* to nourish blood and improve vitality, often also affect uterine tone; and iron is believed to improve both anaemia and uterine tone. You may be prescribed a combination of mineral supplements such as over-the-counter tablets, herbal tablets, or herbal mixtures made up by the practitioner.

Iron supplements

Anaemia can be the cause as well as the result of abnormal uterine bleeding. Some research shows that women who had heavy periods also had an iron deficiency, but not necessarily anaemia. The researchers guessed that the heavy periods were caused by a relative weakness of both the uterine muscles and the blood vessels of the endometrium which were unable to stop bleeding by contracting. This condition is very similar to the lack of uterine tone described by natural therapists. Iron is the most important mineral in cases of heavy bleeding. An info page on iron, including good food sources, is under Minerals in the Self Care chapter.

Vitamin A supplements

Vitamin A is important for healthy endometrial growth and women with normal periods have significantly better levels of vitamin A than women with heavy periods. In a research study, when women with heavy periods were given vitamin A, more than

92 per cent improved. Normal oestrogen levels are dependent on vitamin A.

Vitamin A is only useful for heavy periods affected by a deficiency. It can be toxic if taken for prolonged periods, or by pregnant women.

Enough vitamin K

Crude chlorophyll has been used for heavy periods, although exactly why it can help is unclear. One theory is that chlorophyll contains high levels of vitamin K which is necessary for the normal clotting of blood. Studies have shown it can make the period shorter.

Deficiencies of vitamin K are probably rare because there's a lot of it available in food and your body can make vitamin K if you're not eating it. But to get the goodies, you need to eat dark green leafy vegetables and yoghurt, which will help the bowel bacteria manufacture the vitamin. Steer clear of antibiotics whenever possible.

The flavonoids

The flavonoids are a diverse group of natural compounds in food and are some of the major useful constituents of herbal medicines. Flavonoids improve capillary strength and interact with oestrogen receptor sites to reduce the proliferative effect of oestrogens in the body. Flavonoids found in citrus fruits and buckwheat leaf can be useful for heavy periods.

Plant oestrogens

Plant oestrogens, which are often also flavonoids, can inhibit the effect of oestrogen on the endometrium by taking up 'parking spaces' at oestrogen receptor sites, stopping the stronger body-made oestrogen from causing an overstimulating effect on cells. Studies have shown that when women have a high intake of soya products (plant oestrogens with high levels of some types of flavonoids), they ovulate later and their period tends to get lighter and shorter. The plant oestrogens are explained in the Self Care chapter.

Prostaglandins

Prostaglandins play a major role in triggering a period and imbalances of prostaglandins are implicated in heavy periods and period pain.

The most practical way of improving heavy bleeding is to eat your way to the right prostaglandins balance by cutting down on 'bad' fats and eating the right fatty acids. (See Bad Fats and Good Fats, number 8 of the 20 Diet Hints in the Self Care chapter.)

Herbs

Getting the herbal mix right requires training and experience. A herbalist should prescribe a combination of herbs for functional menorrhagia, choosing from herbs which affect uterine tone and regulate uterine bleeding—the astringents, uterine tonics and emmenagogues; and from the herbs which improve overall vitality, treat the liver, cool excess Heat in the body and help to clear excess oestrogen (a full list is under Herbs in the Natural Therapies chapter.)

These herbs are particularly useful for heavy periods:

- **Uterine astringents.** *Trillium erectum, Equisetum arvense, Achillea millefolium, Tienchi ginseng, Capsella bursa-pastoris* and *Hydrastis canadensis*. The important astringents for heavy periods in adolescence are *Achillea millefolium* (yarrow), *Alchemilla vulgaris* (ladies mantle), *Capsella bursa-pastoris* (shepherd's purse) and *Geranium maculatum* (cranesbill).
- **Uterine tonics.** *Angelica sinensis, Chamaelirium luteum, Rubus idaeus* (raspberry leaves), *Caulophyllum thalictroides, Mitchella repens* and *Aletris farinosa*.

Herbalists recognise a type of uterine bleeding that is accompanied by a lack of vitality, pale facial colour and poor general energy and strength. The uterine and female tonic herbs, especially the Warming herbs *Aletris farinosa* and *Angelica sinensis,* may also be prescribed.

- Exercise moderately.
- Reduce stress levels. (For more info see Stress in The Usual Suspects section at the start of this chapter.)
- If your problem is related to iron deficiency, see the iron info page in the Self Care chapter for low-fat, iron-boosting foods.
- A low-fat high-fibre diet will reduce period flow by increasing oestrogen clearance and regulating prostaglandins balance. Avoid or reduce fats from dairy products, meat, eggs and coconut.
- Eat more fibre. It helps to keep oestrogen levels within the low to normal range. There's more info on fibre in the 20 Diet Hints in the Self Care chapter.
- If bioflavonoid deficiency is the assumed cause of the heavy bleeding, increase your intake of citrus fruits, buckwheat leaf tea, and fruit and vegies generally.
- Eat more 'bitter' green, leafy vegetables to help your liver function.

Uterine fibroids

Fibroids are fibrous, non-cancerous growths of the uterus (don't panic if a doctor talks about fibroid tumours, uterine leiomyomas or uterine myomata: it's just the same thing with scarier names). They affect up to a quarter of women over the age of 35. A fibroid is made of dense muscular fibres arranged in circular layers and surrounded by a layer of compressed smooth muscle cells.

Fibroids vary greatly in size, number, and position. Some grow really big and cause pressure symptoms; others stay small and don't cause any problems. It's rare, but very occasionally fibroids can become cancerous.

There are different types of fibroids. They are usually self-contained, fibrous and covered tumours, benign, and roughly spherical. But some are 'pedunculated', attached to the uterine cavity or the outside of the uterus by a stem or 'pedicle'. In rare cases these can twist on the pedicle (called torsion). This can cause extreme pain. Immediate surgery may be needed. (The ovary can also twist, causing torsion, when misshapen by the presence of a cyst.)

Fibroids may cause few symptoms; occasionally quite large ones are discovered because of a routine examination or ultrasound scan for another reason. Fibroids that don't interfere with fertility or cause unwanted symptoms should be left to their own devices and be regularly monitored. Some measures to reduce too much oestrogen in relation to progesterone can hold their growth steady and reduce the risk of growing more of them.

The ones that need closest monitoring are fibroids which are large, growing on a pedicle or protruding down through the cervix. Fibroids that are growing quickly are at an increased risk of developing into an aggressive type of cancer. Often doctors suggest that they be surgically removed to be on the safe side.

Symptoms

The most common symptom of fibroids is heavy periods. Larger fibroids can cause a feeling like you need to wee a lot, pressure, and a feeling of heaviness, dragging and congestion in the lower abdomen. In rare cases, pressure on the ureter (the tube between the kidney and the bladder) may force a back-flow of urine causing structural abnormalities of the kidney and ureter, and abnormal kidney function. Very large fibroids may cause a bulging stomach. Sometimes fibroids will cause a miscarriage or infertility and in rare cases, they may cause early labour.

Where they grow

Intra-uterine fibroids

These fibroids are found within the uterine cavity and often cause heavy periods. Also called 'sub-mucous' fibroids, some can be removed during a hysteroscopy if they are smaller than 5 or 6 centimetres across. They can extend through the cervix if they are growing on a stem. They can cause problems with fertility because the endometrium around the fibroid doesn't undergo normal hormonal change. This can make it harder for the fertilised egg to implant, and the miscarriage rate is often higher.

Myometrial fibroids
These are fibroids found within the muscle wall of the uterus (the myometrium). Also called intramural fibroids, they can grow at any location within the uterine muscle and vary a lot in size. The main symptoms are usually heavy periods, and, if the fibroid is very big, pressure on nearby organs—for example, the bladder.

Extra-uterine fibroids
These fibroids are on the outside of the uterus. Also called 'sub-serous' they can cause pressure symptoms or heavy periods. Some are found around or on the Fallopian tubes and can interfere with fertility.

What makes them grow

Nobody really knows exactly, but we do know that fibroid growth is dependent on oestrogen: they rarely develop before the first period and almost always shrink after menopause. You are at greater risk of fibroids if you have another condition of oestrogen overactivity, such as endometrial hyperplasia or endometriosis. Lowering 'excess' oestrogen is important for a successful treatment.

Fibroids have also been found to contain larger amounts of the chemical DDT than other uterine tissue. The significance of this is not clear, but DDT has oestrogen-like effects and may in some way initiate the tissue changes.

Related factors

- Pregnancy seems to reduce the risk of fibroids developing and each pregnancy further reduces the risk.
- It's possible that coffee increases the risk of developing uterine fibroids.
- Studies which have investigated the Pill and fibroids have been inconclusive: some studies show a reduced incidence; one study shows a slightly increased rate (not statistically significant); and two others found no change. That's a fat lot of good, then.

Diagnosis

A fibroid could be suspected if you also have these signs and symptoms:

- Heavy periods.
- A sense of congestion in the lower abdomen before and during a period.
- An enlarged uterus discovered by a doctor during a pelvic examination.
- A lower abdominal mass felt by you or your doctor.

An ultrasound scan is used to diagnose uterine fibroids. (Ultrasounds are explained under Screening in The Medical Approach chapter.) They will show up as a shape in or on the uterus. Usually there's a really good view and they can tell you the exact size and position. Ultrasounds are a good way to monitor the growth rate of fibroids.

Some doctors will also want to perform a laparoscopy to make sure that what is seen on the ultrasound is a fibroid. This often happens if the ovaries can't be clearly seen, because the suspected fibroid might really be an ovarian cyst or a cancerous growth.

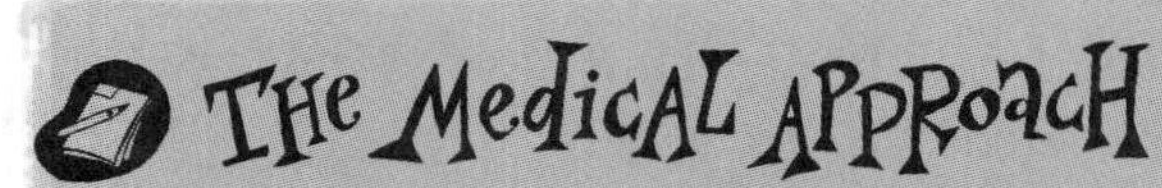

There are three main options for the management of fibroids:

- Observation.
- Drugs to reduce the size of fibroids. These drugs have two different effects, but the overall aim is to reduce the level of oestrogen. The drugs used are Danazol, to boost androgens and suppress oestrogens; and GnRH agonists, which induce a medical menopause. When you stop using the GnRH agonists, the fibroids can grow back—sometimes within two to three weeks. They are usually only used prior to surgical removal. (There's more info under Drugs in The Medical Approach chapter.)
- Surgical removal of the fibroid, called a myomectomy or, more commonly, a hysterectomy, the removal of the uterus (explained under Surgery in The Medical Approach chapter).

Natural therapies

Regulate excessive bleeding

It is often surprisingly easy to reduce the excessive bleeding caused by fibroids and this may be all that you want, especially if you have passed your possible childbearing years, your fibroids are small, or you are against surgery.

You may be prescribed any of the herbs favoured for the treatment of the heavy bleeding called functional menorrhagia. Good ones for fibroids are *Trillium erectum, Equisetum arvense, Achillea millefolium, Tienchi ginseng, Capsella bursa-pastoris* and *Hydrastis canadensis*. Astringent herbs are usually combined with one or more of the uterine tonic herbs to improve the uterine tone and try to normalise uterine function.

Considering the number of women who develop fibroids, the research on treatment and prevention isn't up to scratch. In one of the few trials using herbs to treat fibroids, the herbs *Paeonia lactiflora* and *P. suffruticosa, Poria cocos, Cinnamomum cassia* and *Prunus persica* were given to women with uterine fibroids. Ninety per cent of the women experienced an improvement of their symptoms and in 60 per cent of the cases, the fibroids got smaller.

Regulate relative oestrogen excess

It is important to control relative oestrogen excess because otherwise you might just keep growing multiple fibroids. And if you have them surgically removed without addressing the hormone situation, more might grow.

All conditions related to oestrogen excess, including fibroids, seem to respond to the same sorts of treatment for Too Much Oestrogen in the Hormones chapter.

Reducing fibroid size

Herbs prescribed to treat fibroids and reduce their size include *Calendula officinalis, Thuja occidentalis, Ruta graveolens* and

Tunera diffusa. Vitamin E is believed to reduce fibroid size, but the reasons for this are unclear.

Self Care

- Follow the strategies for reducing relative oestrogen excess: the same ones for self care in the Endometriosis section.
- Eat plant oestrogens (see the Plant Oestrogen section in the Self Care chapter).
- Increase the intake of bioflavonoids (citrus fruits) to reduce heavy bleeding which comes with fibroids.
- Iron is recommended for anaemia or low iron levels, and may also get the periods back on the right track. Prevent anaemia by having enough iron in your diet. (The info page on iron is under Minerals in the Self Care chapter.)

Erratic bleeding

Spotting or bleeding between periods

You might be used to 'spotting'—little bleeds just before or after your period, named for the effect they have on your undies gusset. But if spotting suddenly happens for the first time ever, get it checked out.

Bleeding between periods is usually slight, painless, and annoying, because you may not have a pad or tampon with you. It is also most worrying. The cause is usually hormonal, but spotting after sex can be the big warning sign of cancerous lesions of the uterus or cervix.

Bleeding between periods should always be investigated, especially when:

- it's not part of your usual cycle;
- you're 40 or older;
- it happens after any kind of sex.

Any vaginal bleeding after menopause must be investigated immediately by a doctor no matter how small, because it could be uterine cancer. Other causes of post-menopausal bleeding might be polyps or lesions on the cervix.

Unscheduled bleeding

The fancy name for unscheduled bleeding is metrorrhagia, pronounced metro-rah-jee-ar. It means bleeding at times other than the period. Sometimes it's called inter-menstrual bleeding or threshold bleeding. The bleeding often happens at the time of ovulation, although it may happen at any time during the cycle.

Bleeding between periods is often not a problem—it might be caused by hormonal changes at ovulation or by benign lesions on the cervix—but it *could* be caused by cancer of the cervix or uterus, and until that possibility has been investigated and eliminated as the cause, no treatment should be undertaken. It is vital that you don't just take a drug or herbs to stop bleeding without knowing exactly what is going on.

It's the slight bleeding that can be most suggestive of cancer or other serious problems, many of which must be treated early. So *any* bleeding between periods must be checked out immediately. So, off to the doctor with you and no hiding behind the couch.

Too many periods

Normal periods that happen at intervals of less than 21 days, are called polymenorrhoea (pronounced polly-men-oh-rear). Causes include misbehaviour of the hypothalamic-pituitary unit or the ovary. Often, the problem is to do with ovulation: either it doesn't happen, or it happens too early.

Too often and too heavy

The big word for this is polymenorrhagia (pronounced polly-men-o-rah-jee-ar). This is a combination of menorrhagia (heavy periods) and polymenorrhoea (too many periods). Thank God it doesn't include another complaint as well or we'd be here all day trying to spell it, let alone pronounce it. Any of the factors which cause too many periods or heavy bleeding might be involved in polymenorrhagia.

Common causes of bleeding between periods

Dysfunctional uterine bleeding (DUB)

DUB is caused by a problem at hormone HQ: the hypothalamic-pituitary unit. This often results in hormonal irregularities, erratic bleeding and not ovulating. The dysfunction may last for only one cycle or become entrenched.

Endometrial hyperplasia

The endometrial cells are excessively stimulated by prolonged exposure to too much oestrogen in relation to progesterone. Not ovulating (ovulation guarantees the presence of progesterone) is the usual cause. Endometrial hyperplasia is diagnosed by examining a tissue sample under a microscope. The tissue is collected during a hysteroscopy or dilatation and curettage (D&C) surgery. (They are fully described under Surgery in The Medical Approach chapter.) The condition can lead to endometrial cancer if untreated. Common symptoms are irregular bleeding, spotting, and/or heavy, persistent flow.

Uterine cancer

Cancer of the uterus (commonly of the endometrium) is more likely over age 40. Symptoms include abnormal or recurrent bleeding between periods, after sex or after the menopause. Over 40, these symptoms, however scant or fleeting, should always be investigated.

Polyps

A polyp is an overgrowth of tissue, which is attached by a stem or pedicle. They can happen in the cervix and endometrium. The cells of the polyp are often normal, but can bleed easily. They often bleed after sex or examination by a doctor. Women over 40 with cervical polyps may also have endometrial polyps.

Abnormalities of the cervix

Abnormalities of the cervix can cause bleeding and/or pain.

i) Cervical eversion/ectropion

If the cells which normally line the cervical canal grow down and onto the outer areas of the cervix, the 'overflow' is called a cervical ectropion or eversion. These cells are not as tough as the usual cells of the cervix and usually bleed more easily, especially on contact.

ii) Cervical dysplasia and cancer

Both cervical cancer and dysplasia are detected with a Pap smear. Cervical dysplasia is a 'pre-cancerous condition' which means the cells are changing and may eventually become cancerous *if left untreated*. Dysplasia is more common between 30 and 40 years old; cervical cancer is more common in the fifties. Both conditions cause few symptoms, and by the time bleeding has developed, the condition can be quite advanced. Regular Pap tests can avoid this.

iii) Cervicitis

This is inflammation of the cells of the cervix, usually from chronic infection. Vaginal discharge is a common symptom which may be accompanied by pain or contain brownish blood and have a yukky smell.

Conditions affecting the ovaries

Conditions affecting the ovaries don't always show up as a result of investigating abnormal bleeding. Usually pain is the initial symptom.

i) Ovarian cysts

Ovarian cysts are sacs of fluid in the ovary. They may be a consequence of the normal ovarian cycle. They may be benign or more rarely, cancerous. Over the age of 45, one in three ovarian cysts are malignant, and must be removed quick smart. Some cysts can interfere with the regularity of the period.

ii) Ovulation

Some women experience spotting with pain (would you believe doctors call this mittelschmertz) at the time of normal ovulation. The bleeding is presumed to be caused by the oestrogen changes at mid-cycle, but is relatively rare and should be investigated.

(continued over page)

Hormonal contraceptives

The combined (oestrogen and progesterone) Pill; the sequential Pill (Pills containing oestrogen and progesterone varied throughout the cycle); the Mini Pill (progesterone only) and Depo-Provera (an injection of slowly absorbed progesterone) can all be associated with abnormal bleeding patterns.

Malnutrition or excess weight loss

This may be due to severe illness, unavailable food, inadequate food, eating disorders or excessive exercise. Usually periods stop, although rarely heavier periods may be the result.

Pregnancy

i) Placental malfunction

Bleeding can result from one of three main placenta problems:

- Bleeding caused by abnormal development of the placenta and/or a foetus.
- Bleeding related to a normally developing placenta, which is in the wrong place. This is called a 'placenta praevia'.
- Bleeding caused by a normal placenta dislodging from the uterine wall too early. This is called an 'accidental haemorrhage' and is very painful.

ii) Hydatidiform mole

This results from a malformed foetus, and the pregnancy cannot continue. The tissue secretes large amounts of a hormone which usually causes severe 'morning sickness'. Often heavy bleeding starts about 10–12 weeks into the pregnancy, but will generally continue until all the mole is expelled. As this tissue can become cancerous, a D&C is recommended to remove all the tissue, and hormones are monitored for a year.

iii) Ectopic pregnancy

An ectopic pregnancy is one which has started to develop outside the uterus. The embryo may be in the Fallopian tube, within the fimbriae of the ovary, or in the pelvic cavity. Ectopic pregnancies do not develop normally because there is no endometrium to sustain the developing placenta. If the pregnancy develops in the tube, the tube can rupture. This is dangerous and usually requires emergency surgery.

Dysfunctional uterine bleeding (DUB)

DUB isn't caused by an underlying disease: it's one of those disorders of function where there is a problem with the hormone balance. Everything about the uterus looks healthy, although the endometrium may not show the usual changes caused by progesterone. The disorder usually originates from the hypothalamic pituitary unit misbehaving.

Causes

In many cases of DUB, ovulation is abnormal, or fails entirely. This leads to an imbalance in the hormones—oestrogen is still pumping out, but progesterone production is either far too low or gone altogether. This results in the 'unopposed' oestrogen overstimulating the endometrium (uterus lining) and leads to the characteristic bleeding patterns—an erratic cycle, no obvious signs of ovulation, and irregular or prolonged episodes of bleeding.

In the normal course of events, oestrogen is 'opposed' by the presence of progesterone. The progesterone production and withdrawal maintains the regularity of the endometrial shedding (and therefore the period). When you don't ovulate (or progesterone production is too low), oestrogen continues to stimulate the endometrial cells which grow and thicken. But the absence of progesterone means that the endometrium does not develop the usual structural features of the secretory phase, including special tiny blood vessels to nourish the endometrium and control blood loss once the period starts.

Without the development of these blood vessels, circulation throughout the thickened endometrium eventually fails; and the tissue becomes fragile and starts to break down. This does not happen uniformly throughout the endometrium—some bits are shed while others remain intact, resulting in the spotting and erratic blood loss.

At the same time, the hormonal imbalance may lead to disordered prostaglandins. In a normal cycle, the body slows the blood loss using prostaglandins to increase uterine tone and cause spasm of the spiral arterioles. Without these, you can get really heavy bleeding. This type of DUB is most common when regular ovulation is at its most fragile: among teenagers who have just started to get periods, and around the menopause. It can also be a feature of any condition when ovulation doesn't happen, such as thyroid disease, androgen excess, and obesity. It's often caused by stress.

Diagnosis

As with heavy bleeding, the diagnosis of DUB is a diagnosis of exclusion, so other conditions must be eliminated as the cause of bleeding.

Signs and symptoms highly suggestive of DUB are:

- Age. Women who are establishing their normal cyclical pattern in the first few years of their period, and women whose cycles are slowing down around menopause are more likely to develop DUB.
- Normal uterine size and normal cervix. Because spotting can also be a feature of something wrong with the cervix, a healthy cervix means the spotting is more likely to be DUB. The uterus can get bigger and change shape if you have fibroids or adenomyosis, both common causes of heavy periods.
- A recent history of persistent or severe stress. Because of its effect on the hypothalamic-pituitary function, stress can stop ovulation or disrupt progesterone production.
- A reliable negative pregnancy test. Pregnancy-related bleeding is the most common cause of abnormal period patterns.
- No pain during a vaginal examination or an abdominal palpation by a doctor. Pelvic inflammatory disease and endometriosis are two conditions which can cause symptoms similar to DUB, but they both usually cause pain during an examination.

The Medical Approach

The treatment for DUB is similar to the treatments set out earlier for functional menorrhagia (heavy bleeding). A synthetic progesterone drug, usually Provera or Primulut, is used to try to interrupt the abnormal hormonal pattern and regulate the cycle. Usually a diagnostic curette (D&C) or hysteroscopy is performed on older women to determine whether the bleeding is caused by endometrial hyperplasia or cancer. (There's detailed info on the drugs and surgery in The Medical Approach chapter.)

Natural therapies

The treatment of DUB aims to:

- re-establish ovulation;
- support the luteal phase of the cycle;
- treat stress where appropriate;
- use all or any of the treatments listed under functional menorrhagia as necessary.

Around the time of the first period, erratic cycles are so common that it's usually thought of as being physiological—in other words, a normal feature. So young women with dysfunctional bleeding patterns don't usually require any treatment unless the bleeding is particularly severe and causing other problems. Herbal remedies which are appropriate for erratic bleeding experienced around this time are *Achillea millefolium* (yarrow), *Equisetum arvense* (horsetail), *Rubus idaeus* (raspberry leaves) and *Alchemilla vulgaris* (ladies mantle).

Herbs to re-establish ovulation

In order to re-establish ovulation, it is first necessary to find out why it went away. This may be related to the life stage—around menopause or the first period; or ovulation may temporarily stop because of stress, overexercising, low body weight or a poor diet. Sometimes the exact cause is unknown. (If a doctor ever says to you: 'The reason for your problem is idiopathic', don't faint. Idiopathic is just the secret doctors' language word for 'I haven't got a clue what's causing this'.)

Not ovulating can be caused by complex hormonal irregularities related to the endocrine glands. These conditions are treated by fixing any abnormal function of the other glands, such as the thyroid or the adrenal gland; or addressing a major disruption in ovarian function like polycystic ovaries; or treating the abnormal activity of the hypothalamic-pituitary unit, such as hyperprolactinaemia. An expanded list of the herbs is under Herbs in the Natural Therapies chapter.

- 'Female tonic' herbs are used to re-establish normal bleeding patterns. These herbs may interact with the hypothalamus or the pituitary to re-start ovulation. The most important of these are *Chamaelirium luteum, Aletris farinosa, Dioscorea villosa* and *Trillium erectum*.
- *Trillium erectum* (beth root) contains hormone-like plant substances called diosgenins, which seem to help regulate both the blood flow and the hormone balance. This uterine tonic herb is considered to be 'specific' to the treatment of DUB, which is caused by not ovulating, and can regulate both cycle length and period flow within one to three cycles.

A delicately calculated combination of *Chamaelirium luteum* (helonias) and *Vitex agnus castus* (chaste tree) can be used to treat DUB. Helonias is the herb of choice for the first half of the cycle and for regulating ovarian function. *Vitex agnus castus* has been shown to stimulate ovulation, and is specifically good for problems of the luteal phase of the cycle and hypothalamic-pituitary function. Trials have verified its use in DUB, endometrial hyperplasia, stopped ovulation and 'fixing' cycles less than 21 days long. *Vitex agnus castus* can be used for irregular periods around the menopause, often in combination with *Cimicifuga racemosa*.

- Nervine herbs can calm stress and stop your hormones going feral. The best ones for this include *Hypericum perforatum, Leonurus cardiaca* and *Verbena officinalis*.

Self Care

- Follow the self-care suggestions under functional menorrhagia (heavy periods) listed earlier on.

- Minimise stress. Apart from anything else, erratic and heavy bleeding is stressful in itself and the worry caused by having the symptoms may feed into the stress cycle and worsen the symptoms. Stress management hints are included in The Usual Suspects section at the start of this chapter.

Endometrial hyperplasia

Endometrial hyperplasia is a condition in which the endometrium, the uterus lining, builds up too much. Its name is made up of *endo* (ancient Greek for within); metrial (*metra* is Greek for uterus); *hyper* (Greek for too much) and plasia (*plasticus* is Latin for building up). The overstimulated, 'hyperplastic' cells can progress through a range of changes from being mildly overgrown and easily treated, through to endometrial cancer.

Causes

It happens for much the same reasons as dysfunctional uterine bleeding (DUB)—too much stimulation of the endometrial cells by oestrogen without the balancing progesterone levels. In the case of endometrial hyperplasia, the hormonal imbalance causes the cells to change and become overgrown, and can cause erratic bleeding. The causes are usually not ovulating and erratic cycles.

Diagnosis

A diagnosis is made by taking a biopsy sample of tissue during hysteroscopy surgery under a general or local anaesthetic. (The procedure is explained under Surgery in The Medical Approach chapter.)

The endometrial cells are examined and graded according to the degree of change from normal to abnormal; usually with a three-stage grading of mild, moderate and serious (often called simple, complex and atypical). Cystic hyperplasia is another term used for the least advanced (simple) form of endometrial hyperplasia.

Once the change in the endometrium has been graded, a treatment is decided on which will take into account the severity of the endometrial change, your age, and whether and when you want to become pregnant.

It is important to nail down the underlying causes of endometrial hyperplasia. These include not ovulating in conditions like polycystic ovarian disease, thyroid disease, and ovarian and adrenal tumours. Relative oestrogen excess can be the result of obesity and diabetes.

Other risk factors for developing endometrial hyperplasia include getting the first period at an early age, late menopause, never being pregnant and taking oestrogen drugs without progestogens—a possible hormone replacement therapy (HRT) prescription.

The Medical Approach

The aim of treatment is to remove the abnormal tissue and then establish the usual shedding of the endometrium in each cycle—initially with drugs. The affected endometrium is removed with a curette (D&C) when the hysteroscopy is performed. (These are explained under Surgery in The Medical Approach chapter.) This will not 'cure' the condition unless the hormonal causes of the endometrial hyperplasia are also dealt with.

To fix the abnormal hormonal pattern, gynaecologists usually recommend synthetic hormones to simulate a normal hormonal pattern. Usually, a progestogen pill is taken, ranging from 10 to 21 days so that the endometrium develops like it would in the luteal phase, and afterwards, the drug is stopped to allow a 'period'. Ovulation often starts spontaneously after a few cycles on progestogens. The reasons for this are unknown. (See Drugs in The Medical Approach chapter.) Progestogen drugs are no good if you're trying to become pregnant. If you want to be pregnant, ovulation is usually stimulated by short courses of fertility drugs such as Clomid. Talk to your doctor about side effects.

Endometrial hyperplasia does not always become endometrial cancer, but the risk increases the more the cells are changed. Between 1 and 4 per cent of women with the mildest form—simple or cystic hyperplasia—can develop endometrial cancer; but more than 20 per cent of women progress to cancer if they have the most advanced form and are not treated appropriately.

About 10 per cent of all cases of post-menopausal bleeding are caused by endometrial hyperplasia (up to 20 per cent are caused by cancer). This figure increases if you're obese or you're given oestrogen without progesterone. When oestrogen is given alone, the endometrium is continually stimulated by oestrogen without the counter-balancing effect of progesterone. This danger is explored under HRT in the menopause chapter, Finishing Up.

Natural therapies

Endometrial hyperplasia must be diagnosed by a medical practitioner. Usually, the same doctor will administer medical treatment, but sometimes patients refuse to accept it. A decision to treat with natural remedies should only be made after careful evaluation of all your risks and benefits. The best practical advice in this situation is almost always to follow the advice of your doctor (feel free to get a second opinion).

After medical treatment, natural therapies can be helpful to maintain normal period patterns, reduce the effects of unopposed oestrogens, and reduce risk factors for cancerous change. Overall, the treatment will be similar to that described for DUB above, except that regular, cyclic periods must be re-established quickly, within a couple of cycles. This can be difficult to achieve with natural remedies, which can bring on periods, but not necessarily quickly treat the original cause of not ovulating.

Herbs are explained more fully under Herbs in the Natural Therapies chapter.

- In mild cases of endometrial hyperplasia, some herbs can kick-start ovulation which has been stopped by stress, diet or approaching menopause. The situation must be back to normal within two cycles. Useful herbs to re-establish ovulation include *Chamaelirium luteum, Angelica sinensis, Cimicifuga racemosa, Aletris farinosa* and *Vitex agnus castus*.
- If the stopped ovulation is caused by thyroid or adrenal gland conditions or polycystic ovaries, it may take too long to get it back to normal: this can be dangerous, and a natural therapist should wait until this is dealt with by a doctor before continuing other helpful treatment.
- Emmenagogue herbs may be used to re-establish periods. These herbs are powerful and can cause unpleasant effects if not prescribed or taken properly. They can cause termination of pregnancy, so be positive that you're not pregnant before using them. Popular starters include *Ruta graveolens* (rue) and *Artemisia vulgaris* (mugwort).
- Herbs which come from the astringent group, including *Trillium erectum, Achillea millefolium* and *Capsella bursa-pastoris*, can reduce bleeding.
- To protect the endometrium, you may be prescribed herbs with plant oestrogens and steroidal saponins. There are important restrictions on exactly how to use these herbs and only a herbalist who specialises in this condition should prescribe them.
- Anti-oxidants may be prescribed as many believe they have a protective role against cancerous change. So far there are no scientific trials producing definite evidence of this. Chief among these are vitamins A, E, K and C, betacarotene and a mineral called selenium which seems to work best when accompanied by vitamin E in the body. Supplements with high levels of selenium are only available on prescription, but foods with lots of selenium include whole grains, meat, eggs, brewers' yeast and fish. A supplement with high levels is known as Arizona Garlic.

Self Care

- Stress and diet are often important factors. Excessive exercise; a body mass index (BMI) below the recommended levels; many drugs (both prescribed or social); alcohol consumption, cocaine, and other recreational drugs; and excessive amounts of coffee can all interfere with normal ovulation. All these are covered in The Usual Suspects section.
- See the 20 Diet Hints in the Self Care chapter for foods which help protect against cancer.
- Eat plant oestrogens like linseeds and tofu (more info in the Self Care chapter).

Spotting and the cervix

Bleeding from the cervix is often slight, erratic and painless. Sometimes the discharge doesn't resemble blood at all, but is brownish or like stained clear fluid. It can happen at any time during the cycle, and is more common after poking about, usually after sex or examination by a doctor. Many of the common causes of cervical bleeding are not related to cancer and are easily treated. Bleeding caused by cancer of the cervix is rare if you have regular Pap tests. (For a full explanation see under Screening in The Medical Approach chapter.)

No periods

Even though we might make a joke about the unbounded joy of not having to bother with periods, the 'convenience' might be a warning signal of trouble.

Not that you need to panic if you've missed one period, especially if you've been travelling or stressed. After one missed period, you can afford to wait and see what the next one is like—unless you might be pregnant, in which case, skates on and straight to the doctor.

If you've already started your periods and you then stop for more than six months, you may be told you have amenorrhoea (pronounced ay-men-oh-rear). Basically it just means stopped periods, or no periods. This is not a diagnosis of whatever the problem is—it describes a symptom caused by a condition. The hard bit is finding the cause, because a range of hormonal, physical and metabolic conditions can cause the period to stop.

Needless to say, it is absolutely vital that treatment should only proceed after identifying the underlying problem. Don't let anyone 'treat' you to bring your period back without knowing why it went away. Otherwise, a serious condition could be masked. Polycystic ovarian disease or elevated prolactin levels, which commonly stop periods, may not be accompanied by any other obvious signs. Another danger is that if you don't know you're pregnant—herbs or drugs used to 'bring on the period' could damage a developing foetus.

Amenorrhoea is usually divided into two types for the purposes of diagnosis and treatment: primary amenorrhoea, in which you haven't had your first period by 17, and secondary amenorrhoea when you've had periods, but now they've stopped.

Not getting the first period (primary amenorrhoea)

- Your periods haven't started by age 17;
- Your puberty changes haven't started by age 14; or
- Your period hasn't started within two years of the other puberty changes such as weight gain, budding breasts and hair in grown-up places.

Most common causes

In most cases, girls don't get their first period because of a simple, easily fixed reason, like being underweight and overexercising. Or it might be caused by any of the other culprits responsible for secondary amenorrhoea, which are listed below.

Less common causes

Not getting your first period can also be caused by a number of congenital and hormonal factors. In extremely rare cases, a young woman might not have a uterus or have another congenital abnormality—maybe a blockage in the vagina which stops the blood flow. There are a few hormonal irregularities that can delay or stop the first period.

Diagnosis

The medical diagnosis of why you haven't had your first period follows a fairly routine pattern. In many cases, there is no major physical problem, the onset of puberty has simply been delayed, and periods will come along in their own time. Delayed onset of puberty, however, is a diagnosis of exclusion, and most doctors will want to make absolutely sure there's nothing else the matter. First they check to see whether you have all systems go on the oestrogen front.

If you have any development in the bosoms department, it means that either your ovaries are making oestrogen, or the body is converting androgens to oestrogens in the fat tissues. Full breast development only happens when your ovaries are making oestrogen, so how developed your breasts are (this has nothing to do with actual size) gives important clues to the causes of the lack of period.

Being a normal height for your age can be important because some physical abnormalities are associated with being unusually short. (Of course, being short doesn't mean you will automatically have any physical abnormalities.)

The next step is an ultrasound to make sure you have a uterus and all the right accessories. (An explanation of ultrasounds is under Screening in The Medical Approach chapter.)

If there's still no problem, the next step is to take blood tests to see if there's a hormone problem. Usually the levels of follicle stimulating hormone (FSH), luteinising hormone (LH), and prolactin (the breast-related hormone) are checked. Normal levels of all three are seen in delayed puberty; a high LH with a low FSH is seen in polycystic ovarian disease; a high prolactin level usually indicates a pituitary tumour called a prolactinoma; and a high FSH and LH indicates a possible 'resistant ovary syndrome'.

The Medical Approach

Some of the rare physical abnormalities can be corrected by surgery. If this is not possible (you can't replace a missing uterus) then both doctors and natural therapists should consider counselling options for somebody dealing with their feelings and the health implications. Some of the other medical causes can be treated with hormonal drugs. This is a complicated area of medicine and you'll need to find a specialist. A serious eating or overexercise disorder will also need specialist help. (More info is in The Usual Suspects section at the start of this chapter under Eating Disorders, Diets, and Exercise and also in the chapter called Starting Out: Adolescence.

Natural Therapies

A natural therapist can help you offset the side effects of prescribed drugs, and support you in treating eating or exercise disorders.

The periods stop (secondary amenorrhoea)

- Your period stops for six months or more during any of the years between the first period and menopause; or
- You miss more than three periods in a row and your usual cycle is longer than 28 days.

Common causes of stopped periods (secondary amenorrhoea)

Hypothalamus problems

The hypothalamus usually secretes gonadotrophin releasing hormone (GnRH) in pulses, but a number of conditions can interfere, including:

Stress

Stress, including travel, can stop periods. The oestrogen levels are in the lower range and often ovulation doesn't happen.

Weight loss

Periods can stop if the body fat content drops below 25 per cent. Common causes are being underweight, anorexia nervosa and serious illness.

Overexercise

GnRH is badly affected by prolonged and rigorous exercise and this can stop periods.

Severe chronic illness

Chronic renal or liver failure, and other severe or prolonged illnesses can stop periods because of their effect on the hypothalamus.

Drugs

Some prescribed drugs can interfere with hormones.

Post-pill amenorrhoea

About 80 per cent of women get a period within three months of stopping the Pill, but about 1 per cent will experience long-term post-Pill absent periods. Some of these women have pre-existing conditions, such as polycystic ovarian disease, which haven't been noticed while the Pill caused regular 'periods'.

'Phantom pregnancy'

A phantom pregnancy is usually accompanied by higher than normal levels of prolactin and luteinising hormone (LH), which stop periods.

Hypothalamic lesions

Lesions of the hypothalamus which stop periods are linked to levels of follicle stimulating hormone (FSH) and LH which are too low to stimulate follicle development and oestrogen production.

Uterus problems

Asherman's syndrome

Persistent absent periods and infertility which results from intra-uterine adhesions (scar tissue), usually following D&C surgery (explained under Surgery in The Medical Approach chapter) or from an infection in the uterus.

Narrowing of the cervix

Obstructed period flow caused by chronic infection, or medical procedures including cone biopsy, cauterisation treatment (the destruction of tissue with a hot instrument, or the burning of tissue with a caustic substance), cryosurgery (the destruction of tissue with extreme cold), laser surgery, or irradiation of the cervix.

Pituitary problems

The destruction of pituitary gland tissue can stop periods:

Pituitary lesions

Malignant or non-malignant tumours of the pituitary can stop periods. The most common of these are caused by an increased secretion of prolactin which leads to a condition called hyperprolactinaemia.

Pituitary insufficiency

In rare cases the pituitary tissue can be damaged by lack of oxygen, blood clots or severe haemorrhage (haemorrhage after childbirth causing destruction of the pituitary gland is called Sheehan's syndrome). The FSH, LH and oestrogen levels are all low.

Empty sella syndrome

In this rare syndrome the membrane that separates the pituitary and hypothalamus is either absent or incomplete, and periods can stop.

Not ovulating

A number of conditions can lead to prolonged dysfunction of the ovaries and no periods:

Polycystic ovarian disease (PCOD)

This common condition is characterised by not ovulating, multiple ovarian cysts, an abnormal hormone profile and no periods. There's a whole section on PCOD later in this chapter.

Breastfeeding

Breastfeeding is initially triggered by high prolactin levels which stop ovulation and periods.

Thyroid conditions

An underactive thyroid causes lower levels of sex hormone binding globulin (SHBG) which leads to an eventual increase in oestrogen production. An overactive thyroid leads to a greater conversion of androgens to oestrogens. Both situations can stop periods because they stop ovulation, but once the thyroid condition has been treated, periods start again.

Cushing's syndrome

A syndrome caused by excess corticosteroids and a wide range of symptoms including obesity, thinning of the skin, abnormal fat distribution around the neck and upper back, high blood pressure, diabetes, hairiness and stopped periods. It can be caused by adrenal or pituitary tumours, or cortisone medication.

Congenital adrenal hyperplasia

This is a rare congenital condition where the adrenal gland produces too much androgen.

Androgen-secreting adrenal and ovarian tumours

These very rare, often malignant tumours secrete androgens and can stop periods.

Premature ovarian failure

The ovaries may stop working before you're 40. The causes are unknown: in some cases it may be because of an auto-immune problem or because the ovarian tissue won't respond to FSH and LH.

Destruction of ovarian tissue

Ovarian tissue can be damaged by impaired blood supply. This can stop ovulation and periods.

As you can see, some of the causes of secondary amenorrhoea shown here can be tackled on your own, such as too much exercise and not enough kilojoules. Others are conditions needing specialist medical treatment, maybe with drugs or surgery. A natural therapist will be able to help you offset the side effects of necessary drugs. If you need surgery, make sure you check out the handy hints for preparation and convalescence in The Medical Approach chapter.

Here's some more info on some of the specific causes of stopped periods.

Hyperprolactinaemia

If you have hyperprolactinaemia you have too much prolactin hormone. The most common symptom of hyperprolactinaemia is the production of breast milk, even if you're not pregnant. Other symptoms might include light, irregular periods or stopped periods. Because high prolactin is one of the more common causes of absent periods, women with no periods usually have their prolactin levels evaluated in the first round of medical tests.

Causes

Higher prolactin levels can be caused by abnormal function or stimulation of the prolactin-secreting cells in the pituitary gland. This rise might go on for ages, or happen suddenly and cause only a temporary increase in prolactin. (The only way the menstrual cycle can be altered is when prolactin levels remain persistently elevated. A temporary surge or rise might give an abnormal blood test result, but it won't have a prolonged effect on your periods.)

Prolonged hyperprolactinaemia

Tumours of the pituitary gland, called microadenomas or prolactinomas, which secrete prolactin, are the most common causes. Often the tumours are very small and can't even be seen with a CAT scan, a type of X-ray.

Other causes include an underactive thyroid gland ('hypothyroidism'); surgery or chest wall trauma caused by burns, irritation or shingles; epileptic seizures and spinal cord tumours.

Temporary hyperprolactinaemia

- Too much stress for too long.
- Overexercise, such as athletic training.
- Too much breast stimulation. 'Deer Massage' (a meditative yoga pose which includes prolonged and regular massage of the nipples) can cause irregular periods.

Drugs causing excess prolactin

Some drugs can cause elevated prolactin levels, stopped periods or unwanted breast milk production:

- Major tranquilliser therapy such as the phenothiazines (Largactil, Stemetil, Stelazine and Melleril), and haloperidol (Serenace).
- Anti-ulcer drugs such as Pepcidine, Tagamet, Tazac and Zantac.
- The anti-hypertensive drugs Aldactone and Aldomet.
- High-dose oestrogen oral contraceptive pills.
- Opiates, cocaine and alcohol, especially beer.

Signs and symptoms

- Breast milk production.
- Low levels of both gonadotrophin releasing hormone (GnRH) and luteinising hormone (LH).
- Reduced levels of oestradiol, most androgens and sex hormone binding globulin (SHBG). Adrenal androgens are elevated, usually without causing hairiness.
- Often, low bone density regardless of oestrogen levels.

The Medical Approach

- You will be given a blood test to find out the prolactin levels. The most reliable time to take the blood is during the follicular phase (first half) of the cycle, late in the morning. Breast stimulation, heavy meals and exercise should be avoided before the test. Some endocrinologists take three tests at half-hour intervals to rule out false positive readings.
- When a high prolactin level has been identified, a CAT scan of the pituitary gland is recommended to evaluate the size and presence

of the pituitary tumour. Rarely, very large pituitary tumours might need to be surgically removed because they can damage the nearby optic nerve.

- But in most cases the aim is to re-instate a normal cycle by prescribing bromocriptine (Parlodel) to reduce elevated prolactin, stop lactation and re-instate ovulation, cyclic regularity and fertility (more info is under Drugs in The Medical Approach chapter). Other conditions which are responsible for the elevated prolactin levels, such as hypothyroidism, will also require treatment.
- If you're lactating, but have normal periods, treatment is rarely needed. Your doctor will keep an eye on the condition. However, if the cycle is erratic and long, progestogen drugs can be given at regular intervals and then withdrawn to bring on a period. There's more info on them under Drugs in The Medical Approach chapter.
- Yearly measurements of blood prolactin levels are often suggested to monitor prolactin-secreting tumours. These tumours usually do not increase in size and so repeated X-rays are usually unnecessary. The level of prolactin can decrease over time, even when the tumour size remains constant. Checks are maintained to make sure the tumour doesn't encroach on the optic nerve and damage your sight.

Natural therapies

Some women experience side effects from bromocriptine such as dizziness and seek herbal alternatives; others are inclined to try a more natural approach for their complaints before using medication. But the herbal, vitamin and mineral treatments for hyperprolactinaemia can be quite complex and certainly not as straightforward as taking a drug. In severe cases of hyperprolactinaemia there is also a tendency for herbal preparations to regulate periods successfully for the first few months, and then it becomes more of a struggle.

So, you need to decide in advance what you want from treatment. Herbal remedies make quite useful short-term medications where pregnancy is the aim, and are useful for milder cases. Herbs may not be much chop in the longer term to regulate periods and maintain oestrogen levels when prolactin levels are very high.

Some nutrients help normalise prolactin levels because they boost dopamine levels. Dopamine, a brain chemical, is a prolactin-inhibitor.

Even if you choose to treat the problem with natural therapies, it is still best to keep under the supervision and regular checks of a specialist doctor.

Zinc and vitamin B6

The body needs zinc and vitamin B6 to make dopamine. Zinc may be a good supplement if you have hyperprolactinaemia *and* signs of zinc deficiency or relative dopamine deficiency. There's an info page on zinc under Minerals in the Self Care chapter.

Herbs

A number of herbal formulas commonly used in traditional Chinese medicine have been tested for their effectiveness in the treatment of hyperprolactinaemia. These include Rehmannia Eight Combination (Ba Wei Di Huang Tang) which has been used to improve fertility and Peony and Liquorice Combination (Shao Yao Gan Cao Tang). Peony and Liquorice Combination is thought to act directly on the pituitary gland to counteract hyperprolactinaemia.

Vitex agnus castus, a herb from the European herbal tradition, has been shown to mimic the action of dopamine. *Vitex agnus castus* can be a safe and efficient alternative to drugs for infertility related to luteal phase defects and for premenstrual sore breasts caused by mildly elevated prolactin levels. All herbs must be administered by a specialist herbalist, and there's more on them under Herbs in the Natural Therapies chapter.

Self Care

- Stress can raise prolactin levels. Check out Stress under The Usual Suspects for management hints.
- Avoid beer, which increases prolactin.

Bleeding too lightly

A period is considered abnormal if it:

- goes for less than three days;
- the cycle is more than 35 days;
- the bleeding is very slight or almost absent; and/or
- needs two or less pads or tampons a day.

Having periods which are too light is called oligomenorrhoea. Can you believe these names? Basically it just means light periods (*oligo* is ancient Greek meaning too little, or scant). So oligohypermenorrhoea means heavy periods which are infrequent. (*Hyper* means too much.) And finally, let's get this over with right now, light periods that are also infrequent are called a word that sounds the same, but means the opposite: oligohypomenorrhoea (*hypo* means not enough).

Don't forget you may have a naturally light period which is perfectly healthy for you: light periods are not necessarily a problem. It's usually a temporary thing where you have one or two light periods, unless there's an underlying disorder causing a failure to ovulate.

A lighter period than normal often indicates that you didn't ovulate, or you have a functional disorder caused by overexercise, not eating well or stress.

The Medical Approach

Doctors will often not bother to treat light periods unless you want to get pregnant and your light periods are caused by not ovulating. Some doctors will identify the underlying cause and suggest treatment. Some doctors will suggest the Pill if they suspect your oestrogen is too low to protect your bones.

Usually a fertility drug is used to induce ovulation, often one called Clomid. (Side effects must be discussed with your doctor.)

Natural therapies

- The underlying cause will be identified and treated if possible, for example, putting on weight.
- Herbs to normalise hormone levels and induce ovulation can be used. These include *Vitex agnus castus* and the steroidal saponin-containing herbs such as *Chamaelirium luteum* (helonias) and *Aletris farinosa* (true unicorn root). (It's alright, no unicorns were harmed during the making of this product.) Other useful herbs are *Angelica sinensis* and *Paeonia lactiflora* (peony). There's more detail under Herbs in the Natural Therapies chapter.

Blood quality

Some natural therapists will see light periods as a syndrome called lack of blood quality. There's a bit of history behind this way of thinking.

Over the centuries, traditional medicine observed that people who looked as though they had lost blood and were pale, weak, tired and vague were said to have 'weak' blood; those who were red-faced, overstimulated, irritable and energetic were said to have an 'excess' of blood.

A large number of women's complaints were attributed to blood because women not only lose blood every month and during childbirth, but also were believed to lose the essence of blood when they breastfed. (Many early cultures thought of breast milk as blood with the redness taken out.)

A relatively modern name for weak blood, dating from around Shakespeare's time until the turn of this century, was 'chlorosis'. Chlorosis means 'greenish colour' and was a common diagnosis of young women. The symptoms were fatigue; a yellowish tinge to the Anglo-Saxon face, with dark rings around the eyes and period symptoms such as no periods or heavy bleeding.

The opposite condition, 'plethora', indicated an excess of blood. It was characterised by overindulgence generally and of alcohol in particular, irritability, headaches, and a red face. It was a condition common to the older generation, usually gouty old grumpy men, and was believed to be the precursor to strokes.

A diagnosis of either chlorosis or plethora was cast aside when in modern times it became possible to test for anaemia. Technically, anaemia means a lack of iron in the red blood cells or insufficient numbers of red blood cells. The common causes are lack of dietary iron or excessive blood loss. The term is often used (incorrectly) in common language to describe a number of symptoms including tiredness, an inability to concentrate, paleness, dizziness, or a lacklustre attitude to life.

A natural therapist's diagnosis of poor blood quality (also known as 'blood deficiency' in traditional Chinese medicine, and 'anaemic' or 'nutritionally depleted' by naturopaths) is *not* the same as medical anaemia, but a more complicated syndrome characterised by:

- Exhaustion and poor stamina.
- Unusual debility around the period, and especially afterwards.
- An increased tendency to infection around the period, especially candida (thrush) and recurrent viral infections such as herpes.
- Headaches often with or after the period.
- Dizziness.
- Pale face and tongue.
- Dry skin and unhealthy, lank hair.
- Period irregularities, especially no periods or infrequent periods, occasionally heavy bleeding.

The aim of the treatment is to improve the overall quality and activity of the blood. Iron, though important, is not everything:

- The quality of blood is corrected with diet, nutritive herbs and supplements.

- The general energy levels are improved with the women's tonic herbs.
- In cases of infrequent periods or stopped periods, hormonal regulating herbs are used.
- Assimilation of nutrients is assisted with the Warming digestive herbs and foods.
- Circulation is enhanced with circulatory stimulants and Warming herbs.

Many of the common herbs used to treat abnormal bleeding are also nutritive herbs and are high in the blood-building and anti-haemorrhagic nutrients like iron, vitamins A, K and C, and folic acid. Some important examples are *Rubus idaeus* (raspberry leaves) and *Petroselinum crispum* (parsley leaves).

Chamaelirium luteum, *Aletris farinosa* and *Angelica sinensis* as well as *Rubus idaeus* are general female tonics and assist with regulation of all aspects of the menstrual cycle.

Anaemia is related to blood quality and is a common complaint affecting women who have periods. An info page on anaemia and getting enough iron is under Minerals in the Self Care chapter.

Ovarian cysts

Ovaries are complicated little organs with one major job to do—assembly and dispatch. Each month one ovary makes an egg and sends it down the Fallopian tube chute to the uterus in case the ovary owner wants to use it to get pregnant. But as well as egg dispatch, ovaries are responsible for a very intricate and constant series of hormone production. So each ovary is made up of complex tissues which deal with these various functions.

It's not so unusual for this busy ovarian tissue to start doing something abnormal, so ovarian cysts are also quite common. The main thing to know is that the word 'cyst' doesn't necessarily mean a problem at all, and it certainly doesn't automatically mean cancer. Most cysts are completely harmless wee things, requiring no treatment, and you won't even know you have them. At the other end of the scale, cancerous tumours can develop, and these must, of course, be surgically removed.

There are many different kinds of cysts with different structures and behaviours. For example, the weirdest type of common ovarian cyst contains teeth and hair (more of this *X-Files* type behaviour later).

If the ovarian cells which produce hormones for the natural cycle develop abnormally, it can create a cyst which pumps out large amounts of hormones—more than you need. This can cause temporary side effects like more facial hair. Some cysts come with painful conditions like endometriosis; other pretty sneaky ones may spontaneously develop and wither away without ever causing symptoms.

Often you only discover you have an ovarian cyst because of a routine pelvic examination, or during an unrelated examination or ultrasound. Sometimes pain during penetrative sex can be a warning sign, and very large cysts can cause pressure symptoms, a 'bloated' stomach and discomfort. Cysts range in size, if we are to use the medical profession's favourite fruit analogy, usually from the size of a sultana to the size of a grapefruit. (Occasionally there'll be some weird story from an overseas newsagency specialising in amazing stories about a 47-kilo ovarian cyst being removed and the less said about that sort of caper the better.)

Which cyst is which?

An ultrasound will detect most ovarian cysts and a doctor can sometimes make an 'educated guess' about the type because some types of cysts are usually solid, semi-solid or fluid-filled. Many of the different types of cysts can be benign, malignant or 'borderline', and it is usually not possible to tell which one you've got without surgery. Some cysts can be left and kept under observation, but if in doubt, a surgeon will want to go in and remove them.

The most reliable method of telling whether a cyst is malignant, benign or somewhere in between, is to examine it under a microscope during an operation, or after a cyst's removal, in a pathology lab. Cysts are removed under general anaesthetic, during a laparoscopy or laparotomy operation. (Procedures as well as preparation and recovery hints are fully explained in The Medical Approach chapter.)

The main thing about ovarian cysts is to find out which kind you're dealing with, so that you and your health practitioner can accurately plan what to do next. Because of the small possibility that an unidentified cyst might be cancerous, this is no time for airy-fairy guessing games. At the very least an ultrasound exam, or more likely a laparoscopy should be performed for peace of mind.

Benign cysts

There are heaps of benign ovarian cysts. The most common ones are the physiological cysts and those which come with polycystic ovarian disease (PCOD).

Both of these develop because of a disturbance to ovulation. They're by far the most common kinds of cysts you might need to have attended to, so there's heaps to know about them, including how they can throw your hormones out of whack. More later in this chapter.

Other less common varieties include cystadenomas, fibromas, dermoid cysts and Brenner cysts. Many are symptom-free unless they rupture, or cause the ovary to become twisted (called torsion). But even though these cysts are usually not cancerous, they usually have to be surgically removed because most of these benign cysts can have a cancerous form and a definitive diagnosis of when a cyst is cancerous can usually only be made in the laboratory after it is removed. They could also become twisted on a stem and cause pain or rupturing, needing emergency surgery.

Physiological cysts

Physiological cysts are the most common cysts, and they usually don't need treatment or surgery. They are also known as 'simple' or functional cysts. They are not to be confused with the 'functioning cysts', which 'function' by producing hormones. (You'd think they could think up some less confusing names.) Physiological cysts are caused by abnormal development of the egg in the ovary—not by abnormal cell growth. There are two sorts of these cysts, follicular and luteal, named because of the time they appear in the menstrual cycle.

Follicular cysts

Follicular cysts, which are common, are formed due to a deviation of the normal ovulation. They develop from a developing follicle (egg sac) which—oops—turns into a cyst instead of an egg.

In most cases the cysts are small, cause few symptoms, and may be accidentally discovered. They generally require no treatment and are usually re-absorbed without causing any problems, and other egg sacs come along and do the right thing. Occasionally these cysts may rupture, but since they are small and don't often contain blood, they cause little trouble and usually require no further treatment.

Luteal cysts

Luteal cysts develop in the second phase of the cycle. Big ones can cause dull pain, but most of the time they are only discovered because of a routine examination. They require no treatment and will usually be re-absorbed by themselves.

Sometimes, a luteal cyst will rupture. If small ones do, the pain is generally pretty mild and stops when the period starts. But if there's a rupture of a large, blood-filled luteal cyst, it may cause serious pain and be confused with ruptured ectopic pregnancy or something else.

Luteal cysts may interfere with progesterone production and cause irregularities in the cycle. The progesterone stimulates the lining of the uterus and can delay a period or make the cycle longer or shorter. Luteal cysts usually disappear after one cycle, and everything will return to normal without any treatment.

Cysts that probably should be surgically removed

Hormone-producing (functioning) cysts

Hormone-producing cysts, also known as functioning cysts, can produce male or female hormones and therefore can interfere with the menstrual cycle or fertility. (They are usually diagnosed because of their effects on the period.)

Some rare cysts which produce androgens (male hormones), can cause side effects such as male-pattern hair growth, deepening of the voice, decreased breast size and the development of a more male body shape. Surgical removal of the cyst should fix all of these problems except for the voice changes. You'll just have to sound sexy for the rest of your life and, sadly if you're a professional singer, move to another section of the choir.

Cysts which produce oestrogen are the most common. They can cause irregular and heavy bleeding and abnormal cell changes in the endometrium (uterus lining) which can progress to endometrial cancer. All of these symptoms are related to prolonged excess levels of oestrogen. These cysts vary in size, but are often quite small, and should be surgically removed.

Serous and mucinous cystadenomas

These types of ovarian cyst can grow to very large sizes and torsion (that twisting on the pedicle thing) can be a problem. The serous cysts are filled with a thin liquid, and the mucinous ones contain a much stickier mucus-like substance. Rupture of either type is likely to cause pain, but the mucky stuff causes more irritation of the pelvic lining and is more likely to cause adhesions (healing scars which can bind organs together). Serous cysts do not affect ovulation, but they rarely re-absorb by themselves so the best idea is to have them surgically removed, given the greater mess that might have to be operated on if they rupture. (Serous and mucinous ovarian cysts have a rarer, malignant form called a cystadenocarcinoma. You can't tell if it's the nastier version on an ultrasound. This is another reason why doctors will want to get them out.)

Fibromas

Fibromas, as you may have guessed, are fibrous. They are often solid and sometimes produce excess oestrogen. A proper diagnosis of fibromas must be done with a microscope during or after an operation. Because they rarely go away of their own accord, and can get bigger and cause pressure or torsion problems, it is safest to have them surgically removed.

Dermoid cysts (teratomas)

Dermoid cysts form as a result of abnormal multiplication of the cells which make the egg in an ovary. These egg-producing cells have the potential to create different types of tissue normally found in anyone's body, because they may end up being used to make a foetus, if fertilised by a sperm.

Erratic growth of these cells in dermoid cysts can produce many different structures, including hair, teeth, bones and skin fragments. (That's the weird bit.) This is because the cells are getting way ahead of themselves and trying to make bits of a person.

Obviously these bits are not things that one wants hanging around in an ovary, so dermoid cysts are best removed surgically. Dermoid cysts can be on a pedicle, can become malignant and won't go away by themselves. They rarely rupture but when they do it can be incredibly painful.

Once you understand what a dermoid is, you can stop worrying that your body is creating something from the *Alien* movie. If you develop a dermoid cyst, don't be too freaked out—it is quite common after all, and it's not as bizarre as Michael Jackson's face.

Brenner tumours

These are usually small and benign, but can sometimes become malignant. They can happen at any age and sometimes cause irregular or heavy periods, but are more common after the menopause. It's usually best to have them surgically removed, especially after menopause when they are more likely to be cancerous.

Malignant cysts (ovarian cancer)

Ovarian cancer is quite rare, but usually develops insidiously without symptoms, so the cancer can be advanced before anybody knows about it.

The good news is that the earlier ovarian cancer is diagnosed, the greater the chances of survival. And the early surgical removal and treatment of a cancerous cyst may result in a complete cure.

To further confuse the issue, ovarian cysts can be 'borderline'—neither benign nor malignant, but somewhere between the two, and some benign ovarian cysts may progress to becoming malignant. Some tumours might start elsewhere and then spread to the ovary. Your best protection against ovarian cancer is vigilance, and swift surgical intervention to be sure of anything that looks like it could turn nasty.

If you're over 40 you should have an annual internal examination. We all should have an internal examination when we go for the usual yearly or two-yearly Pap test. Pelvic ultrasound screening can also reduce the risk of ovarian cancer. All these procedures are explained under Screening in The Medical Approach chapter.

The Medical Approach

Physiological cysts are diagnosed with ultrasound. They rarely require treatment but some women develop these cysts so regularly that the Pill is suggested as a treatment to suppress ovulation. More info on the Pill is under Drugs in The Medical Approach chapter.

The three most common strategies when a cyst is found are:

- surgical removal;
- hormonal treatments which can prevent some cysts from forming; or
- 'wait and see'.

Treatment obviously depends on what the complications might be for an individual type of cyst left to its own devices. Complications can include rupture, twisting of the ovary, interference with the regularity of the cycle, destruction of ovarian tissue, the spread of cancer, and infertility.

Many cysts require no treatment. If the cyst is small, and most likely to be benign and will re-absorb of its own accord, it's safe to wait and see. This is especially likely for young women who develop benign physiological cysts which usually re-absorb within two cycles.

But when any cyst is present for more than two cycles, surgery is often recommended because benign and trouble-free cysts don't usually hang around this long. The Pill may be recommended for recurrent problem cysts or for some cases of polycystic ovarian disease (PCOD) because it prevents ovulation, which is the source of these cysts. Long-term use of the Pill is also associated with a lower risk of developing ovarian cancer.

Surgical removal of a cyst is advised if it is judged to be a likely culprit for complications or serious illness: cysts which continue to grow, fail to re-absorb or which might be malignant. Some women seek natural treatments to 'dissolve' or 'shrink' the cyst because they're frightened of or opposed to the notion of surgery. This is not a good policy—treating ovarian cysts without specific knowledge of their type is asking for trouble.

'Torsion' can happen when the ovary containing the cyst twists and cuts off its own blood supply, causing death of the ovarian tissue. Torsion of ovarian cysts can cause severe pain and will require immediate surgery. Torsion can also happen when the cyst itself twists on its stem, or 'pedicle', and this can lead to rupture.

Large cysts, especially those larger than 5 centimetres across, can rupture at any time causing pain and adhesions, and should be surgically removed. The blood-filled cysts of endometriosis (called endometriomas) tend to grow with each period and are prone to rupture, even when quite small, and should also be surgically treated. Growing or large ovarian cysts, too, are removed because they can go completely feral, destroying parts of the ovary and even causing the entire ovary to atrophy and stop ovulation or hormone production.

If malignancy is suspected, swift surgical removal is essential. Ovarian cancer is a concern for all women. Although the incidence is very much less for younger women, one in every three ovarian cysts in women more than 45 years old are cancerous. In this age group, when a small benign-looking cyst is discovered the doctor may wait for one cycle, but if it persists or if there is any doubt about the type of cyst, the doctor should suggest immediate removal.

Ovarian cysts which appear after the menopause are suspicious (because ovulation has stopped, ovarian cysts should not form) and there is a high likelihood of malignancy. They should be removed as soon as possible. (The presence of some malignant cysts can be tracked by blood tests, which is useful because you can avoid repeat operations or ultrasounds to try and see if a cyst is still there.)

Natural therapies

A trained herbalist can help with preventing more simple cysts from occurring, but should not attempt treatment of an undiagnosed cyst. A therapist is usually not worried about simple cysts unless they happen often and interfere with the cycle or cause pain. *Chamaelirium luteum* (helonias) will usually prevent the formation of recurrent cysts. It's believed to normalise ovarian function, including ovulation and is also used for infertility caused by erratic ovulation. The way that it works is not fully understood because, unlike the Pill, it doesn't stop ovulation. It should be prescribed by a herbal specialist.

Self care

If you must have surgery, check out how to prepare and recover from an operation in The Medical Approach chapter.

Polycystic ovarian disease (PCOD)

Here's the confusing part: there's this thing called polycystic ovaries, which literally means any condition causing many cysts in the ovary or ovaries. And then there's this whole other thing called polycystic ovarian disease (PCOD), which is much more complicated, because it covers a whole lot of specific conditions or syndromes which also cause multiple ovarian cysts.

As you can imagine, there is a fair bit of confusion about the two terms because many writers, doctors and natural therapists do not differentiate between polycystic ovaries and polycystic ovarian disease.

According to ultrasound examinations, up to one in five women have multiple ovarian cysts. Some of them have both normal cycles and periods and experience no problems; others may have a range of symptoms including irregular menstruation or abnormally light periods.

All of these women have polycystic ovaries—ovaries which have many cysts, *but only those with additional hormonal irregularities have polycystic ovarian disease*. So anyone with many 'simple' cysts on their ovaries has polycystic ovaries. Those who have lots of cysts on their ovaries *and* hormonal abnormalities have polycystic ovarian disease (PCOD). This section deals only with PCOD.

People with PCOD have a tendency to produce too much androgen (male hormones) and to ovulate erratically. Other symptoms of PCOD can be no periods, no ovulation, male-pattern hairiness and obesity. To add to the guessing game, women with PCOD might have none, any or all of these complaints.

Making a diagnosis of PCOD is further complicated because these symptoms just mentioned can also happen to people who don't have PCOD at all. Women with similar symptoms might have something else entirely, like a misbehaving thyroid gland.

Diagnosis

PCOD is usually suspected if you have developed irregular periods or stopped periods, you're carrying around extra weight, can't seem to get pregnant and look more moustachey than usual—'male-pattern' hair growth. An ultrasound of the ovaries will detect multiple cysts. Before a firm diagnosis of PCOD can be made, all of the other possible types of endocrine abnormalities need to be excluded as causes. This usually involves a physical examination, blood tests and X-rays in addition to the ultrasound. (More ultrasound info is under Screening in The Medical Approach chapter.)

Causes

Although it is now generally agreed that PCOD originates in the ovary, a number of other factors seem to make important contributions. Putting on extra weight can trigger hormonal changes that can kick a symptom-free simple cysts condition into a full-on case of PCOD. It has been suggested that other endocrine glands like the thyroid might also be implicated in leading to PCOD in some women. PCOD may also be inherited. Around 40 per cent of the women in families with PCOD will have the condition, but not all of them will develop symptoms.

Abnormal ovarian function

Women with PCOD have been found to have low levels of ovarian oestrogen (oestradiol) and high levels of ovarian androgens. (Basically—the girly hormones are being outflanked by the blokey hormones.) The androgens produced within the follicle (the bit that makes the egg) seem to prevent ovulation and normal egg development. The end result is that the eggs become cysts instead, so that's why ovulation doesn't happen. Some women with PCOD have one ovary that's normal and one that's polycystic.

Androgen excess

Androgens, made in the ovaries and the adrenal glands, usually circulate in small amounts in the blood of all women without causing any 'masculinising'. If you've got PCOD, however, you've got too many blokey hormones—not as many as blokes have, but enough to cause a hormone imbalance and the symptoms of PCOD. (There's more info on androgen excess in its own section below.)

Excess weight gain

Various bits of the body convert androgens into an oestrogen called oestrone by a process called aromatisation—not to be confused with lighting smelly candles and having a lavender bubble bath. One of the parts of the body which aromatises is fatty tissue. So if you are overweight, there are more fatty tissues converting androgen into more and more oestrone. This maintains really high levels of oestrogen in the body all month long, instead of the natural cycle causing the normal ups and downs of oestrogen throughout the cycle.

Some women control the severity of PCOD and the regularity of their menstrual cycle by reducing their overall weight. Many women with PCOD and obesity have problems with insulin resistance.

Here's some good news: if you have PCOD you'll probably take to being thin better than other women. You can probably maintain your bone density even when your Body Mass Index (BMI) is low, and continue to ovulate (or start to) when you're thin. Women with 'normal' ovaries function best in the reproductive department and maintain bone density when there's a heap of food around—the origin of the exaggerated, roly-poly earth mother image. A Body Mass Index (BMI) result of 21 can often maintain normal cycles if you have PCOD. (See Being Underweight in The Usual Suspects section for how to calculate your BMI.)

The adrenal glands

Another theory is that PCOD can be started because the adrenal glands are pumping out too many androgens, which are then faithfully converted to oestrone by the fatty tissue. These high, constant oestrone levels suppress the egg-making follicular hormone, and encourage too much luteinising hormone which in turn tells the body to make even more androgens—and so it's a vicious circle.

Sex hormone binding globulin

High levels of androgen and obesity also suppress the sex hormone binding globulin (SHBG), a protein which transports both oestrogen and testosterone around the body. Normally, the SHBG 'babysits' the natural testosterone. When SHBG levels drop, the testosterone runs wild, causing acne and male-pattern hair growth.

Signs and symptoms

- PCOD is the most common cause of not ovulating: about 75 per cent of women with PCOD develop infertility (if you don't make the eggs, you can't get them fertilised).

- About 60 per cent of women with PCOD have excess body hair.
- About half will not have periods.
- Around 40 per cent are overweight.
- Nearly a third have abnormal bleeding patterns.
- About 20 per cent develop 'male' characteristics such as a deeper voice and changes in body shape.
- About 15 per cent have the basal body temperature changes which indicate ovulation.
- About 10 per cent have regular period cycles.

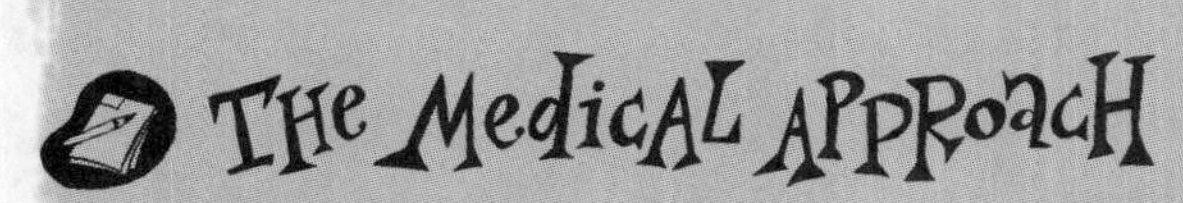

Reduce the risk of endometrial cancer

If periods have stopped, periods should be brought about to protect the endometrium from too much cell build-up which can eventually become cancerous—it's the endometrium which bleeds away during a period.

Doctors prescribe cyclic hormones like the Pill, or small doses of progesterone for seven to ten days each month after which the 'period' will come on. The progesterone, either taken alone or in the Pill, initiates changes in the endometrium which are similar to those in the normal cycle. (There's more on these drugs in The Medical Approach chapter.)

Induce ovulation with drugs

Fertility drugs, such as Clomid, are used if you want to get pregnant. Side effects should be discussed with your doctor.

Reduce hairiness

The most common drugs prescribed are Androcur (cyproterone acetate) or the Pill called Diane (can you BELIEVE manufacturers called a Pill *Diane*? What are they thinking? Do you reckon there's a prostate drug called Bruce, for God's sake?) The hair often grows back when the person stops the drug.

Natural therapies

The tendency to develop PCOD cannot be 'cured' but hormones can be regulated so that symptoms are minimised. If you have bad PCOD, natural remedies may not be strong enough to control your feral hormones. Combining natural remedies and drugs might be more useful, especially when there is serious risk of endometrial change or severe masculinising effects from androgens.

Natural therapists share the same three aims as the medical approach, using different means. The emphasis of natural treatments will depend on the combination of the symptoms and your idea of a successful outcome.

Reduce the risk of endometrial cancer

For the endometrium to be adequately protected, you need regular periods. These intervals vary depending on your weight and age. If you're within the normal weight range, and aged 35 or less, you should have at least three periods every year. Older women, particularly if they're overweight, should have at least six a year (until the menopause, obviously).

Obese women, who are likely to have more problems with PCOD, should be having a period each month if they can. For this reason, the Pill may be your best treatment option to protect the endometrium if you're obese and at increased risk of endometrial hyperplasia or cancer.

Herbs which can bring on periods and other natural remedies which may be useful to protect the endometrium are outlined under Endometrial Hyperplasia in the Erratic Bleeding section.

Stimulate ovulation if you want to get pregnant

Some herbs are believed to be able to normalise ovulation, and can be prescribed by a professional herbalist with specific experience in this area. *Chamaelirium luteum* is a beauty as it is also used in preventing ovarian cysts. *Cimicifuga racemosa*, best known for use against menopausal symptoms, also gets the menstrual cycle into gear because of its effect on luteinising hormone (LH). It is particularly useful for PCOD with hops and peony.

The other helpful group of herbs are the 'female tonic' herbs. This group are usually 'oestrogenic' and contain phyto-oestrogens or steroidal saponins. They exert a much weaker effect than oestrogen and may kick-start ovulation by increasing the levels of follicle stimulating hormone (FSH). Included in this group are *Dioscorea villosa* and *Aletris farinosa*. *Vitex agnus castus* should be cautiously prescribed for this condition because although it stimulates ovulation, it may increase luteinising hormone which you definitely don't need.

Reduce excess hair growth

If you're worried about sprouty bits, your target is your androgen levels. See the section on androgen excess, below, for treatment details.

Training the other feral hormones

Luteinising hormone

Too much luteinising hormone (LH) causes too much androgen around the place, and when LH levels fall, so do androgens. Three herbs have a direct impact on luteinising hormone: *Cimicifuga racemosa* (black cohosh), *Humulus lupulus* (hops), and *Lycopus virginiana* (bugleweed). Hops and black cohosh are especially good—hops when stress and nervous tension accompany PCOD. Both seem also to inhibit the effect of oestrogen. *Lycopus virginiana* is usually given to treat hyperthyroidism, but will also reduce the levels of LH as well as follicle stimulating hormone (FSH). It should only be taken short term, and not if you're trying to ovulate properly again. Remember, don't self-prescribe.

Blood sugar abnormalities

Women with PCOD are prone to blood sugar abnormalities which develop as a result of obesity and 'insulin resistance'. In this condition, insulin production continues (unlike in diabetes), but the levels become very high because the insulin can't get glucose into the cell the way it's supposed to, so the body is fooled into thinking it needs more insulin.

The priority is to lose weight and help the insulin to get into the cells. The nutrients which help are magnesium, zinc (info pages on these are under Minerals in the Self Care chapter), manganese and chromium. Herbs you may be prescribed include *Gymnema sylvestra* (gymnema), *Galagea officinalis* (goat's rue), *Trigonella foenum-graecum* (fenugreek), and the bitters.

Regulating the blood lipid levels

About three-quarters of women with PCOD have blood fats ('lipids') and blood sugar abnormalities which require treatment, and some also have thyroid gland abnormalities or hyperprolactinaemia as well. The general principles of blood fats regulation involve eating stuff like the bitter herbs, high-fibre foods, and legumes like lentils and soya products, and reducing animal fats. More on Bad Fats and Good Fats, number 8 of the 20 Diet Hints in the Self Care chapter.

Androgen excess

The androgens are a group of hormones, found in both men and women, that have masculinising effects. Women usually have much lower levels of androgens that men. When these blokey hormones get out of control in women, it can cause erratic or stopped periods.

Causes

A number of gynaecological and other conditions can lead to excess androgen production. The common conditions include diseases of the ovaries, adrenal gland disorders, prescription drugs including Dilantin, some of the progestogens such as Duphaston and Danazol; the corticosteroids and corticotrophins; and the anabolic steroids,

Hairy problems

such as Deca-Durabolin. Increased androgen is also linked to obesity, Cushing's syndrome and being post-menopausal.

The anti-epileptic drug Dilantin is particularly linked to increased male-pattern hair growth (hair on the upper lip, around the nipples, spreading pubic hair beyond the 'bikini line' and up to the navel, heavier and thicker hair growth on the arms and legs). Most of these drugs can also interfere with period flow and the regularity of the cycle.

Signs and symptoms

- Irregular or stopped periods.
- Excess hair growth, known as hirsutism. Not always caused by high androgen levels. The amount of hair on your body is usually genetic.
- Excessive scalp hair loss, which is referred to as androgenic alopecia, or male-pattern baldness, which is also genetic. The hair loss might be a generalised thinning or a 'balding spot' on the crown. The hair can get thinner and finer quickly, or the loss can be spread over time. It doesn't result in complete baldness.
- Acne can get worse or suddenly appear.
- Increased male-pattern hair growth and a delayed first period in puberty; and very obvious changes in the amount and coarseness of body or facial hair on adult women, especially along with period irregularities. (Nearly everybody gets a few more hairy bits as they get older.) Hair loss and acne might come along for the ride.
- In severe, rare cases there might be 'virilisation', such as enlargement of the clitoris and reduced breast size. Usually, androgen-producing tumours of the ovary or adrenal gland are responsible for the extremely high androgen levels. Some drugs such as Danazol can also cause virilisation.

Diagnosis

The first step is to test the blood for an elevated testosterone level and the levels of the carrier protein, sex hormone binding globulin (SHBG). Serum testosterone is the best indicator of ovarian androgen production and SHBG indicates how much testosterone is able to exert androgenising effects. The ovaries make more androgens if you have polycystic ovarian disease. Some ovarian cysts also produce androgen.

Testing for the androgen called DHEA sulphate is the most reliable test. When there's a suspicion of adult-onset adrenal hyperplasia, or androgen-producing adrenal tumours, it can detect abnormal adrenal androgen levels. If you develop adult-onset adrenal hyperplasia you are more likely to be short, with elevated blood pressure, period irregularities and some extra tufty bits in the hair department.

Some women have normal androgen levels but an increased sensitivity to their androgens. This tendency is thought to be inherited. It causes similar symptoms to those caused by elevated androgen levels and responds to the same treatments.

The Medical Approach

The treatment of androgen excess depends on the causes. Obesity requires loss of weight; post-menopausal women are often prescribed HRT; drugs can be withdrawn or changed; congenital adrenal hyperplasia and adult-onset adrenal hyperplasia are treated with low doses of dexamethasone, a corticosteroid drug. Adrenal or ovarian tumours will usually require surgical removal.

Some types of the Pill can be used to treat androgen excess. A contraceptive Pill called Diane, which contains an anti-androgen, is used specifically for androgen excess which causes either acne or hirsutism. Some of the new 'third generation' Pills—which contain the progestogens norgestimate, desogesterol and gestodene have low androgen potency (Femoden, Marvelon, Minulet, Triminulet and Trioden). The use of these types of Pill, however, can increase the risk of blood clots and they're not for everyone. (There is more info on the Pill under Drugs in The Medical Approach chapter.)

Many Pills contain a progestogen called levonorgestrel, which has androgenising effects—in most cases it's not the Pill to be on if you already have androgen excess. Check with your doctor. The amount of progestogen in the Pill used will influence its androgenic potential. Triphasil and Triquilar usually don't make androgen excess any worse, for example.

Other progestogens with androgenising effects such as Duphaston, Primulut and Danazol are also discussed under Drugs in The Medical Approach chapter.

Natural therapies

Again, the treatment depends on the cause. Women with polycystic ovarian disease (PCOD) will need advice to help regulate hormonal balance and re-establish regular periods. After the menopause, you can use vegetarian diets and plant oestrogens to increase SHBG and reduce the masculinising effects of androgens. (There's a whole section on plant oestrogens, and protein info for vegetarians in the Self Care chapter.)

Too much male-pattern hair growth or hair loss caused by androgens can be difficult to control with herbs. The *Smilax* species (sarsaparilla) and *Turnera aphrodisiaca* (damiana) seem to block the effects of androgens by competitive inhibition, but drugs are faster and more reliable. When excess hair growth or loss is a serious problem, drugs first, followed by herbal remedies for maintenance, can be the best combo.

Another method is to increase the rate at which androgens are converted by the body to oestrogens. Peony and Liquorice Combination, a formula used in traditional Chinese medicine, is suitable for too much androgen made in the ovaries, but its effects are short term.

The adrenal gland contribution to androgens may be modified by adaptogen herbs including *Eleuthrococcus senticosus* (Siberian ginseng) and *Panax ginseng* (Korean ginseng). The nervines, a group of herbs used to moderate the effects of stress (see Stress in The Usual Suspects section for details), may also be helpful. *Humulus lupulus* (hops) which is a nervine and has the additional benefit of lowering luteinising hormone is an important herb for PCOD.

When excess hair growth is the primary concern, treatment must be continued for many months, and in some cases indefinitely. It is important that the chosen herbal remedies are considered safe for long-term administration. It is vital that you work with a trained herbalist with a specialty in this area, and (all together now) don't self-prescribe.

Self Care

This is not a condition for self-treatment. The advice of a practitioner with knowledge in this area is essential. There are some things you can do to help, though.

- If you're obese or have PCOD, reducing weight or maintaining an ideal weight will help to control androgen levels. Regular meals, a low fat intake and more fibre will help. (Hints on diet are in the Self Care chapter.) Losing weight, and a high fibre and plant oestrogen-containing diet increases the levels of sex hormone binding globulin which helps to bind androgens so that they are less available.
- Reduce stress with long, slow distance exercise, relaxation techniques or meditation (see under Stress in The Usual Suspects section).

Endometriosis and adenomyosis

Endometriosis is a mystery. No-one knows for sure why it happens, but plenty of people will tell you their pet theory—whether you're interested or not—such as 'having a baby cures it' (not necessarily true) or 'it means you'll be infertile' (not necessarily true) and 'you'll be right; my cousin Shazza had endo and now she's got nine kids' (not necessarily true; and poor old Shazza).

You can't really prevent 'endo' or its close relative, adenomyosis, because there's a mixed bag of theories about why it happens, and who's most likely to get it. It's hard to diagnose because it causes heaps of different symptoms, and because some doctors assume the pain is period pain which will 'settle down', especially in younger women. And its hard to treat because endo is different in each person. Decisions about treatment are complex and sometimes the best course of action is anybody's guess. Despite the anecdotal Shazza factor, predictions about future fertility are almost impossible.

As a matter of fact, if your endo doctor says there is nothing to be done, or 'My dear girlie, I know exactly what will cure you, and I understand exactly the extent of your endo without looking inside you and I'll have you cured in a jiffy and give you buckets of babies', then run away. Also run right away if your natural health practitioner says, 'I have a secret theory about endo that nobody else knows about. It happens because you are dehydrated/not eating enough essence of moose antler/not comfortable with your feminine side (etc).'

Having endo is difficult enough without dealing with the smug or narrow-minded shockers out there. You may well find that a combination of medical and natural solutions works best for you. Find somebody who says, 'I have a lot of experience in the field, this is my specialty. I can make educated guesses and try various things and we'll work together to find the best treatment for you.'

But don't get too depressed! Lots of people do get over endo, lots of other people will always have it but manage the pain, and there's a lot we do know and that might help. This is the condition that led to the meeting of your authors—Kaz took her endo along to see Ruth, and believe us when we say we've really been through it! Let's start with what it is.

What is it?

Normally, the endometrium lines the inside of the uterus and is expelled, looking like blood, during each period. When you've got endometriosis, this endometrial tissue starts to grow elsewhere in the body. Usually the endometrium doesn't travel very far, and is found mostly in the pelvis.

One of the main problems with endo is that the endometrial cells in the wrong place keep trying to act like they're in the uterus getting ready in case an egg wants to implant. So each month they grow, and then bleed away again, basically causing new implants and getting bigger. If you could see the endometrial implants, they would look like cysts of dark blood—and doctors often call them 'chocolate cysts' although how they can face a Mars Bar after that is a mystery, too.

Endo causes pain because these 'cysts' or 'implants' are growing in the wrong place and causing pressure and bits to stick together which shouldn't stick together, and blockages where they shouldn't be, all mostly in the pelvis and on all the most delicate reproductive gear we've got, like Fallopian tubes, and that's why it can lead to infertility. But having endo doesn't mean you're automatically infertile, because it depends on how much damage has been done to which parts and how sneaky the body can be to get around it.

Endo is usually diagnosed after a long search for what's causing pain or difficulty in getting pregnant. It is the cause of up to 80 per cent of pelvic pain or infertility. Endo also tends to come back: about half of all women with endo develop it again within five years of successful treatment.

ENDOMETRIOSIS can be on the ovaries, the Fallopian tubes, the outside wall of the uterus, the uterine or ovarian ligaments, the bowel, the ureters, the tube leading from the kidney to the bladder, or the bladder itself, or the pouch of Douglas which is the space between the uterus and the bowel. It can be on the vagina, cervix or vulva. Some people have even found it on their eyelids and navel and other distant places. It's pesky stuff.

The name endometriosis comes from the ancient Greek for within, *endon*, and the word for uterus, *metra*. The *osis* bit on the end is Greek for process, in this case, a disease process. We'll just call it endo.

ADENOMYOSIS is more specific: endometrium growing between the fibres of the muscular wall of the uterus. (*Adeno* is ancient Greek for glandular.)

Symptoms

Adenomyosis and (especially) endometriosis are wildly varying diseases (but you can call them disorders if you like), with symptoms ranging from really severe and near constant pain, dragging feelings in the pelvis, very painful penetrative sex, abnormal bleeding, shocking premenstrual tension, and infertility, all the way down to not a single symptom in sight.

The symptoms suggestive of endo, starting with the most suggestive, are:

- really bad period pain;
- difficulty getting pregnant;
- pain during sex, particularly during penetration;
- pain getting worse toward the end of periods;
- pain before periods and at ovulation;
- pelvic pain on one side;
- a mother or sister with endo.

If you've got all these symptoms you've probably hit the endo jackpot. Getting your first period at an early age, long periods (more than seven days) and heavy *periods* are associated with an increased risk of endo. (Long and irregular *cycles* are associated with a lowered risk.) If you describe all these symptoms and related factors and your doctor says, 'It's just a slight head cold' or 'Nothing to worry about there, missy' make sure you're out of the surgery in two seconds flat. Some of us can spend years getting a diagnosis. If you suspect endo, make sure you get a referral to a specialist—in this case, a gynaecologist at the very least.

Pain

There's no relationship between the severity of endo and the severity of the pain. There seems to be no rhyme or reason about the kind of pain, when it comes, or how bad it gets. About one-third of women with endo have no pain.

The kind of pain is often described as congestive and heavy, or a dull, dragging sensation in the pelvis. During the period, the pain can become sharper, more crampy. For some women, the pain is severe enough to cause fainting, vomiting and diarrhoea. Many women report pain during sex or during bowel movements. There might be random pain throughout the month; at ovulation; before, during or after the period; or all the time. The symptoms are all over the shop.

Hormonal imbalance

If you have endo you probably also have symptoms of PMS including anxiety, mood swings, bloating, breast soreness, constipation, food cravings, and headaches. Interestingly, all women with endo are strikingly beautiful. Alright, sure we made that bit up, but it did cheer you up for a minute there, didn't it?

Cycle length and period flow

Some women with endo have long cycles, but a short cycle with a heavier period is common. The flow is characteristically slow to start and may be thick, brown to black and tarry at first. Irregular cycles, spotting, and/or mid-cycle bleeding can be common.

Diagnosis

Some symptoms you describe may indicate the need for a pelvic examination. The doctor will feel for the pelvic organs and whether they're moving freely or have likely 'adhesions', when cysts or scar tissue has stuck the organs together.

Sometimes, if the doctor can't get enough information this way, you might be referred for an ultrasound examination or look-around laparoscopy surgery. (All of these procedures are explained under Screening and Surgery in The Medical Approach chapter.)

Ultrasound imaging will not reveal endo in the pelvic cavity, but it can usually be relied on for an operator to see adenomyosis or endo cysts in the ovaries. Endo cysts, being made of blood, appear on the ultrasound monitor as darker shapes than other fluid-filled cysts.

Definitive diagnosis

A laparoscopy procedure under general anaesthetic is the only way that a diagnosis of endometriosis can be absolutely confirmed. The operation is usually known as a 'look-see' when any major gynaecological problem is suspected, but often, if endo is found, it will be treated at the same time (more on this shortly). (Hints for getting ready and recovering more quickly from the op are in The Medical Approach chapter.)

Who's got it

Most estimates suggest that between 1 and 10 per cent of women have endo. But this might be a conservative estimate because usually, only women who have pain or infertility have investigative surgery—which is the only foolproof way to diagnose it. Doctors doing surgery for other reasons who also have a look round for endo find that more like 15–20 per cent of women have it. The trick is that a lot of women don't have any trouble or pain from their endo and never even know it's there.

Some researchers believe there are various types of endo, some not as severe as others, because only some women develop endometriosis that causes pain or infertility. Other researchers think it's your individual health which determines the extent of your endo symptoms. Women with a good immune system and inflammatory responses may prevent the endo getting a hold in their bodies without even knowing it.

What it does

About 60 per cent of women with endo develop cysts in the ovaries (ovarian cysts) which vary from microscopic spots to a cyst the size of a tennis ball. When small, the endo growths look a bit like blood blisters and are reddish-blue, or brown if the blood is old. Both ovaries are usually affected. The ovary usually tries to contain the growth of the endometrial tissue by creating a capsule around it, and a cyst is formed. These cysts are either called endometriomas, 'chocolate cysts' or endometrial cysts, and are filled by endometrial blood shed at each period. Even when small, these cysts can rupture and spill their contents into the pelvic cavity.

Unruptured cysts keep growing within their thickened capsule. The endo tissue inside still responds to hormonal change in the same way as normal endometrium and bleeds with each period, causing the cysts to get bigger every month. Eventually the blood becomes thick, sticky and dark brown.

There may be increasing pain as the cysts become larger and press on other organs, blood vessels and nerves. Occasionally, cysts wither away because the internal pressure deprives the cyst of a blood supply and it atrophies. Former atrophied cysts can be identified by the little white scars they leave on the ovarian tissue.

Alternatively, the cyst may grow painlessly, but the risk of rupture multiplies as the months go by. When really large cysts rupture, they usually cause symptoms of acute abdominal pain and shock which has to be treated by immediate surgery. This rush-to-the-hospital situation is relatively rare because cysts almost always rupture before they get big.

Even a very small amount of the blood shed during this kind of rupture will cause inflammation and pain. These common, smaller cyst ruptures usually happen during or just after a period, and are a prime suspect in causing endo pain.

Endo can be anywhere in the pelvis as well as the ovaries. Favourite endo sites are the aforementioned laddishly-named pouch of Douglas, the uterine ligaments, which are like tent-ropes which tether the uterus in the right place, and the peritoneum. (See the Anatomy section if you need more info.)

The 'raspberry-like' implants, or endometriomas of varying number and size can be reddish-blue or brownish-black. As the endo gets worse, the implants tend to merge together and form larger islands of endometrial implants.

Adhesions

The endo tissue will usually 'menstruate' for some months at each period, but as the disease advances, scar tissue develops as the body tries to isolate the irritating intruder and 'wall off' the problem area. Fibrous, solid lumps form over the tissues and organs that have become invaded by the endometrial implants: the adhesions (scar tissue).

Adhesions usually solidify over time and become thick and fibrous. If the endo just keeps getting worse, the body makes more and more adhesions. The tissue and organs near the endo get progressively covered and plastered down by scar tissue. Eventually the pelvic organs can become one large immoveable mass. Any movement of these constricted organs, for example, during sex or an examination by a doctor, can cause pain or discomfort.

Adhesions can also be caused by internal healing after an operation.

Causes: the theories

Almost everyone who gets endo gets it when they are producing oestrogen and menstruating regularly. But other factors must be needed to cause endo, or we'd all have it.

Theories include having too much oestrogen; a retrograde flow of period blood backwards through the Fallopian tubes and out into the pelvis which is then not dealt with by the immune system; a cellular change within the uterine wall; an imbalance of the prostaglandins and leukotrienes which can cause problems with ovulation, fertilisation, embryo development, and the function of the Fallopian tube. The wrong levels of prostaglandins and leukotrienes can also make the period pain worse. (There's more on prostaglandins in the Hormones chapter.)

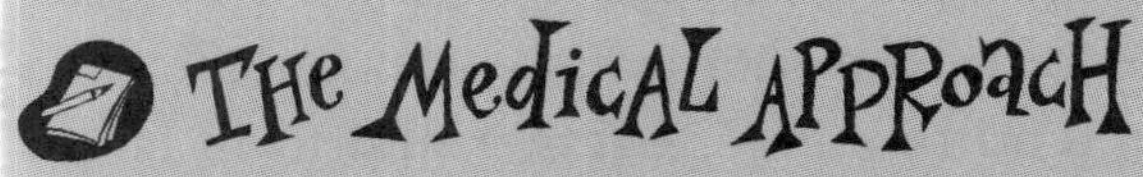

Drugs

Drug treatment of endo aims to:

- reduce the volume of period flow (the Pill);
- create a pregnancy-like state (the progestogens, Provera, Danazol or the Pill when given continuously so the patient does not ovulate or have any periods; or
- cause a temporary menopausal state (the GnRH agonist range of drugs).

Which drug to choose depends on your medical history, the severity of your endo, which drugs you can tolerate easily and whether or not you want to get pregnant. These drugs, and the prostaglandins-inhibitors used for the treatment of period pain are explained under Drugs in The Medical Approach chapter.

Surgery

All the surgical procedures mentioned here, and hints for preparing and recovering from an operation are in The Medical Approach chapter.

The most common recommendation is for a laparoscopy during which endometrial lesions and cysts will be removed. If the patient has given prior permission, this can be done at the same time as the diagnosis is confirmed, so you don't have to undergo surgery twice. (There's not much worse than waking up after an operation and being told, 'Yes, there's something in there that should come out, so as soon as you've recovered from this op, let's just go in again!' as once happened to the flightier author of this book, who changed to another doctor at the speed of light.)

Endo cysts and patches can be destroyed by the surgeon using different methods: burned away with diathermy electrical current; vaporised by lasers and/or cut out with a scalpel. Laser laparoscopy surgery for the treatment of pain caused by endometriosis is very successful. In one study of pain relief following laparoscopic laser, just over 62 per cent of women said their pain was reduced or gone.

Surgical treatment of endo will not necessarily increase fertility. Similar pregnancy rates were shown for women who had just had a look-see laparoscopy and those who had laser removal of endo during a laparoscopy. Several studies suggest that neither the medical nor surgical treatment of mild endometriosis improves the fertility rate any more than does having no treatment at all. In cases of severe endometriosis, laser treatment seems to improve fertility more than laparotomy (pelvic operation with a larger incision) or diathermy burned off removal of endo.

Occasionally, some women will need microsurgery to remove adhesions from the pelvic cavity or the tubes; and really serious endo or endo causing pain that refuses to respond to any treatment may require a hysterectomy. This is obviously not a decision to be taken lightly and should be considered only as a last resort.

The natural therapist's treatment of endo aims to:

- bring down relatively high levels of oestrogen;
- improve the immune system;
- regulate prostaglandins;
- ensure normal uterus function and period flow; and, if asked,
- improve fertility.

The big factors here in deciding on treatment are the amount of pain and whether you want to get pregnant. Some categories of herbs, such as the emmenagogues, can't be given to someone who wants to be or is pregnant. And if the pain is really severe, then knocking that on the head has to be the first priority.

Many of the complaints linked to endometriosis are covered in detail elsewhere in the book. For instance a whole section is devoted to the management of period pain, another to the treatment of heavy periods, and another to PMS. To get a whole picture of endo, make sure you ferret out the Natural Therapies approach for each of the other relevant sections.

Reducing oestrogen

Too much oestrogen causes PMS-type symptoms and the abnormal production of endometrium. Oestrogen levels are influenced by a range of factors, including 'competitive inhibition' with plant oestrogens, and dietary changes and exercise to improve oestrogen clearance.

The natural therapist's aim is to keep oestrogen within normal limits, rather than reduce the levels below normal which is the aim of some medical treatments such as GnRH agonists.

A list of helpful ways to reduce oestrogen is under Too Much Oestrogen in the Hormones chapter.

You may not respond properly to dietary or herbal manipulation of oestrogen. Some people's hormones are so feral you can't kick-start them back to right levels without drugs. If you're one of these people, start with the drugs—you may be able to come off them later. You can do all of the other natural therapy treatments except for taking specific herbal remedies for hormone regulation. You can't start that until you come off the hormone drugs.

Improving uterine tone

Herbs may be given to improve 'uterine tone', which is the strength, and ability to spasm, of the uterus. Uterine tone is mainly regulated by prostaglandins balance, and is responsible for having an easy period.

All the herbs mentioned here are explained fully in the Herbs section of the Natural Therapies chapter. They should only be prescribed by a specialist herbal practitioner and not given by novices or self-administered. Personally I wouldn't know a spasmolytic from a grand piano if it were up my left nostril, which Ruth informs me is unlikely.

Uterine tonics initiate regular and orderly uterine contractions and regulate uterine tone. *Angelica sinensis* (Dang Gui) is the principal herb used for endometriosis; *Caulophyllum thalictroides* (blue cohosh), *Chamaelirium luteum* (helonias) and *Rubus idaeus* (raspberry leaves) are good, too.

Emmenagogues have an expulsive effect on the uterus, and can speed up or 'bring on' the period flow. They are indicated for congestive symptoms which include heavy dragging pain, especially when the period is late. They should always be prescribed with the uterine tonics.

Spasmolytics reduce uterine muscle spasm, relieve pain and ensure orderly uterine evacuation. (Sounds like some kind of fire drill.) The most important ones for endo include the *Viburnums, Paeonia lactiflora, Corydalis ambigua* and *Dioscorea villosa*.

Prostaglandins regulation

The essential fatty acids found in oily fish have the greatest impact on period pain and retrograde flow caused by prostaglandins or leukotriene imbalance. (Essential fatty acids are explained under Bad Fats and Good Fats, number 8 of the 20 Diet Hints in the Self Care chapter.)

The herbs *Tanacetum parthenium* (feverfew) and *Zingiber officinale* (ginger) also have prostaglandins-inhibiting effects and can improve period pain. Feverfew is a Cold herb, ginger is Hot, and as most period pain is made worse by cold, feverfew is often combined with ginger.

PMS

Endo and PMS often go together. See the whole section on PMS in this chapter.

Mood swings

Many people with endo get episodes of depression and irritability. Common symptoms are feeling overwhelmed, tearful and irritable; feeling inadequate and as though everything is too much; inappropriate tiredness; irritability and 'on a short fuse' all the time.

Counselling is probably the best way of dealing with 'reactive depression'. Herbalists may also recommend *Hypericum perforatum*, the B complex vitamins, and the common nervines such as *Avena sativa, Scutellaria laterifolia* and *Passiflora incarnata* are useful.

Pain

The emphasis comes off painkillers and onto underlying reasons for the pain. See the Period Pain section for more detail. All of the herbal and other remedies treat the *cause* of the pain—the prostaglandins imbalance, the uterine muscle spasm, and the inflammatory responses. Fish oils have the most impact on period pain caused by prostaglandins and leukotriene imbalance. In some cases of endo, much of the pain is from the bowel (more of which later).

Infertility

Some people who are still infertile after medical treatments will try natural therapy as a last resort. All of the problems of endo-related infertility need to be treated to provide the most stable environment for conception to take place. They include prostaglandins imbalance, luteinised unruptured follicle syndrome, failed ovarian follicle development, infrequent ovulation, immune dysfunction and adhesions. Also, you'll probably need to have sex at some point.

Fish oils, star flower oil and evening primrose oil alter prostaglandins and leukotriene levels and may be capable of improving fertility. Evening primrose, from between 2 and 4 grams daily, and/or fish oils also between 2 and 4 grams daily, can be taken as supplements. (Essential fatty acids are explained under Bad Fats and Good Fats, number 8 of the 20 Diet Hints in the Self Care chapter.)

Immune system irregularities

Calendula officinalis is a good herb to normalise the immune system. It stops muscle spasm, reduces period bleeding, and reduces inflammation. It is useful when there is dull, congestive pain with heavy bleeding; and in any case of period disorder with altered immune function. (All of these factors are common to endo.)

Ovulation problems

In endo, ovulation can be delayed or the egg might not develop normally in the follicular phase. Or, you can develop luteinised unruptured follicle syndrome, in which the follicle develops but the egg isn't 'expelled' from the ovary. This is often linked to lower than normal progesterone levels. All these conditions are associated with infertility caused by an ovulation problem or early miscarriage.

Chamaelirium luteum (helonias) is known as a herb to regulate ovarian function during the follicular phase. It is used for ovarian cysts and for infertility. *Vitex agnus castus* is also useful for infertility caused by not ovulating, and for problems of the luteal phase. It is a difficult herb to use, and like others mentioned, should never be self-prescribed because it can overstimulate ovarian follicles. You could end up with having all your eggs in one basket, so to speak.

Other herbs known to enhance fertility, although exactly why is unknown, include *Aletris farinosa* (true unicorn root) and *Angelica sinensis* (Dang Gui).

Adhesions

Vitamin E is great for stopping the formation of adhesions. Doses of 500–1000 International Units (IU) of vitamin E each day can be used to prevent adhesion formation, although doses at this level should be supervised. If you're about to have an operation or you've just had one, give the large doses of vitamin E (more than 500 IU) a miss for a while, because there's a slight chance it will encourage unscheduled bleeding.

Exercise

Exercising often helps, especially exercise first thing in the morning and of the 'long slow distance' variety. If you exercise rigorously during your period you have an increased risk of endo, perhaps because it contributes to retrograde flow. Regular exercise may mean a reduced risk of endo because it probably reduces the rate of oestrogen production. So, don't throw yourself around quite so much during the period (and no hanging upside down from the monkey bars) but otherwise regular exercise probably won't hurt, and is likely to be a real help.

Irritable bowel syndrome

Quite frankly there's nothing pleasant about having a grumpy bottom. Irritable bowel syndrome often accompanies endo, and can make period pain even worse. Because some of the symptoms of endo are so similar to irritable bowel syndrome, you mightn't realise you have bowel spasm instead of endo pain itself.

Endo and irritable bowel syndrome often happen together. Maybe this is because rogue prostaglandins can cause muscle spasm in both the bowel and the uterus, and it is also possible that the bowel reacts to the irritation in the pelvic cavity by going into a reflex spasm with the uterus. Maybe when one bit of the body goes into spasm, all the rest decide to go out on strike in sympathy.

The irritable bowel syndrome diet in the Self Care chapter, and especially the seed breakfast, will help. The seed breakfast also has the advantages of being rich in trace minerals, calcium and the essential fatty acids which help to balance the prostaglandins.

Constipation

Constipation is a common problem before a period. It aggravates period pain and slows down oestrogen clearance through the bowel.

- Eat bitter green vegetables and dietary fibre and drink lots of water.
- Most laxatives bring on spasms of the bowel to push everything along, and this is exactly what you *don't* want, as a reflex spasm in all of the organs in the pelvic cavity can hurt like hell. You might need to take herbal extract mixtures containing bitters to maintain regular bowel habits, but these should not contain any of the anthraquinone laxatives.
- Steer clear of painkillers with codeine: it often aggravates constipation.

General hints

- Cut out coffee: drinking two cups of coffee or four cups of tea a day is linked with higher risk of infertility due to tubal disease or endometriosis.
- Cut out alcohol: women who drink more alcohol are more likely to have endo. Even moderate alcohol consumption, if it's also associated with ovulatory disorders or endo, is implicated in a lower fertility rate.

- Eat more fibre, yoghurt and bitters (green, bitter-tasting things like some lettuces and the bitter herbs). Hints on all these are in the 20 Diet Hints in the elf Care chapter. Care for your elf. I ask you. Why didn't my mother let me do typing lessons?
- Functional hypoglycaemia—getting light-headed and fainty between meals—often aggravates mood swings or depression. A hypoglycaemic diet is included in the Self Care chapter.
- Stay on a low-fat, high-fibre diet high in essential fatty acids. Tests have suggested that fish oils and Gamma-linolenic acid (GLA) are useful in treating both the inflammation and the severity of endo and even infertility. Star flower, fish and evening primrose oil may contribute to a reduction in inflammation and also improve fertility. Women with endo who have period pain or problems with fertility will probably benefit more from fish oils than evening primrose oil (or similar). Doses of between 2 and 4 grams daily are recommended. See Bad Fats and Good Fats, number 8 of 20 Diet Hints in the Self Care chapter.)
- Eat often from the cabbage family of vegetables.
- Eat plant oestrogens like soya beans and lignans such as linseeds to help keep oestrogen levels lower. (A plant oestrogen section is in the Self Care chapter.)
- See under Stress in The Usual Suspects section for hints on calming down.
- Breastfeeding is useful in curbing endo. Mind you, it's best to have a baby first. Full-term pregnancies tend to decrease the risk of endo, and the risk gets lower with each following full-term pregnancy. *This does not mean* that pregnancy will 'cure' endometriosis. Anyway, trying to cure endo is not a good reason for getting pregnant. And some women who have had lots of kids still get endo.
- Consider your contraception. Intra-uterine devices (IUDs) have been linked with an increased incidence of endometriosis, possibly because they encourage retrograde flow and alter prostaglandin levels.

Researchers investigating the Pill and endo were unable to arrive at any firm conclusions. Some studies report an increased risk, others a reduced risk, and still others no change. Helpful, isn't it? In another study of more than 17 000 women, the incidence of endo was lower in women *currently* using the Pill, and higher in *former* Pill users, compared with women who had never taken the Pill.

Here's how the Pill might influence the risk of endo: the extra oestrogen could increase the risk (although the amount of oestrogen in Pills has been dropping steadily for 30 years); the extra progesterone might decrease risk; and the lighter periods experienced on the Pill might cut out some retrograde flow.

- Read the bit about the liver in the Natural Therapies chapter and follow the ideas for a healthier liver.
- Finally, make sure of good reliable professional back-up. Endo is too complicated to be taken on alone.

Chapter 6

FINISHING UP

Menopause

Any woman over 50 who has a tantrum or forgets her car keys is liable to be labelled 'menopausal'. The typical stereotype is a neurotic, grumpy old bag plagued by insomnia, struggling through her day being constantly overwhelmed and humiliated by hot flushes that leave her feeling faint and liable to whack somebody over the noggin with her handbag. Well on her way to being incontinent, she couldn't be bothered with sex, young people, or new-fangled ways of cooking peas. In some people's minds, menopause is even linked with dementia.

The real 'typical' menopausal woman may have some temporary problems with menopausal complaints like hot flushes, but they don't stop her from getting on with her life. Being 50-something isn't old, but for all sorts of complex reasons, women have somehow confused ageing and menopause. Images of old women often show them as fearful, or gossiping, or senile. Many people lump together the years between menopause and death with the tag 'post-menopausal woman'; they imagine a rather batty 98-year-old, rather than a dynamic 50-, 60- or even 70-year-old.

And of course there's the implication that if you've got wrinkles, they're not beautiful character lines tracing a history of life and accumulated experience, but an appalling misbehaviour in the Trying To Look Like A Supermodel stakes. Getting 'old' is seen as a bad career move in a society which worships youth. All this can build up a fear of ageing.

Making menopause a time of positive change rather than a major freakout is a matter of planning. Preparing for mid-life with a good diet, lifestyle, exercise program and especially attitude, will determine how you experience menopause—and what comes after.

What is it?

Menopause literally means stopping menstruation. The word is made up of the trusty, rusty old Greek: *meno* (monthly) and *pausis* (to stop). You won't know menopause has happened until a whole year has passed since the date of your last period—the actual date can only be decided retrospectively, by counting backwards. Medically recognised menopause actually happens on one distinct date (forget Tupperware, now you can have a menopause party).

The medical term for what we usually mean by 'menopausal' or 'going through the menopause' is 'climacteric', or 'peri-menopausal'. The peri-menopause, like puberty and the years when the menstrual cycle starts to become established, is characterised by irregular periods, hormonal fluctuation, and sometimes, an emotional roller-coaster. We're just going to call it 'menopausal'.

When to expect it

Menopause between the ages of 45 and 55 is considered normal. Most women in Australia become menopausal between 48 and 53. Thinner women are much more likely to have an earlier menopause than women who are heavier. Being very overweight may delay the onset of menopause until well into the fifties.

Early menopause

Premature menopause is when you have your last period before you're 40. The ovaries may stop working before the usual time, menopause might be brought on for medical reasons, or triggered by surgery or illness. Nobody really knows why some women's ovaries suddenly take early retirement. Some people say it happened to them during a period of extreme stress. Another theory is that the body makes a mistake and produces antibodies to ovarian tissue, causing premature ovarian shut-down. Auto-immune diseases, and in rare cases, mumps can also bring on the menopause.

Medically-induced menopause

Relatively new drugs can bring on a 'temporary menopause' in treating some cases of endometriosis and uterine fibroids. These drugs are called gonadotrophin releasing hormone agonists (GnRH agonists). The most common brand is Zoladex. The menopausal state is reversed when the drugs are stopped.

While on the drugs, the changes are usually the same as any natural menopause: bone density loss, vaginal dryness, hot flushes and mood changes. Although the condition can be reversed, it can be much harder to regain the bone density once off the drugs.

Menopause can also come on after radiation therapy for cancer, particularly of the pelvis. Sometimes this is not deliberate, but the changes are often permanent. The ovarian tissue degenerates and fails to work in the usual way, and menopause is the result. The herb *Angelica sinensis* (Dang Gui) may help to protect the ovary from the effects of irradiation. It must be properly prescribed by a herbalist.

Some drugs used in the treatment of cancer are of necessity pretty strong stuff. They include cyclophosphamide, chlorambucil, mechlorethamine and vincristine. These drugs can potentially cause menopausal symptoms and their use may be associated with permanent infertility and menopause. Tamoxifen, used as an anti-oestrogen in the treatment of breast cancer, can also cause menopause-like symptoms.

Surgically-induced menopause

Surgically-induced menopause is rarer now that drugs achieve the same result. In the past, it was more common to have a hysterectomy operation in which the ovaries and uterus were both surgically removed. (If you let them, surgeons will refer to this as a bilateral salpingo-oophorectomy.)

This operation, or the surgical removal of the ovaries only, will immediately create a menopausal state. This type of surgery may be performed for very severe endometriosis, oestrogen-dependent breast cancer, ovarian tumours or ovarian cancer.

According to medical wisdom, a hysterectomy which takes the uterus and leaves the ovaries shouldn't cause any interruption in ovarian activity—but up to a third of women who have this surgery do have menopausal symptoms.

If menopause isn't brought on immediately by a hysterectomy, on average, it will come on five years earlier than in women who still have their uterus. Ovarian shut-down is thought to happen earlier because of the alteration in ovarian blood supply after the surgery. A controversial, unproven theory claims that tubal ligation ('having your tubes tied') may also be associated with premature menopause for much the same reasons.

Normal stage or a disease?

Some doctors believe menopause is a 'deficiency' disease, characterised by a lack of oestrogen, and comparable to other disorders caused by hormone deficiency such as diabetes, Cushing's disease and hypothyroidism.

Hormone deficiency diseases, they claim, are states which can be reversed or held off by replacing a hormone. This mob says that medication should replace the deficient hormone and return the body to 'normal'. They are big fans of hormone replacement therapy (HRT) and believe that *all* post-menopausal women, having outlived the functional lives of their ovaries, are diseased and in need of continued medical attention until they die.

For these doctors, menopause is just like other hormonal disorders, such as diabetes, but has the peculiarity of affecting *all* women at about the same time in their lives. It's a bit much to say that every single one of us is biologically faulty and in need of treatment and medication. (Not to mention a Bex and a good lie down.)

Some doctors have introduced an air of vagueness and contradiction into this debate. In her book for the mid-life woman, *Menopause*, Dr Miriam Stoppard writes 'While I believe that the menopause is a normal stage in a woman's life, I also believe that it is a true deficiency state . . .'. She also endorses HRT.

Natural therapists view menopause as a normal transition, although people may need supportive treatment for any rogue symptoms. Rather than telling all mid-life women they are diseased, most natural therapists and many doctors encourage menopausal women to adopt positive lifestyle changes, good eating patterns and a positive attitude to the changes.

The pros and cons of HRT are discussed later in this chapter.

Positive thinking

Researchers in one study found that levels of hormones were not the relevant factor in what sort of menopause a woman had. The important elements were being physically well, exercising moderately, having a positive attitude to menopause and feeling happy. Exercising, even once a week, was associated with fewer menopausal 'side effects', and so were positive relationships and friendships. Changing your diet can reduce some menopausal symptoms.

The changes

Hormone levels

The hormonal changes usually come on slowly. About two to three years before ovulation stops, levels of oestrogen and progesterone decline gradually, sometimes in association with irregular periods. When hormone production changes gradually, fewer menopausal symptoms may be the result. (This may be one reason why 'naturally' menopausal women tend to have a much easier time of it than women who get the menopause in one big hit brought on by surgery or drugs, or an early end to ovary function.)

Lots of hormonal variations, not just declining oestrogen, cause physical and biochemical changes. The most common ones include changes in the menstrual cycle, hot flushes and the dreaded PMS-type mood swings.

FSH and LH

Basically what happens is that the ovaries which run the menstrual show start to retire and this results in the changes in hormone balance. During the menstrual cycle, oestrogen usually holds down levels of follicle stimulating hormone (FSH). As oestrogen declines, the FSH level rises. (FSH levels in blood are sometimes used as a biochemical indicator of menopause.) Luteinising hormone (LH) also increases.

Both LH and FSH are released in small bursts about every hour to an hour and a half. It has been shown that the 'bursts' of LH coincide with hot flushes.

Oestrogen

The dominant kind of oestrogen in post-menopausal women is the oestrone converted from androgens in the fatty tissues, because the ovaries have stopped making oestradiol—which is about 12 times stronger than oestrone. Higher levels of oestrone may contribute to the increased bone density and lack of menopausal symptoms experienced by heavier women.

Testosterone

After menopause, the ovaries continue producing the same levels of testosterone as they always have. Testosterone is an androgen (male hormone) and is probably responsible for some of the facial hair and male-pattern baldness in some post-menopausal women. Oestrogen would normally balance it all out.

To offset the effects of this continued testosterone, you need more sex hormone binding globulin (SHBG), a carrier protein. Vegetarian diets and diets with a high plant oestrogen content increase SHBG. (The plant oestrogen diet info is in the Self Care chapter.)

Progesterone

Progesterone production is all over the shop around the menopause because ovulation happens less often and less regularly. This can cause mood changes and irregular periods.

Menstrual cycle changes

Before menopause, the menstrual cycle is usually regular and the period flow is one you're used to. Gradually, you'll notice changes in the period flow or its regularity. The period may come more often (which is very boring), but more often the cycle length increases because ovulation is winding down. This means you still get periods, but at longer and longer intervals. This stage may last for a few months or for a few years. During this phase, you might think it's all over—but be warned. You can still get pregnant.

Other symptoms can include heavier periods, hot flushes and night sweats. Blame your oestrogen levels. If you get symptoms which are similar to PMS, try the suggested remedies for PMS D in the PMS section of the When Things Go Wrong chapter.

Some women stop having periods all of a sudden; others may have normal periods further apart; some have surprise 'flooding'. This is sometimes referred to as the 'transitional phase' because it represents the stage immediately before menopause. Finally, periods stop completely and you become officially menopausal.

Diagnosis

Common tests

There are a few ways to tell whether menopause is approaching. Single tests are not all that reliable and are generally added to any symptoms you're getting to make a diagnosis. Sometimes the symptoms are the best indicators anyway.

Blood tests for levels of FSH are not infallible, but are often used to diagnose menopause. High levels of FSH indicate declining levels of oestrogen. FSH levels often fluctuate around the menopause and can give misleading results. The FSH levels will remain consistently high once you have become menopausal, but by then you won't need a blood test to tell you.

Sometimes the blood levels of oestrogen and progesterone are measured to see whether they are within the normal limits, but this is an even more unreliable test than the FSH level and in most cases a waste of time and money.

The vaginal walls can show early changes which are caused by the declining oestrogen levels. When examined by a doctor, they might look thinner and drier, and sometimes bleed. These signs are generally quite late, but you might develop them early if you have symptoms of chronically low oestrogen (low body weight, a strenuous exercise regime, or a very high-fibre diet).

A menstrual diary in which you also record other symptoms will be a great help. (The menstrual symptom diary is under A Normal Period in the When Things Go Right chapter and can be photocopied for continual use.) Often doctors will prescribe HRT on the basis of symptoms even if blood tests are normal. If the symptoms improve, they are assumed to be related to the menopause. Natural therapists will also prescribe on the basis of symptoms and will usually try to regulate hormone levels and establish normal period patterns.

When to see a doctor

Even if you're coping fine with menopausal symptoms and don't think you need any help, you need to see a doctor if you have:

- any vaginal bleeding, no matter how slight, coming a year or more after the last period
- bleeding after sex
- persistently heavy periods
- any unusual spotting or bleeding which worries you
- mid-cycle bleeding or bleeding between periods
- unexpected pain associated with periods or bleeding.

Managing the symptoms

Erratic periods and the endometrium

If ovulation becomes erratic, the cycle length and regularity of the period will have an effect on the endometrium (cells lining the uterus). The endometrium tends to be exposed to lower levels of oestrogen for longer periods of time, and to be exposed to little or no progesterone (which is only produced once you've ovulated).

As a result, the endometrium tends to bleed more easily, and periods can become really heavy. Spotting is common and in rare cases, the endometrial cells can undergo cancerous changes. These changes are explored in Endometrial Hyperplasia under Erratic Bleeding and Dysfunctional Uterine Bleeding (DUB) in the When Things Go Wrong chapter.

Hot flushes and sweats

This is the symptom which most women find the most 'embarrassing'. Sitting in the middle of a business meeting or arguing over the washing machine repair bill, some women are given a horrible reminder of uncontrollable adolescent blushing. Some of the modern rewriting of menopause suggests that women just call them 'power surges'. Although most of us are more likely to think, 'Bugger power surges for a joke. I'm not an electrical sub-station, I just want my body to behave itself.'

About three-quarters of all menopausal women experience some form of hot flushes; and about one-third of them will seek treatment. Two Australian studies indicated that almost 40 per cent of the menopausal women experienced 'troubling' hot flushes, but not all women took medication or sought help for their symptoms.

Flushes are likely to be as different as the women who have them. Some have fleeting hot and sweaty feelings; others might be drenched with sweat, feel uncomfortably hot, go red in the face and/or have heart palpitations. Sometimes hot flushes come with headaches, a sense of increased pressure in the head, vagueness, transient chills, fatigue, dizziness or nausea.

The body usually adjusts to the changing hormones after about a year and the hot flushes disappear completely. In very rare cases they will last for five to ten years after the period has stopped.

Flushes are caused by oestrogen decline, and a surge of luteinising hormone (LH). Hot flushes are more severe if you are very thin, probably because body fat helps to make extra oestrogen. Women who become menopausal suddenly, or at a younger age than usual, often

Hot flushes

experience severe hot flushes. Maybe the body's not prepared for the sudden loss of oestrogen.

After a flush there is often a slight drop in temperature caused by loss of body heat from sweating. Temperature fluctuations can cause the on-again, off-again problem with clothes and lead to a serious disturbance in sleep patterns—thrashing about, in other words.

Lately, there has been speculation that hot flushes are not just a nuisance and that they may serve a positive role. One theory is that the increase in body temperature sets the stage for a healthier old age by burning up toxins and stimulating the immune response (similar to the increase in immune activity when we have a temperature caused by a cold or the flu). Another is that they represent surges of creative and positive energy. You little sub-station, you.

The Medical Approach

The medical treatment of any menopausal symptom is almost always hormone replacement therapy (HRT)—and hot flushes respond well to this medication. Somewhere between 60 and 90 per cent of women with hot flushes who are treated with HRT improve dramatically. In view of the lack of information on the long-term effects of HRT, natural remedies may be more appropriate unless there are compelling reasons why HRT should be considered. The pros and cons of HRT are explored later in this section.

Natural Therapies

Natural remedies are prescribed after taking into account all the factors that might contribute to the menopausal symptoms—including lifestyle and medical elements.

The need to differentiate between the differing triggers for hot flushes has long been accepted in herbal medicine. It makes the treatment more complex, but much more likely to bring relief of the symptom *and* the cause.

Herbs

Herbs containing plant oestrogens have been used for centuries for the management of hot flushes and other oestrogen-related symptoms. All plant oestrogens are many times weaker than synthetic, laboratory-made oestrogens or the oestrogens made in the body. But a menopausal woman produces very little oestrogen of her own, so the plant oestrogens become more dominant, and can do some good.

Of particular interest to herbalists is *Cimicifuga racemosa*, long recognised and used in the European, American Indian and Chinese traditions for menopausal symptoms. It has been the subject of a number of open and double blind trials in Germany where many medical doctors routinely prescribe it for menopausal symptoms. The results are very good, especially for hot flushes and vaginal dryness.

Anxiety

Anxiety or worry can bring on a hot flush and a number of herbs are useful. They include *Hypericum perforatum*, for flushes associated with anxiety depression states; *Humulus lupulus* (hops), for flushing and insomnia; *Tilia cordata* (lime or linden flowers) and *Leonurus cardiaca* (motherwort) for menopausal symptoms which are accompanied by palpitations; and *Verbena officinalis* (vervain) for anxiety associated with thyroid dysfunction.

Fatigue and overwork

The herbal adaptogens most commonly used are *Panax ginseng, Eleuthrococcus senticosus, Codonopsis pilosa, Glycyrrhiza glabra* and *Astragalus membranaceus*.

Night sweats

Humulus lupulus (hops) contains oestrogen-like substances and is good for night sweating. In some cases, simply improving the quality of sleep with herbal hypnotics will put a lid on hot flushes. *Valeriana officinalis, Scutellaria laterifolia, Passiflora incarnata,*

Avena sativa and *Matricaria recutita* are commonly available either as teas or in tablets.

Severe sweating

The two herbs which are useful for menopausal sweating are *Salvia officinalis* and *Astragalus membranaceus*, and they are usually combined with the other remedies for flushing. One common Chinese formula for sweating associated with weakness contains *Astragalus membranaceus, Codonopsis pilosa, Angelica sinensis, Cimicifuga racemosa, Atractylodes macrocephala* and *Bupleurum falcatum*.

Salvia officinalis (garden sage) is oestrogenic and improves circulation to the brain.

Supplements

Vitamin E

Studies in the 1950s showed vitamin E is useful for menopausal symptoms. In clinical trials, doses ranged from 10 to 100 milligrams a day (100 IU is equivalent to 67 milligrams). Vitamin E reduces the severity of hot flushes and other symptoms associated with menopause. Between 100 and 500 IU a day is the usual dose. (Women with blood pressure or heart problems should get medical advice before using vitamin E.)

Vitamin C and the Bioflavonoids

In the early 1960s, the bioflavonoid hesperidin, derived from citrus fruits, was shown to reduce the severity of hot flushes, but more research is needed to know why. Sometimes moderate to high doses of vitamin C seem to help too, maybe by increasing the viability of oestrogens in the body.

Evening primrose oil

Many women find that evening primrose oil is useful for a variety of menopausal symptoms, including flushing, mood changes and fluid retention. The dose range to try is between 1 and 3 grams daily, but studies have shown it's not much better than a placebo. If symptoms improve with evening primrose oil then you probably had PMS rather than menopausal problems.

Evening primrose oil is also rather expensive and the other herbs and supplements are often more cost-effective for menopausal women. Diet can also be altered to take in more essential fatty acids. (See Bad Fats and Good Fats, number 8 of 20 Diet Hints in the Self Care chapter.)

Self Care

- Dress to reduce the severity of the symptoms. It is most useful to wear a bikini under a fake fur coat. Oh, alright. Try light and loose-fitting clothing from natural fibre, such as cotton; it's much less likely to aggravate sweating. Try a lighter layer underneath a jacket or cardigan you can shrug off and cotton night gear, and you can sleep on a towel or folded sheet you can throw out of the bed if it gets wet, rather than having to change the sheets.
- Avoid food and drink which seems to aggravate hot flushes. They include coffee, excessively spicy foods and alcohol. Drinking or eating foods that are extremely hot can also trigger a flush and simply eating foods at a lower temperature can help. If you love going out for a curry and a few drinks, get ready to hurl your cardie on and off all night.
- Here's a simple home remedy for the treatment of hot flushes and sweating: Chop about six fresh sage leaves and soak overnight in the juice of a lemon. In the morning, strain and drink the juice diluted with water to taste. Two weeks of this mixture will usually control flushing and sweating, and also improves digestion and concentration. It should not be continued for longer than two weeks. You can have another round of it after two months.
- Eat 'plant oestrogens'. Eating just 100 grams of tofu and 2 dessert-spoons of freshly ground linseeds (use a clean coffee grinder) every day can reduce hot flushes and vaginal dryness. Researchers have also seen a link between eating foods with high levels of plant oestrogens and lower rates of oestrogen-dependent cancers. (More info on the plant oestrogens is in the Self Care chapter.)

Dryness

Declining oestrogen levels can dry out the tissues of the vagina, vulva, and urethra, or the eyes and mouth. A range of symptoms might be experienced from none at all, to varying degrees of burning, dryness and irritation. Vaginal, vulval or urinary tract symptoms can play havoc with your sex life and general comfort.

Vaginal dryness, thinning of the vaginal walls and urinary symptoms usually happen after menopause, but sometimes happen before it. Like other menopausal symptoms, there is a large variation in symptoms. Vaginal dryness during sex can cause mild discomfort through to pain.

Less oestrogen can also lead to increased alkalinity of the vagina which can cause irritation, itching or infections. About 40 per cent of women over 55 have some dryness and about half of these report moderate to severe symptoms. The severity seems to be connected to dietary factors, body weight and stress.

When urethral tissue is affected by declining oestrogens, recurring problems can include weeing all the time, a burning sensation, cystitis, and incontinence. These complaints require active treatment, and all women who develop urinary tract symptoms around the menopause, or later, should consider mucous membrane change as a potential cause: only treating the urinary tract infection will almost certainly mean it will keep coming back.

The Medical Approach

Vaginal dryness, soreness, and painful sex can be treated with oestrogen-containing creams, tablets or pessaries. They should be used at night and their benefits and cautions are outlined under Not Enough Oestrogen in the Hormones chapter.

Collagen disorders which affect other tissues such as bones, the pelvic organs and the skin, are increasingly being treated with oestrogen pills.

And doctors will usually prescribe HRT.

Natural therapies

Natural therapists recommend creams for vaginal dryness. An aqueous cream (like plain old sorbolene) from the chemist or vitamin E cream can be used as a base to which herbs and oils are added. This can be made at home: 10 millilitres of infused oil of *Calendula officinalis* (marigold); 30 millilitres of olive oil; 20 millilitres of the oil of evening primrose in 75 grams of aqueous cream. Apply two or three times daily to the vulva and inside the vagina. If you make a large batch, store it in the fridge.

Oestrogenic herbs can also be used in creams, since oestrogen is well absorbed through the skin. Middle Eastern women reportedly use a poultice of *Trigonella foenum-graecum* (fenugreek), but the pungent odour makes it rather antisocial and would probably put you off your curry. Using a water-based lubricant, such as 'Wet Stuff' during sex will also help. It's available from ordinary old chemists and supermarkets or those shops which sell mysterious battery-operated items and black leather French maid's uniforms with optional thonging.

For collagen health throughout the whole body, including bones and skin, vitamin C and the bioflavonoids (usually rutin or hesperidin) are essential. Silicon, zinc and the vitamins B6, B12, A, K and folic acid are also important. Sometimes supplements are required, but a balanced diet is the best way to get nutrients.

Self care

- Eat plant oestrogens, especially linseeds (see under Plant Oestrogens in the Self Care chapter for more info).

'PMS'-type symptoms

Women in their forties with PMS symptoms are often told, or believe that they are 'menopausal'. Symptoms related to hormone fluctuations are not necessarily menopausal unless you also have irregular periods—and even then there may be other causes. Some of the 'menopausal symptoms' like hot flushes, migraines and palpitations are experienced by women in their twenties and thirties—not to mention men—who are not menopausal, and who are not automatically prescribed HRT.

One study of recently menopausal women showed that although hot flushes increased when periods stopped, symptoms like sore breasts, irritability, excitability, depression and poor concentration improved after the period '[which] suggests that these symptoms are more likely to be related to periods than to the menopause.'

Evening primrose oil capsules are commonly recommended or self-prescribed for these symptoms even though they are no better than placebo for true menopausal symptoms when scientifically trialled. Evening primrose *is,* however, useful for PMS and so if you feel better on the capsules you've probably got PMS symptoms rather than menopausal ones.

So, if you are 40-something, with fairly regular periods, and no hot flushes or vaginal dryness, don't just assume a problem is caused by oncoming menopause. You might respond better to remedies for PMS. See the suggestions under PMS in the When Things Go Wrong chapter.

Mood changes

About one in ten women experience depression, anxiety or feelings of inadequacy around menopause, but there is some dispute about why it happens. Some researchers have shown that these symptoms are related to hormone changes, others found these symptoms were more common when women had pre-existing problems such as depression, difficulties with coping generally, or PMS. We could call these the 'I don't want to go through menopause' theory and the 'hormone theory'.

According to the 'I don't want to go through menopause' theory, women with a negative attitude to menopause or ageing, were much more likely to experience problems. This theory says that any mood changes are caused by attitude, not hormones.

The hormone theory reckons that stress caused by mood changes may lower oestrogen levels and aggravate menopausal symptoms, which then causes more stress. In one study, menopausal women recovering from depression had higher levels of oestrogen as they improved. Sleep deprivation due to hot flushes is believed to be another cause of depression. When oestrogen levels are increased, sleep patterns return to normal.

Treatment for mood swings is varied because the causes are often diverse. You might be depressed before your period because of hormones, or you might be depressed before your period because the bank manager keeps shouting at you. When PMS is the cause, symptoms will happen before the period.

Whatever the choice of treatment: vitamin, herb, drug, or counselling, it is far better that the cause of the depression or mood swings be found rather than prescribing something to lift the mood temporarily.

The Medical Approach

Some doctors commonly prescribe HRT, believing that it alleviates the mood changes associated with menopause. It doesn't, however, appear to be any better than a placebo in having an effect on mood. It does improve flushing and vaginal symptoms and this might cheer you up.

Anti-depressant drugs or sedatives should rarely be needed, not least because so many people have become dependent on them and they don't go to the root of the problem. Doctors may also suggest counselling.

Natural Therapies

- *Hypericum perforatum,* a herb which has been compared to tricyclic anti-depressants in effects, has a long history of use for menopausal complaints which are associated with anxiety or depression. Herbalists refer to this plant as a nervine, specific to the management of menopausal complaints. Again, make sure you get to the cause of the problem and don't just take an anti-depressant, herbal or otherwise.

- Tired women often think that their symptoms must be due to menopause. In reality, they may be due to any of the usual causes of fatigue including hypoglycaemia, iron deficiency, adrenal exhaustion, too much exercise or depression. Women who are well, but tired all the time, respond to combinations of the appropriate herbs for the nervous system, adaptogens and vitamin B complex, along with appropriate dietary changes and increase in exercise. *Eleuthrococcus senticosus* (Siberian ginseng) at doses of 500 milligrams to 1 gram twice a day combined with a standard vitamin B complex tablet twice daily, is often effective. Herbs are more fully explored in the Herbs section of the Natural Therapies chapter.

Self Care

For all types of mood changes, simple lifestyle changes, such as exercise, stress management techniques, yoga, and meditation are helpful. Sometimes depression, anxiety or self-esteem problems will require the skills of a counsellor.

B vitamins, particularly vitamin B6, or any of the other remedies used for PMS, are helpful for mood changes. For mood changes that might be PMS, have a squizz at the PMS section in the When Things Go Wrong chapter.

Migraines

Premenstrual migraines can get worse approaching the menopause. The headaches are often thought to be caused by blood sugar fluctuations, and the rapid decline in oestrogens just before a period. The oestrogen freefall can trigger a blood vessel spasm, which causes the headache.

The regime described for premenstrual migraines in the PMS section of the When Things Go Wrong chapter—almost always in conjunction with the prescription herb *Cimicifuga racemosa* (black cohosh)—can help symptoms of fluctuating oestrogen levels. Increasing the amount of plant oestrogens in the diet is also useful—more info on them is in the Self Care chapter.

Hormone replacement therapy (HRT)

The accepted medical reasons for using hormone replacement therapy (HRT) are for the treatment of hot flushes, vaginal dryness and for women who have an increased risk of developing osteoporosis or heart disease. Some doctors, however, prescribe HRT for *any* symptom experienced by menopausal women, including depression, mood swings, insomnia and migraines, lost socks, barracking for Richmond and wondering if you paid the butcher.

Australian women are among the highest users of HRT in the world, despite a barrage of conflicting media coverage of risks and benefits. There simply isn't enough information on the long-term use of some of the different types of HRT to confidently predict the eventual effects. That information will eventually come from the women who are taking HRT now. And the ones who don't.

Types of HRT

HRT can be given as an oestrogen pill with or without progesterone; as an oestrogen-impregnated patch; as a vaginal cream or pessary; or as an oestrogen implant with or without testosterone.

Tablets

Oestrogen only

The 'natural' oestrogens are favoured over the 'synthetic' because they cause fewer liver-related side effects, they are metabolised quickly and exert weaker oestrogen effects (and therefore are less of a problem for long-term use), and they are associated with a lower incidence of breast cancer.

The 'protective dose' is usually recommended to protect the bones and heart, but is included only as a guide—many factors will alter the dose needed by each individual. The dose range is the usual extent of individual prescriptions by doctors or recommended on the packet.

- **Premarin.** A potent conjugated ('natural') oestrogen made from (euwww!) pregnant horse urine. It also contains oestrone and smaller amounts of oestradiol. Daily dose range: 0.3–1.25 milligrams. Protective dose: 0.625 of a milligram.
- **Progynova.** (Oestradiol valerate). Easier on the liver than some forms of oestrogen. Daily dose range: 1–4 milligrams. Protective dose: 2 milligrams.
- **Ogen.** (Piperazine oestrone sulphate). Oestrone is the second-most potent form of oestrogen. Daily dose range: 0.625–2.5 milligrams. Protective dose: 1.25 milligrams.
- **Ovestin.** Made from oestriol, the weakest form of body-made oestrogen. It needs to be given in large doses, but has little effect on the endometrium and often means minimal vaginal bleeding. Daily dose range: 1–4 milligrams. Protective dose: 2 milligrams.

Oestrogen and progesterone

- **Trisequens.** Packaged like the Pill in a blister pack, the first group of tablets taken in a cycle are oestrogen alone, the next are oestrogen and progesterone and the final group contain very low levels of oestrogen. You'll probably have a 'period' while taking the final oestrogen ones.

Progesterone (progestogens)

At larger doses progestogens are used to transform the endometrium so that it will shed when the drug is withdrawn after about ten days—causing a 'period'. At smaller and continual doses, the endometrium tends to shrink and is thought to be less prone to cancerous change.

Patches

Oestrogen is easily absorbed through the skin. The patches are usually a multi-layered, plastic-coated and adhesive small 'bandaid' which has an outer waterproof layer; a drug reservoir with the oestrogen; an inner membrane through which the drug is released; and then glue. The patch is usually stuck to the stomach or a buttock.

Patches are usually changed every three or four days, or each week, and must be applied to a different area each time. They sometimes cause skin irritation which is reduced if the alcohol in the patch is allowed to evaporate prior to application (waving the patch around after removal of the adhesive cover ought to do it). Oestrogen absorption through patches is accelerated if body temperature rises and you sweat. Take it off while you throw yourself around.

Estraderm is the oestradiol patch of different strengths (2, 4 and 8 milligrams), which release 25 micrograms, 50 micrograms and 100 micrograms respectively over three to four days. (There is also a seven-day patch called Climara.) The 50 micrograms dose is equivalent to 0.625 of a milligram of Premarin and is favoured as the protective dose.

Creams and pessaries

Vaginal creams or pessaries containing oestrogen are used for the dryness, irritation and chronic, recurrent urinary symptoms associated with low oestrogen. The oestrogen in these creams is absorbed through the skin and causes blood oestrogen levels to rise. The newer creams do not need to be used with progesterone, because they contain oestrogens which do not overstimulate the endometrium.

Oestrogen creams and pessaries are usually recommended to be used every day for about three weeks, and then only about twice weekly. A break every three months for one month is usually recommended, or a progestogen drug (often Provera) is given for 12 to 14 days every second month to bring on a 'period'.

Ovestin

Available as a cream or pessaries, it contains the weaker oestrogen, oestriol. It's inserted into the vagina at night, while lying down, for maximum absorption. Ovestin is for mild to moderate oestrogen deficiency symptoms.

Vagifem
(What brilliant marketing genius thought of *that* name?) This is a pessary which contains oestradiol, a stronger oestrogen. The treatment regime is similar to that described for Ovestin. Vagifem is used for moderate to severe oestrogen deficiency symptoms.

Implants
Implants are small 'tablets' of oestrogen which are injected under the skin by a doctor with a special instrument. The oestrogen is gradually absorbed into the bloodstream and the implant needs replacing every four to eight months or when symptoms return. If you still have a uterus you should take progesterone as well to protect the endometrium. The implants are usually oestrogen alone, but sometimes oestrogen and testosterone are used, especially if you find you've lost interest in sex and would like to crank it up again.

Possible side effects

- Combined oestrogen and progesterone treatment can bring on PMS-like symptoms such as breast soreness, pain or swelling. You might be tempted to stop taking progesterone because of these symptoms, but don't forget taking oestrogen alone is associated with an increased risk of endometrial cancer.
- In rare cases blood pressure can increase after starting HRT and so a repeat visit to the doctor who prescribed the drug should be arranged a few weeks after you start on the drug.
- Oestrogen, either too much or too little (depending on your susceptibility) can cause the blood vessel spasm which leads to migraines. Some women on HRT develop migraines, others experience total relief from migraines. Progesterone can be implicated as well and a change of dose and type of HRT is probably worth considering.
- Oestrogen-dependent conditions such as fibroids and endometriosis can be aggravated by HRT, and so some people will need to go off it.
- If you're on HRT and develop bleeding between periods, after sex, or when not normally expected, immediately go to the doctor. A

hysteroscopy and biopsy of the endometrium will be needed to rule out endometrial cancer. (Hysteroscopy is explained under Surgery in The Medical Approach chapter.)

Breast cancer

Does HRT give you an increased breast cancer risk? It depends. Which you may have guessed from the conflicting media coverage. When oestrogens are given for more than ten years, the risk of breast cancer seems to increase.

In most cases, the increase is apparently small, but as one American researcher points out: 'A relative risk as small as 1.2 increases your chance of developing breast cancer each year from 1 in 250 to 1 in 200.' One European study showed an increased risk of 1.5 after 20 years and another showed 1.7 after nine years.

The jury is still out on whether there is an increased risk of developing breast cancer if a woman on HRT has pre-existing conditions which may predispose her to a higher risk anyway, such as a history of benign breast disease or a family history of breast cancer. At this stage researchers are unable to say either way, although some studies have shown an increase in risk in long-term users.

Another unresolved issue concerns oestrogen and progesterone given together long term. It was believed that progesterone would 'protect' breast tissue in the same way that it protects endometrial tissue from the overstimulation of cells by too much oestrogen, which can cause them to become cancerous. But some researchers have suggested an increase in breast cancer rate even with this combined approach.

In ten years, oestrogen and progesterone will have been used together for long enough and by enough women to make a firmer statement on the combined effect. We can't see the big picture yet.

Endometrial cancer

You increase the risk of endometrial (uterine lining) cancer if you take oestrogen drugs without progesterone. The risk increases the longer you stay on the oestrogen-only regime, and remains higher for five or more years after stopping the treatment.

Despite adequate medical guidelines, these potentially dangerous combinations of HRT are *still* prescribed for women by some doctors. A survey of 2000 Melbourne women on HRT in 1995 found that 26 per cent of women still with a uterus were prescribed oestrogen without progesterone.

There are two ways of taking progesterone with oestrogen so that the endometrium is protected. Progesterone can be taken for a short period of time and then stopped, causing a 'period'; or a low dose of progesterone can be taken continuously, which leads to endometrial 'shrinkage'.

Bones

Oestrogens, including the Pill, have a positive effect on bone density, and long-term prescriptions of HRT can be used to prevent or treat osteoporosis. When HRT is given to comparatively young post-menopausal women (between 50 and 75 years old) for 10 to 20 years, the fracture rate is down by nearly half. Consider HRT if you have a substantial fracture risk but be aware that when you stop, any positive effect will be lost within a few years. Because of concerns with long-term HRT use, increasing calcium and exercising may be better all-round options.

Heart disease

Some researchers believe HRT reduces risk of heart disease, others are not so sure and believe the issue requires further investigation. There are other ways to reduce the risk of heart disease without taking a pill, including a low-fat high-fibre diet. If you have a blood fat disorder that runs in your family you should consider HRT as well as dietary changes.

Gall bladder disease

Women on the Pill and HRT are more prone to gall bladder disease than other women. (Pills need to be processed by the liver before they pass into the bloodstream and this can cause stones to form in the gall bladder, because the bile becomes more concentrated.) An oestrogen patch avoids this possibility because the oestrogen is absorbed straight into the blood from the skin.

Reasons to avoid HRT

The contra-indications for HRT include:

- Known or suspected pregnancy.
- Known or suspected cancer of the breast.
- Known or suspected oestrogen-dependent cancer.
- Undiagnosed, abnormal vaginal bleeding.
- Active thrombophlebitis (inflammation of a vein with clot formation), or diseases associated with blood clotting abnormalities including recent heart attack or stroke.
- Liver, kidney, or pancreatic disease, and diabetes. (You may experience a worsening of these conditions or additional side effects from HRT.)

Checklist for the mid-life woman

- A monthly breast self-examination. Most doctors also recommend a mammogram every two years for women over 50.
- A yearly internal gynaecological examination including a Pap test (explained in the Screening section of The Medical Approach chapter).
- Weight-bearing exercise for a minimum of 30 minutes at least every second day.
- Calcium intake: 1500 milligrams a day. (Read the calcium info page in the Minerals section of the Self Care chapter.)
- Magnesium intake: 800 milligrams a day. (Read the magnesium info page in the Minerals section of the Self Care chapter.)
- Maintain your body weight at the middle to upper level of ideal weight to protect your bones.
- A yearly blood pressure check, more often if it's high.

- Book in for a bone density check if there's a strong family history of osteoporosis, or you have many risk factors. Re-check in two years.
- A cholesterol check in your mid-fifties. Repeat as directed by your doctor if there's a family history of heart disease.

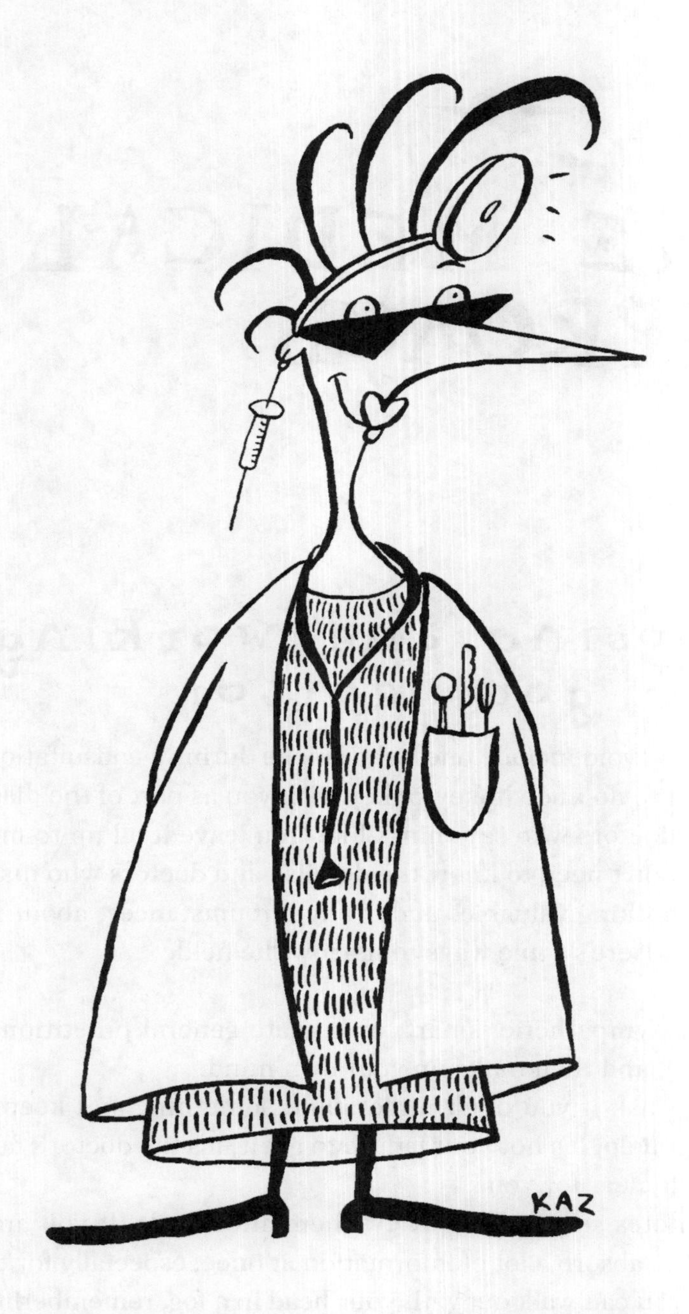

'I'm afraid you've got myxomatosis'

Chapter 7

THE MEDICAL APPROACH

Choosing and working with your doctor

Doctors to avoid include ones who smoke during a consultation, ones who want to do nude hokey-pokey with you as part of the diagnostic process, doctors who say things like 'You leave it all up to me, little girl, you don't need to know the details', and doctors who insist that there is nothing valuable, under any circumstances, about natural therapies. Here's some ways to narrow the field:

- Find a sympathetic, smart, up-to-date general practitioner. Ask around, and then make up your own mind.
- Always ask if you don't understand something and keep asking until you do. It's not your failure to get it, it's the doctor's failure to make it clear for you.
- Take notes so you can review them afterwards. If you are being asked to absorb a lot of information at once, especially for the first time, you can walk out with your head in a fog, remembering afterwards only the bit where you think the doctor said, 'I'm afraid you've got myxomatosis'.

- First consultations with a specialist are usually half an hour, to allow the doctor to fully explore your medical history. Follow-up consultations will vary.
- Get a second opinion, or extra opinions, if you are unsure or unhappy with any recommendation by a general practitioner or surgeon.
- Always tell the doctor anything you think is relevant to your condition. This definitely includes other medications, herbs or supplements like vitamins you may be taking.
- Always follow the instructions on medicine exactly. Just because 10 milligrams makes you feel better, it doesn't mean 20 milligrams will be twice as good.
- When choosing a specialist for your particular problem, do as much research as you can about their experience, expertise and manner. Don't be afraid to try a few out before you decide.
- Find out if your surgeon is experienced in the latest specialised techniques, or is more of an all-round gynaecologist. For complicated conditions, such as endometriosis, polycystic ovarian disease (PCOD), or high prolactin levels, seek the advice of a gynaecologist, gynaecological surgeon or endocrinologist who specialises in your problem.
- If you have surgery, the surgeon may visit you after the operation while you are still groggy. You may not remember the surgeon's report later. To be fully informed about what happened during your operation, and the implications for the future, get somebody to take notes for you then, organise a telephone call for a better time, or insist on an appointment as soon as you're up.
- Always tell the practitioner if you are pregnant, trying to get pregnant, wouldn't mind getting pregnant or are not perfectly strict with contraception.

Screening

Any full check-up will involve a breast examination, a Pap test, a pelvic examination, and blood tests which are taken by the doctor or nurse and analysed in a pathology lab. Here's what to expect and when to request a particular test:

Pelvic examinations

When

Every year. (And yes, you still need pelvic exams if you're a lesbian or celibate.)

Why

Pain on movement of the organs, or other tell-tale signs such as an organ feeling 'fixed' when it's supposed to be more mobile can indicate endometriosis, infection or adhesions. It can also detect unusual swellings, enlargement of the ovaries, uterine fibroids, pregnancy and tumours.

What

There are usually two stages to a pelvic 'exam'. Both are performed while you lie on your back on the couch in the doctor's office. It's okay to ask for a nurse to be there too. Here's the hard bit: with all that ferreting around going on down there you're supposed to relax. It's not exactly a calming experience, but it shouldn't hurt unless you tense up or there is something wrong. Sometimes the doctor will ask you to put your feet into 'stirrups'. (Try and resist the urge to say 'Giddy-up'.)

The doctor, wearing latex gloves over clean hands, will use a sterilised metal or plastic instrument called a speculum to very gently 'jack' open your vagina a little way so the doctor can look up the vagina and see the cervix. This is also a good time to have a Pap test, a case of 'While you're down there . . .'

For the full pelvic exam, the doctor will put two fingers inside the vagina so the tips of the fingers are in the area at the top of the vagina between the cervix and the wall of the vagina. The doctor's other hand will be placed on your lower abdomen. The doctor very gently wiggles fingertips to jostle some of your organs to feel if they are the right size and shape. The uterus can be felt between the hands and, if you are relaxed (well, *relatively* relaxed), it is fairly easy to tell whether it is in the normal place, the right size and can move easily.

Now go and buy yourself a cup of tea and some chocolate cake.

Pap test

When

Once every two years regardless of your sexual preference, unless your doctor advises you to have one more often.

Why

A Papanicolaou smear test (named after the doctor who invented it) is used to screen for changes to the cells on the cervix, which may proceed to cervical cancer if untreated.

What

See the speculum procedure above in the pelvic exam section. After this, the doctor inserts a tiny, skinny wooden or plastic spatula to gently scrape cells from the surface of the cervix. The cells are then smeared onto a glass slide, given a squirt with hair spray (well, it looks like hair spray but they reckon it's a fixative) and sent to a pathology lab for examination. (A new way of getting cells on the slide is being researched.) The procedure should be painless, but can be a little uncomfortable.

The cervical cells are examined under a microscope in a lab and graded according to the type of cells and whether they have undergone any changes. Pap tests can be inaccurate. When changes in cells are found in a Pap test, a colposcopy is often suggested. A colposcopy is a procedure in which a doctor looks up the vagina with a special telescope to see the cervix.

Breast checks

When

Every month after each period by you and an annual check by a doctor. Most women detect breast changes themselves. They know the 'normal' feel of their own breasts and are in an unique position to detect change and detect it early.

Why

You're looking for lumps or any changes in breast tissue. About

80 per cent of breast lumps are not cancerous, but even when a breast lump is caused by cancer, the earlier it is found, the better the outlook.

What

Breast examination involves two phases: visual and physical examination of the breast tissue. Do it after every period, and after menopause, once a month. You need to get to know—intimately—the feel of your breasts and report ANY changes to a doctor. Now we could print a very involved chart here, but really, we'd prefer you went to the doctor and got a lesson in how to do it properly, because it's easy once you know how. To jog your memory, pick up a pamphlet while you're there or get one from the anti-cancer council in your State or Territory (contact details are at the back of the book).

Ultrasound

This is a type of imaging using high-frequency sound waves to show the inside of the pelvis. An ultrasound for endometriosis or adenomyosis is performed with the same equipment that's used during pregnancy to get an image of the foetus. You will be lying down for the procedure.

Either the ultrasound operator will slide a little probe like a computer mouse around on the outside of your bare stomach, or if that won't get a good enough view, they will put a probe inside the vagina. The probe is usually shaped like a smooth pen with a small bulb shape on one end. It's not too big, and may be slightly uncomfortable when they move it around slightly, but it shouldn't hurt.

The image is projected on a small screen. The ultrasound operator will be able to explain to you what is being seen—otherwise, you're thinking the TV's gone on the blink or something and they're going, 'Ye Gads! It's an ovarian follicle!'.

Blood tests

Drink lots of water before you have blood taken. Otherwise it can be harder to draw blood efficiently. Make sure you arrange a time to call or visit the doctor for the results.

Drugs

The bottom line is that many prescribed drugs are strong and even toxic, to deal with the problem they target. The body can sometimes use a little help, either with something from a natural therapist to offset side effects, like a mineral or vitamin supplement, or by finding another drug or brand of drug that you tolerate better. Always talk to your doctor if you are having a rough time: there are often alternatives.

Hormone drugs

The Pill

There are many different types of oral contraceptives including Pills with variable oestrogen and progestogen levels (Triphasil and Triquilar), or those with the same levels throughout the cycle (Brevinor, Microgynon). Some also contain androgen-blocking agents (Diane) and are used for acne and excessive male-pattern hair growth; some are progestogen-only Pills (the mini Pills such as Micronor and Microlut). A lot of factors need to be considered when prescribing the Pill. Each different brand or type of Pill can have its own effects on individuals. If you have any difficulties see a gynaecologist.

Good points

If taken properly, the Pill is pretty good contraception, but other good side effects may include reduced rates of ovarian and endometrial cancer, benign breast disease (not breast cancer), benign ovarian cysts, pelvic inflammatory disease, period pain, heavy periods and anaemia. Today's low-dose Pills are much safer than the earlier Pills which had much higher doses of hormones.

Bad points

The less jolly side effects of the Pill can include blood clots, stroke, and heart attack, especially for smokers. It can cause period changes such as breakthrough bleeding or spotting, and some women experience androgenic blokey hormone effects, including the weight gain and acne which are associated with the progestogen (synthetic progesterone) in the Pill.

A small number of women develop long-term loss of periods after coming off the Pill—estimated to be about 1 per cent after the first year.

Some women on the Pill also report an increase in mood swings, depression and loss of interest in sex. These symptoms are more common in the first couple of months of taking the Pill and may go away after that. Doctors usually advise taking one Pill for two months before trying a new brand of Pill which might be better tolerated.

Warnings in the Mims and PP Guide (medical books which describe what drugs should be prescribed for, what the drugs do, and when they shouldn't be used) say that oestrogen can make fibroids get bigger. However, it has been shown that fibroids do not necessarily increase in size when women take the Pill, that periods become lighter and that blood-iron levels increase. If you have fibroids and you want to take the Pill, talk to a gynaecologist.

The Pill can cause increased pigmentation of the skin which is known as chloasma or melasma. This usually shows up in patchy, light brown areas on a pale-skinned face and becomes much darker with exposure to the sun. It is probably caused by oestrogen—it also can happen in pregnancy, or in women with high oestrogen levels. Stopping the Pill does not necessarily mean that it will go away completely, although it does tend to fade. Use sun block religiously, and you can lighten the pigmentation with safe skin creams or 'peels' that contain glycolic acid. Doctors sometimes recommend creams containing hydroquinone or acne medication.

Why it's used

Apart from its use as a contraceptive, the Pill is often prescribed for heavy periods. It usually reduces bleeding by thinning the endometrial lining. The Pill can also be used for period pain, especially when you need a contraceptive as well, or if prostaglandins-inhibitors like Naprogesic and Ponstan haven't worked for you. The Pill improves period pain about 90 per cent of the time because it stops ovulation and holds down the prostaglandins which cause muscle spasm.

The Pill improves PMS symptoms in some women, has no effect in others and makes some women worse. The Pill's control of some women's PMS is probably because it stops ovulation and balances the hormones.

Taking the Pill reduces the amount of period blood, and so lowers the risk of developing endometriosis. The latest Pills have much lower levels of oestrogen and seem to reduce the amount of both normal endometrium *and* the amount of endometriosis. Even better results are found when the Pill is used continuously (without a break for 'periods') to create a pretend pregnancy state. If it works, the Pill is better than the other drugs for endo because the side effects of those are much more serious, such as a decrease in bone density.

However, the Pill is not as effective for advanced endometriosis and is not suitable for women who want to become pregnant (der). In one study, most women had a return of endo symptoms within six months of stopping the Pill. The pregnancy rate of women who have endo is also low following the use of the Pill.

Things to take while on the Pill

- The Pill influences a number of nutrients. You'll need more of vitamins B2, B3, B6, folic acid and zinc, but less iron because of the smaller blood loss at the period. If you are on the Pill, a daily B-group vitamin is a good idea, especially one with a B6 level of between 25 and 50 milligrams. (You may be prescribed a larger daily dose.) This may also help with depression and mood changes associated with the Pill.
- Depression can also be tackled by trying a Pill with a lower oestrogen dose.
- Herbal diuretics, especially dandelion leaf tea, can help with fluid retention symptoms. One or two teaspoons a cup, twice daily (not before bed) is the usual dose. Vegetable juices with parsley and celery can also have a diuretic effect, and there are herbal diuretic tablets. Beware of diuretic drugs which can strip the body of potassium. Cut down on salt in food.
- Many women also report that evening primrose oil (between 1 and 3 grams a day) is useful for many of the symptoms such as fluid

retention that they experience while taking the Pill. Diet can also be altered to take in more essential fatty acids. (See Bad Fats and Good Fats, number 8 of 20 Diet Hints in the Self Care chapter.)

- The blood copper level increases when women are on the Pill and may be partly responsible for the mood changes. High copper levels can lead to a zinc deficiency and zinc supplements may be needed, especially by vegetarians and vegans. A zinc information page is included in the Minerals section of the Self Care chapter. The usual dose of zinc is 15–30 milligrams a day.
- Women who smoke and take the Pill can take 100 IU of vitamin E every day to reduce the risk of blood clot formation (but usually not if you have a pre-existing heart condition or high blood pressure). But quite frankly, you are taking a helluva risk smoking while on the Pill. Even women in their twenties and early thirties can have strokes.

A balanced diet will help to prevent nutrient deficiencies while on the Pill (for a balanced diet see the 20 Diet Hints in the Self Care chapter).

Things to watch out for while on the Pill

- Blood levels of vitamin A increase while on the Pill, so vitamin A supplements including cod liver oil, should never be taken with the Pill. The absorption of betacarotene (the precursor to vitamin A) from food, however, may be lower and so you should eat plenty of orange and yellow vegetables.
- Some drugs can make the Pill a less powerful contraceptive, including some anti-epileptic drugs, some antibiotics and the anti-fungal medication, Griseofulvin. Some drugs are cleared more slowly from the body when women are on the Pill. Theophylline, the anti-asthma drug, is one of these.
- Painkillers with paracetamol, like Panadol, reduce the rate at which oestrogen is naturally cleared from the body and may lead to higher levels and more side effects from too much oestrogen.
- Women on thyroid hormones (such as Tertroxine) may need to increase their dose if they are also prescribed the Pill. Some sedatives, tranquillisers and anti-depressant drugs may not work as

well; others seem to have a stronger effect, such as the tricyclic anti-depressants Tofranil and Melipramine. If you are on the Pill or prescribed the Pill as well as *any* other drug, discuss the possible effects with a doctor or at the local chemist.

When to stop the Pill

Symptoms or conditions which indicate that the Pill should be stopped immediately include blood clots, high blood pressure or serious headaches. Smoking while on the Pill increases the risk of developing those problems. Post-Pill absence of periods is not usually treated by doctors until you want to get pregnant, when doctors will prescribe fertility drugs like Clomid. (Side effects should be discussed with your doctor.) Until this time, the usual recommendation is for women to go back on the Pill to maintain their bone density because oestrogen levels are lower when you don't ovulate.

Progestogens

The commonly used progesterone-like drugs or 'progestogens' come from two classes—medroxyprogesterone acetate such as Provera, and norethisterone such as Primulut N. Both progestogens are used in the Pill, and are also prescribed for bleeding irregularities, endometriosis and for the menopause. (You may have heard of Depo Provera. This just means an injection of Provera—depo means injected—lasting three months. It is advertised by manufacturers as an easy, long-term contraception. There are other reliable tablet forms of contraception which have less side effects. These can be stopped if side effects are a problem.)

Progestogens are often prescribed for heavy periods, even if the patient doesn't have irregularities in progesterone production. When you stop taking the drug, it causes complete shedding of the endometrium, which often stops the abnormal bleeding. These drugs need to be given for about 21 days—usually from Day 5 to Day 25 of the menstrual cycle. They are usually prescribed for between one and three menstrual cycles, but sometimes for longer. The androgen-like side effects and abnormal cholesterol levels associated with Primulut and the norethisterones restrict their use to no more than 6–12 months.

Menopausal women taking oestrogens and who have not had a hysterectomy need progestogens. There's more on this in the Menopause section.

Provera and Duphaston (dydrogesterone) are the common progestogens used for endometriosis and can either be taken in the last part of the cycle, or taken continuously to create a pregnancy-like state with no period. About 30 per cent of women have spotting and breakthrough bleeding until the drug starts to work or the dose is adjusted. These drugs are relatively inexpensive (compared to some of the others used for endometriosis) and can give significant pain relief to some women without serious long-term side effects.

Possible side effects

Progestogen side effects can include nausea, bloating, acne, breast tenderness, weight gain and mood changes involving a lot of sudden, unexplained shouting (alright, maybe it was just me) which may be related to the blokey hormone effects of the drugs. The medroxyprogesterones such as Provera have fewer blokey hormone effects. Primulut and other norethisterones have mild oestrogenic, anabolic (growth promoting) and blokey hormone effects.

Provera and Duphaston can cause side effects in some women that are a real drag, or should we say drag queen, including increased hairiness, mood changes and a deeper voice. All the symptoms should go away after the drug use stops, except for the deepening of the voice. Singers and actors and people who want to sound like Betty Boop beware: use another drug if you can.

Fertility is not improved as a result of using progestogens. The return to a regular cycle may be delayed for many months and there are no studies assessing the return rate of endo after progestogen use.

What to take with progestogens

When side effects from progestogens are a problem, the B vitamins, herbal diuretics or evening primrose oil, and essential fatty acids in the diet can sometimes reduce symptoms. For doses see the recommendations under the Pill, above.

Danazol (danocrine)

Heavy stuff, Danazol needs to be carefully prescribed after careful consideration of the risks and benefits for each individual. For endometriosis, Danazol is prescribed in high doses (between 200 and 800 milligrams a day) to stop ovulation, suppress the period and cause the endometrium (both inside and out of the uterus) to shrink. Spotting can be a problem and is usually managed with a dose change.

On the helpful side, Danazol improves period pain and other pelvic pain and causes atrophy of endometriosis implants. It seems to have beneficial effects on the immune abnormalities, is better than other progestogens in improving fertility, and does not have an adverse effect on bone density.

Danazol is sometimes used when abnormal bleeding has not responded to other treatments, but usually only when surgery is ruled out, or when there are long waiting lists for hysterectomy in a public hospital. (Alternatively, you could chain yourself to the nearest health minister until you get into hospital.) The Danazol dose is between 200 and 400 milligrams daily. It has also been used to treat breast tenderness and cystic breast changes; and to improve lethargy, anxiety, and hunger frenzies associated with PMS. For these conditions, it is used at daily doses of around 200 milligrams which cause less side effects and tend not to stop the period.

Possible side effects

Danazol is another progestogen which can cause pronounced blokey hormone effects such as male-pattern hair growth, deepening of the voice, weight gain, acne, and changes like smaller breasts, and an overgrown clitoris. These are reversible when drug use stops, except for a deeper voice, in some cases.

Severe and life-threatening strokes or thromboembolism (blood clots), and increased pressure inside the skull have also been reported with the use of Danazol; and long-term use may cause serious toxicity including jaundice and hepatitis. Some women find it also causes severe mood changes and symptoms like PMS. Some people take it with no trouble.

What to take with it
Side effects from Danazol are difficult to control, especially at the higher doses required for the treatment of endometriosis. However, trying the supplements suggested for the Pill (see above) can sometimes make the difference between being able to stay on the medication comfortably and feeling like you want to bite strangers in the street: 50–100 milligrams of vitamin B6 and 400–800 milligrams a day of magnesium seem to be particularly useful.

Progesterone

The hormone progesterone (not the progestogens, such as Provera and Primulut) has been used for some time for PMS symptoms. Progesterone cannot be taken in a pill because it is very quickly broken down in the liver. So it has to be taken as either a vaginal pessary, a cream, an injection or a slow-release implant inserted under the skin.

Progesterone has many enthusiastic supporters for its use in treating PMS and breast soreness even though controlled trials fail to show a better than placebo effect. It is most effective during cycles where the menstrual cycle has been disrupted, possibly because the progesterone levels caused by the drug are enough to stop ovulation.

Hormone replacement therapy (HRT)

HRT is explored in detail under menopause.

Hormone-blocking drugs

GnRH agonists

We pause for a short message about how the body works. The hypothalamus gland in the brain releases a hormone called gonadotrophin releasing hormone (GnRH). GnRH tells the pituitary gland to start pumping out important hormones which drive the menstrual cycle—luteinising hormone (LH) and follicle stimulating hormone (FSH).

Drugs with a similar chemical structure to GnRH are called GnRH analogues. GnRH analogues either mimic the action or stop you making your own GnRH. When taken continuously, a GnRH analogue stops ovulation and is then called a GnRH agonist—agonist means a competitor. These drugs are mainly used to treat endometriosis and fibroid cysts.

The GnRH agonists are often used to shrink fibroids and the amount of blood vessels which surround them before a myomectomy (surgical removal of a fibroid). This is useful simply because it reduces bleeding and makes it easier to remove a smaller fibroid. Another advantage is to reduce heavy periods before the op, which allows you to deal with any anaemia before surgery. Unless surgery follows the use of the GnRH agonists, the fibroid will grow again when you stop taking the drugs.

When taken for endometriosis, the drugs induce a temporary menopausal state. GnRH agonists are equally effective as Danazol in reducing the symptoms and the size of endometrial implants, and the side effects are said to be less severe.

Endometrial cysts usually return to their initial size four months after stopping drug treatment, making some sort of additional treatment necessary. GnRH agonists have no extra benefits in improving fertility.

GnRH agonists have also been trialled in combination with the Pill for premenstrual symptoms. These sorts of treatments are controversial because they're pretty heavy drugs, and are reserved for really feral cases of PMS. They are very occasionally used for abnormal bleeding which has failed to respond to other treatment.

GnRH agonists cannot be used as pills because of their chemical make-up. Instead, they are either given as a injection (Zoladex), usually once a month; or as a nostril spray (Synarel). They cause a menopausal state and stop periods during their use. Ovulation usually comes back within about a month of stopping the drugs.

Possible side effects
Menopausal symptoms such as hot flushes, dry vagina and headaches are common, and some women have difficulty with sex because of vaginal dryness and some women, come to mention it, find themselves less than interested in the whole idea of sex.

There is an early and significant bone density loss after starting on GnRH agonists. Radial bone density (measured in the wrist) is not affected, but the bone density of the spine shows significant changes. For some women, this may not be reversible and should be considered as part of their decision to use GnRH agonists. Oestrogen and progesterone given together might prevent bone density loss, but aggravate the condition that GnRH agonists were prescribed for.

Some people will develop ovarian cysts in the first two months of treatment with GnRH agonists, especially if they have a previous history of polycystic ovarian disease. These cysts will often disappear themselves as the treatment progresses, but can grow large enough to require surgery or going off the drug.

What to take with GnRH agonists
- Women who take GnRH agonists should ensure that their calcium and magnesium intake is high enough. Information pages on calcium and on magnesium are included in the Minerals section of the Self Care chapter.
- Plant oestrogens can help offset menopausal symptoms brought on by using the drugs (more info is under plant oestrogens in the Self Care chapter).

Bromocriptine
Bromocriptine (the most common brand name is Parlodel) corrects prolactin levels that are too high, and stops the production of breast milk. It reinstates ovulation, a regular cycle and fertility when women have hyperprolactinaemia. Prolactin-secreting tumours can decrease in size with continued use and because bromocriptine improves oestrogen levels, it is always considered when there is a risk of low bone density.

Bromocriptine has also been used to treat PMS, but this treatment has been questioned. Breast soreness is the only symptom to consistently respond and the drug often causes unacceptable side effects.

Women on bromocriptine continue or start to ovulate. If you don't want to get pregnant you'll need to use a 'barrier contraceptive', like a diaphragm or condoms. The inhibitory (dopamine-like) effect on the hypothalamus is only temporary and most women with hyperprolactinaemia who stop the drug will again stop having periods.

Possible side effects
These include nausea, vomiting, dizziness, headaches and a blocked nose. They are usually only transitory and can be reduced if the drug is taken at night, or the drug dose is built up slowly. Many women don't tolerate this drug well.

Tamoxifen

Tamoxifen is a synthetic anti-oestrogen drug which is used for women with oestrogen-responsive breast cancer and (controversially) for pre-menstrual breast pain.

Long-term use of this drug is associated with a higher risk of endometrial cancer and uterine polyps. Other side effects include hot flushes; vaginal dryness, itch or discharge; menstrual changes when women are pre-menopausal and bleeding in post-menopausal women.

Prostaglandins-inhibitors

These drugs inhibit the prostaglandins which cause the heavier periods and period pain from increased uterine muscle spasm. They can be bought without a prescription from a chemist. Aspirin is a well-known prostaglandins-inhibitor, but is not much chop for period pain. Some of the newer, more effective ones are Ponstan, Naprogesic, ACT 3 and Nurofen.

Prostaglandins-inhibitors are absorbed quickly and can reduce pain in about half an hour. They can be used for the relief of period pain, including the moderate to severe period pain associated with endometriosis. Some women only use them when they have pain, others prefer to start to take them before the expected onset of the period.

There seems to be no difference in effectiveness if the drugs are taken before the start of the period, but it's best to get on to them early if vomiting accompanies pain. Keep the dose in the lowest effective range.

Women who have heavy periods, and who continue to ovulate seem to respond better to these drugs than women who are not ovulating. The drugs also seem to work better in combination with the Pill or progesterone tablets, and some doctors recommend these treatments be combined.

Ponstan has also been used to treat mood swings, fatigue, headache and the general aches and pains which accompany PMS.

You shouldn't take these drugs for longer than seven days at a time, so they're no good for the many women who experience PMS for more than a week before their period.

Prostaglandins-inhibitors do not actually reverse the prostaglandins imbalance which causes heavy periods, pain or PMS and will have to be used indefinitely until the cause(s) of the imbalance are found and dealt with. Prostaglandins-inhibitors only control symptoms while they're around. This is not a very alluring prospect, especially since there are many side effects.

Possible side effects

About a quarter of people using prostaglandins-inhibitors have problems with the gastro-intestinal system. Symptoms can include nausea, vomiting, stomach pain, indigestion, diarrhoea, heartburn, abdominal cramps, constipation, abdominal bloating and wind. These drugs should always be taken with food to try to minimise the risk of gastric ulceration. Steer clear of them if you have a history of gastro-intestinal disease.

A number of other complaints can be aggravated by the use of prostaglandins-inhibitors and they may cause problems if you have poor liver function, asthma, clotting disorders, lupus, and heart disease. Prostaglandins-inhibitors can mask the signs of infection and should not be taken when period pain is known or suspected to be caused by pelvic inflammatory disease.

What to take with them
Slippery elm can help to prevent gastric ulceration associated with these drugs. One teaspoon mixed into apple juice, or into equal quantities of apple juice mixed with yoghurt, and taken at the same time as the drug, helps to protect the stomach lining.

Diuretics

Diuretics have been one of the most commonly prescribed drugs for bloating and breast tenderness associated with PMS thought to be caused by fluid retention. The results of trials using different types of diuretics have been conflicting, and due to a tendency for some women to bolt down more tablets than they should, they're not so often prescribed. Some diuretics deplete potassium, so check with your doctor about potassium supplements.

Anti-depressants and anxiolytics

A variety of anti-depressants and anxiolytics (anti-anxiety drugs) are sometimes used for mood disorders associated with period problems, particularly PMS and around menopause. As a general rule it's best to stay right away from them. They treat only the symptoms if they treat anything at all, and you can become dependent without getting to the cause of the problem.

In some cases the depression gets more entrenched. The minor tranquillisers, such as the benzodiazepines (Valium) may add to the fatigue and lethargy often associated with hormonal changes.

Anaesthetics

If you're having general anaesthetic you will need to stay in hospital for a minimum of four hours and maybe longer, depending on what procedures you undergo. Anaesthetics are evolving all the time, and have been since they used whisky or a swift blow to the noggin. 'General' anaesthetics will render you unconscious for the duration of the surgery. Different 'generals' are used—anaesthetists often have their own favourites.

Some people react badly to anaesthetics—if you have a second operation after a bad experience recovering from anaesthetic, find out what you had last time and tell the anaesthetist to try something different.

It's increasingly popular to skip the 'pre-med' relaxing shot of pethidine or other drugs, such as Scopolomine, used to dry up secretions. It's now believed that people recover more quickly from anaesthetic after an operation if they don't have a pre-med. Never lie to your anaesthetist about how much you weigh, how much alcohol you drink or how many cigarettes you smoke. This will affect the amount of anaesthetic and drugs you need during surgery.

Surgery

If you've gotta, you've gotta, but don't be afraid of getting a second opinion, or more if you like, before you agree. Except in emergency situations, surgery should be seen as a last resort. Surgery can be necessary for proper diagnosis and/or treatment. In this section we explain the most common gynaecological procedures.

Whatever surgery you're having, make sure you read the hints below about preparing for surgery and better recovery. These days you can be shovelled in and out of hospital so fast, you'll need all the help you can get in recovering. (Don't feel you have to go home the same day, and if you do, make sure somebody can care for you properly. If you're going home alone or to a houseful of screaming kids who need looking after—don't be bullied and insist on the extra day in hospital. The after-effects of general anaesthetic are not to be sneezed at.)

Good pre-operative strategies can make all the difference to recovering quickly and easily from even a major operation.

Hysteroscopy

Reason

To have a look around the inside of the uterus. A diagnostic hysteroscopy is used before *any* treatment to exclude serious conditions when abnormal bleeding or other worrying symptoms are present, especially when women are over 40. Small procedures such as the removal of polyps or fibroids can be performed at the same time.

Anaesthetic

A general anaesthetic in hospital is recommended by most doctors because, unless you've given birth, your cervix will be too small to pass the instrument through without considerable discomfort. Sometimes a hysteroscopy is performed with a local anaesthetic in the specialist's rooms.

Procedure

A hysteroscope is a small pencil-sized instrument which is inserted into the cervix and through which the inner cavity of the uterus can be seen. The uterine cavity is inflated with gas or fluid so that a good view is possible and extra procedures may be performed. The doctor should be able to see if any parts of the endometrium appear to be diseased.

Time

About half an hour. If a general anaesthetic has been used, there's a four-hour recovery time in hospital. You can probably go home on the same day.

Laparoscopy

Reason

A look around the pelvic organs, usually searching for problems like blocked Fallopian tubes, endometriosis or cysts of some kind. Many kinds of treatment may be performed at the same time, such as removal of cysts, and laser destruction of endometriosis implants.

Anaesthetic

General, in hospital.

Procedure

The surgeon makes two or more small incisions to insert the look-around instrument, called a laparoscope. This thin, pencil-like instrument has fibre-optics through which the operator can view the inner organs. There is usually one incision under the navel and another just above the pubic bone.

The abdomen is usually filled with a gas so that it is pumped up with an 'air' making it easier for the surgeon to see each individual organ, and there's more room to move the laparoscope around. At the end of the procedure, most of the gas is forced out, but some stays in the abdominal cavity and can cause pain or discomfort until it eventually dissipates, which can be after a few days. The pressure of the gas affects nerves, and can cause 'referred' pain in the shoulders.

Minor surgical procedures can be performed during a laparoscopy, such as removing patches of endometriosis with laser (which vaporises) or diathermy (burning off with electrical current), the removal of small ovarian cysts, and the removal of adhesions. These procedures usually only involve a day in hospital; and pain and post-operative complications are minimal because the incisions are small.

Time

Sometimes you can go home the same day, sometimes the next day, depending on what had to be done. A quick look around is one thing, but additional surgery like laser treatment will add on to your recovery time.

Recovery time is usually a few days depending on the extent of the additional surgery and the type of complaint treated. Even though the external wounds can be quite small, the internal organs might take a while to recover. Pain is a good indicator of how much to do and when rest is needed. Listen to your body. See the advice below on pre- and post-op care: it's important.

Laparotomy

Reason

For more extensive surgery than a laparoscopy can handle. Often, to remove large cysts, endometriosis, or to do some repair work to help with fertility.

Anaesthetic
General, in hospital.

Procedure
A laparotomy involves an abdominal incision, usually just above the pubic bone and can include removal of extensive and hard-to-reach adhesions, removal of larger ovarian cysts, diathermy (burning off with electrical current) or laser (vaporising) of extensive and difficult-to-reach endometriosis, or for reconstruction and micro-surgery of reproductive bits. For example, a laparotomy is usual when emergency surgery has to be performed for a ruptured ectopic pregnancy.

Time
A laparotomy can take from between half an hour and several hours, depending on the type of surgery to be performed. Recovery time is longer than after a laparoscopy because the abdominal wounds are more extensive and so is the internal surgery. You may be in hospital a few days to a week.

Endometrial ablation

Reason
Usually to counter heavy periods. The preferred outcome is that only a little or no endometrium is left behind.

There are many critics of this procedure, and disadvantages include a high failure rate. Periods often continue, especially when the patient has adenomyosis. For some though, when all other treatments have failed, this procedure offers a possible alternative to the conventional hysterectomy.

Anaesthetic
General, in hospital.

Procedure
An endometrial ablation is destruction of the lining of the uterus (endometrium) either with a laser or by cauterisation. A

hysteroscope (see above) is inserted through the vagina and cervix and into the uterus to perform the operation.

Time
Usually half an hour to three-quarters of an hour.

'D&C' (dilation and curettage) or curette/termination

Reason
Usually performed after a miscarriage to make sure all tissue is removed, and to reduce the risk of haemorrhage. It is also the surgical procedure used for pregnancy termination. (There is a way of causing an early termination by the use of a hormonal drug, but that drug has been effectively disallowed in Australia by the Federal Government, meaning women who need a termination are denied a choice between surgery and a tablet.) Curettes are also used to remove the endometrium to test it for cancerous or pre-cancerous cells in a laboratory. A D&C can also be performed for diagnostic reasons.

Anaesthetic
General, in hospital. Some doctors will use a local anaesthetic injection to the cervix.

Procedure
The surface of the endometrial lining of the uterus is scraped away with a surgical instrument. The surface begins to grows back straight away and is back to normal within a few weeks.

Time
Usually about ten minutes.

Myomectomy

Reason
To surgically remove one or more fibroids without removing the

uterus. This can be a difficult operation to perform. Some points for and against myomectomy and hysterectomy are discussed below.

Usually a gynaecologist will recommend that a fibroid be removed in these cases:

- Fibroids larger than a 12–14 week pregnancy.
- Fibroids that are growing.
- Fibroids associated with heavy bleeding.
- The fibroid is pedunculated (attached to a stem).
- The fibroid interferes with fertility.

Surgery or not?

Size is often quoted as a reason for removing a fibroid, whether it is causing symptoms or not. In direct opposition to this recommendation, a recent comment in the *American Journal of Obstetrics and Gynecology* suggested that regardless of size, the presence and severity of significant symptoms 'should be the most important considerations in the individualization of treatment strategies'. In other words, if it's not causing problems, leave it alone.

Fibroids are also blamed for problems with fertility and removal is sometimes suggested before you try to get pregnant, just in case. It is unlikely, however, that the fibroids will affect fertility and conception rates. The same study showed that there was an increased rate of caesarean section when a woman has fibroids, particularly if they are situated in the lower portion of the uterus, but no change in fertility rate. Women with fibroids have an increased risk of severe bleeding following childbirth caused by the fibroid interfering with uterine contractions.

Myomectomy or hysterectomy?

For women past their childbearing years or those who don't want to get pregnant, a hysterectomy is usually recommended. For others, a myomectomy may be suggested.

Some surgeons are reluctant to perform a myomectomy, especially for women who don't want to have (more) children. It's difficult for even the most experienced surgeon to predict how easily a fibroid can be removed. You could bleed severely, and this may mean that a hysterectomy will have to be performed anyway, and under less than optimum conditions. Sometimes the exact location of the fibroid will only be discovered during the surgery. It may be in a position where it is difficult to reach, or surrounded by delicate structures. It may be fed by more blood vessels than usual.

Other reasons for not wanting to perform a myomectomy are that the fibroids may grow back or the heavy period bleeding associated with the fibroid prior to its removal may not stop. An unspoken reason for suggesting hysterectomy is the common medical opinion that women who do not intend to have a child have no need for a uterus. A hysterectomy may be offered first and a myomectomy discussed only if you mention it.

This decision is often difficult for many women. When a hysterectomy has been advised, but is not a suitable option, a second opinion from a gynaecologist experienced in the technique of myomectomy is advisable. Removal of fibroids using laser is reported to reduce bleeding at the time of surgery, reduce the risk of adhesions and improve the fertility rate of women wanting to conceive.

Sometimes a hysterectomy may be the only option. A myomectomy might just be too risky, complicated or unpredictable. There may be too many fibroids (although we know of a 45-year-old whose gynaecologist removed 42 fibroids rather than perform a hysterectomy!) or there may be other gynaecological reasons why a hysterectomy is a better option.

Both hysterectomy and myomectomy are elective procedures and so it is possible to arrange an auto-transfusion (where a woman gives her own blood some days before the operation and then is transfused with this blood during the procedure if needed). If you give blood for an auto-transfusion, take iron supplements and increase your daily intake of iron-containing foods (see the info page on iron in the Minerals sections of the Self Care chapter).

Anaesthetic

General, in hospital.

Procedure
It is usually performed through a laparotomy incision. The fibroids are cut out with a scalpel and care must be taken to stop all the bleeding.

Time
The procedure usually takes up to two hours.

Hysterectomy

Reason
This procedure is a last resort in several conditions including really severe, unresponsive endometriosis, heavy periods, fibroids, the severe pain and bleeding associated with adenomyosis and other serious gynaecological conditions, and some cancers. Sometimes doctors talk about a 'partial hysterectomy' (removal of the uterus but not the ovaries).

Anaesthetic
General, in hospital.

Procedure
A hysterectomy is the removal of the uterus, but the removal of the uterus *and* Fallopian tubes *and* ovaries is generally also known as a hysterectomy. Its technical term is bilateral salpingo-oophorectomy. (Sometimes you really do have to worry about doctors. Oophorectomy indeed.) A 'total hysterectomy' usually means that the cervix is taken as well as the uterus, and a 'sub-total' hysterectomy usually means the cervix is left alone. Make sure you understand exactly what your doctor means when the word hysterectomy is used. The operation can be done by making an incision in the stomach and cutting out the uterus; or by entering the body through the vagina with surgical instruments, cutting away the uterus, and pulling it out through the vagina. (Sorry to get a bit graphic, but that's what happens.)

A hysterectomy for endometriosis will probably be done through an abdominal incision if there are multiple adhesions which make vaginal removal too difficult.

For conditions which are oestrogen-dependent, such as severe and non-responsive endometriosis and some types of cancer, the removal of the uterus and ovaries is often recommended. Removing the ovaries can prevent or slow growth of these oestrogen-responsive tissues but, of course, means you will become menopausal.

Time

This is a *major* operation. It usually takes three-quarters of an hour to an hour, but can take several hours depending on possible complications. You will probably be in hospital for between five and ten days.

Preparing for surgery

The following pre-surgery hints will help you to improve wound healing and reduce wound infections; assist with getting up and around again as quickly as possible; and cut down on the common discomfort of bowel problems after surgery, caused by your inside bits being disturbed.

The hints will help in any abdominal surgery, including hysterectomy, myomectomy, laparoscopy, laser surgery, laparotomy or caesarean section. Check them with your surgeon.

- Give up smoking—for good if you can, but at least for two weeks before the operation. This will reduce your risk of post-operative chest infections.
- A few dietary changes in the *week before surgery* can help to prevent or reduce the symptoms of bowel problems afterwards.
- The seed breakfast should be started about one week before the operation and continued as soon as solid foods can be eaten after surgery. (The seed breakfast recipe is in the irritable bowel syndrome diet in the Self Care chapter.)
- Eat daily salads of grated raw carrot and beetroot or a medium-sized cooked beetroot.
- Yoghurt or cultured milk drinks colonise the bowel with healthy

bacteria and cut down on painful wind. Drink or eat about one cup a day of yoghurt with live cultures and no sugar. (Jalna, Hakea and Gippsland are good brands with low-fat options.)

- Avoid refined sugars which tend to increase bowel fermentation and wind.
- Avoid foods which usually cause you wind or constipation or diarrhoea.
- If you already have irritable bowel syndrome or suffer from sensitive bowels: in the week before the op, have three to six cups daily of a special herbal tea combination. Make up a jar with equal parts of *Melissa officinalis* (lemon balm), *Matricaria recutita* (chamomile) and *Mentha piperita* (peppermint tea). Use 2 teaspoons of the mixture for each cup of tea. Take it with you to hospital, and continue taking it for the week after the operation.
- Post-operative nausea is relieved by common ginger root. The usual dose is between ½ and 1 gram every four hours, in tablet form, or between 10 and 20 drops as a fluid oral extract. Organise to take this to the hospital with you to start using as soon as you can after the surgery, but check with the medical staff first.
- Get your muscles going. Poor muscle strength and agility can slow down recovery because getting out of bed and walking around is much more difficult. Weak leg and abdominal muscles can be improved by specific exercises such as yoga exercises, squats, walking, sit-ups and gym work. About a month is usually needed to dramatically improve muscle strength, but even a few days before the op is better than nothing.
- Vitamin C has been shown to improve wound healing time. Start at least one week before surgery on about 2 grams a day and keep going for three to four weeks afterwards.
- Make sure you're getting enough zinc. A lot of women don't. Zinc supplements also have a beneficial effect on wound healing, but probably only in zinc-deficient people. Start a good zinc supplement, such as around 75–150 milligrams of zinc chelate a day with food for two or three weeks before the operation and continue for about two weeks afterwards. (There's an info page about zinc under Minerals in the Self Care chapter.)

- Vitamin E, which prevents internal scar tissue formation (adhesions), is great when fertility must be conserved following surgery. Doses of around 100–250 IU should be taken two weeks before the surgery but stopped two days before the operation. This a relatively small dose, because of a very slight risk of increased bleeding during surgery. Once you can eat again after the operation you can take doses of around 400 or 500 IU a day until you're recovered. This will reduce the risk of post-operative blood clots. Vitamin E cream can also be rubbed into the wound to speed up healing and reduce scarring.

Recovering from surgery

People have forgotten how to convalesce. With the increase in laser surgery, and the resulting shorter hospital stays, some patients are sent home the day after surgery or even the day of the operation.

Many women start housework, child care or go back to work within days of surgical procedures and then wonder why they spend the rest of the year feeling so awful. The financial strains on the average household also mean that many people feel they 'can't afford' to convalesce properly.

Don't take too much notice of standard doctors' predictions of 'you'll be back at the gym in a week' or 'you'll be up and walking by tomorrow'. Everybody is different. Our completely unscientific, informal survey of women who have had abdominal surgery revealed that almost all of them took longer to recover than their doctors suggested they would, and felt there was something wrong with their constitution, not with what the doctor told them.

Any surgery can take longer than expected, with much intrusive moving around of your inside bits. The standard recovery prediction then becomes even less relevant to you, but sometimes you won't be given a re-assessment of your convalescent time.

Recovery times vary considerably between individuals and are influenced by factors such as smoking, lack of previous fitness, an inability to take it easy and let the body heal, having to get up and look after the kids or go back to work before you're ready, as well as more surgery than was originally planned.

It's better to be guided by pain and stamina and to do a little more every day than to resume former levels of work and exercise too quickly. In other words—go by how you feel, not by a standard information sheet given out by the hospital, which will often be based only on averages or best-case scenarios and written by somebody with no first-hand experience.

When the body is under stress or recovering from an illness, it needs heaps more nutrients than usual. Unfortunately, this often happens just when you've lost your appetite. (Any stress, whether it be from surgery, difficult times, a car accident, or too much work, has a similar effect on the body's need for nutrients.)

Being physically active after the procedure improves recovery time and stamina, and reduces the risk of blood clots and respiratory infections. This does not mean you can start doing aerobics the day after. It means you start shuffling around in your slippers as soon as you can and build up from there.

- Your recovering body needs a boost of protein, the B vitamins—particularly vitamin B5 (pantothenic acid)—vitamin C, potassium, magnesium and zinc. You can have a daily vitamin B complex tablet which has 50 milligrams of B5 and B6, with a multi-mineral supplement and 1–2 grams of powdered vitamin C until you feel on top of things again.
- To keep energy steady, eat small but frequent meals of complex carbohydrate (potato, rice, bread, oatmeal and pasta), combined with *small* amounts of protein such as yoghurt, cheese, tofu, hommos, tuna or egg until your normal appetite and bowel function comes back.
- Avoid any food which acts as a 'body stressor', such as caffeine, refined sugars and huge strawberry daiquiris, until you've recovered.
- Some exercise is vital. Exercise every second day allows for one day of recovery after energy expenditure. As strength improves, exercise every day will increase stamina and a sense of wellbeing.

Exercise should be taken at a much slower pace. People tend to overestimate their capabilities so a good rule of thumb is to start at *half* the level you imagine you could comfortably manage *now*; if it is too little, no harm will be done. Long slow distance exercise is best—especially walking.

- Simple, easily digested soups and 'energy drinks' provide concentrated nutrients.
- Have one serve of a cooked green *leafy* vegetable such as spinach, Chinese cabbage or silverbeet every day during the recovery period.
- Never skip breakfast and have a cooked breakfast (porridge, egg on toast, cooked rice cereal, vegetable soup) at least every second day.
- Use the 'suggested menus' given for the hypoglycaemic diet in the Self Care chapter.

Soups are useful recovery foods. The best types are ones based on grains, especially barley and rice; legumes, such as tofu, orange lentils, fresh soya beans and red kidney beans (but not if they give you wind); or root vegies like potato, carrot and sweet potato.

Chicken broth

Yes, the old stand-by, traditional comfort food. Use free-range chicken carcasses. The broth can be prepared with a particular flavour. For example, Thai (lemongrass, lime leaves, galangal, and chilli), or Western (celery, bay leaves, onion, carrot and peppercorns).

High-protein drinks

High-protein drinks are useful meal substitutes or for between meals, particularly if you don't feel hungry and you're having trouble digesting.

Almond Smoothie

2 dessertspoons almond meal

1 teaspoon rice bran

1 teaspoon wheatgerm

Blend with 1 cup commercial soya milk (Bonsoy, Aussie Soy, Vitasoy)
1 teaspoon malt extract
or
½ cup yoghurt ½ cup fruit juice

Berry Drink

½ punnet blueberries, strawberries, raspberries or other berry fruit in season
½–¾ cup yoghurt or soya milk (yoghurt and berries tend to be fairly tangy and may not be to everyone's liking)
1 dessertspoon almond meal, ground cashews, or seeds (the 'seed mix' for irritable bowel syndrome is suitable)

Blend together until smooth.

Tofu Drinks

50 grams soft tofu

Blend with any of the following combinations:

6 dried apricots (soaked overnight in a cup of water) and the water they have been soaked in
2 dessertspoons almond meal
1 teaspoon slippery elm powder
or
1 banana
1 teaspoon slippery elm powder *or* 1 teaspoon rice bran
1 dessertspoon almond meal
1 cup fruit juice
or
1 glass freshly squeezed orange juice
1–2 dessertspoons almond meal *or* ground cashew nuts *or* 'seed mix'
1 teaspoon slippery elm powder

Chapter 8 NATURAL THERAPIES

Choosing and working with your natural therapist

Natural therapists to avoid are ones who have to work sitting under a pyramid for the 'vibes'; ones who insist that they are 'healers' (Blue heelers, maybe); ones who explain that most of their knowledge is based on 'intuitive' messages from the Great Beyond, and ones who say there is no value, under any circumstances, in scientific medicine. Here are some hints on how to narrow the field:

- Familiarise yourself with the different disciplines of natural therapy explained in this section, and decide which kind of practitioner might suit you best.
- Find out what professional qualifications the therapist has, how recent their training is and how they keep abreast, and what professional organisations your therapist belongs to.
- Many natural therapists prescribe herbs. It is best if herbs are prescribed by a full member of the National Herbalists' Association of Australia.

- Your practitioner should, at least, be affiliated to the major governing group for their discipline. (The National Herbalists' Association of Australia requires 700 hours of relevant study for membership; equivalent State bodies also require 700 hours, the Australian Natural Therapists' Association requires 700 hours' study in an approved course; and the Australian Traditional Medicine Society requires a specific number of hours for each discipline.)
- Regardless of their qualifications, you have to like and trust your therapist. Don't be afraid to shop around.
- Try to find a natural therapist who specialises in your problem.
- Any treatment must target the underlying cause, not just the symptoms: you need a full diagnosis as well as treatment. For example, if you have heavy bleeding, don't accept a preparation to stop it without knowing the gynaecological cause. If you simply mask important symptoms, you might be hiding an underlying problem that your body is trying to warn you about. This means you may have to have medical tests, then return to the natural therapist armed with the results.
- Some crucial examinations are not performed by natural therapists and referral to a doctor is needed. The results of the tests can be used by a natural therapist, or a doctor, or both, as a base for their diagnosis and treatment. These include routine screens like Pap tests and breast exams; gynaecological examinations which are performed vaginally and involve internal 'examination' of the pelvic organs; pathology tests such as blood tests, swabs or urine tests; radiological examinations such as ultrasounds and X-rays; and diagnostic operations such as a laparoscopy. These procedures are explained more fully in The Medical Approach chapter.
- Be suspicious of practitioners who prescribe vast amounts of herbs or supplements from their clinic at inflated prices. Four different preparations is a fairly average prescription. If you go home with a plastic bag with 15 different pills, powders and potions, a bunch of pussy willows and seven sacks of dandelion tea, you should be asking why you need it all. It is quite proper for a natural therapist to dispense from their own clinic, just make sure that if they sell

you over-the-counter products, for example, Blackmore's, that their price is competitive with say, your local supermarket. This goes for health food shops too.

- Be wary of any doctor or natural therapist who has a hard and fast pet theory which they apply to all situations—examples of these are people who claim that most disorders, from period pain to exhaustion are caused only by the liver, or stress, or dehydration, or toxicity, or the fact that the moon in June was in Pisces.
- Always tell the natural therapist anything you think is relevant to your condition. This definitely includes other medications you're on, including drugs, herbs or supplements (including vitamins).
- Always follow the instructions on herbal prescriptions and supplements exactly. Never assume that just because something is 'natural' you can take as much as you want to, or vary the recommended doses. Like drugs, under some circumstances, herbs can be dangerous.
- If you are not happy with the results of treatment, seek a second or further opinion.
- Don't expect a natural therapist to be able to 'cure' everything. There are some conditions which are not satisfactorily treated by natural methods.
- Always tell the practitioner if you are pregnant, trying to get pregnant, wouldn't mind getting pregnant or are not perfectly strict with contraception.

Natural therapies

The holistic philosophy

All areas of medicine, including science, have become more interested in the holistic philosophy with its emphasis on the body and mind and a belief in the body wanting to heal itself.

The holistic approach is all about treating individuals with conditions and not just about treating diseases. But it is more than that. It is also about listening to a person's own take on their health. For example, let's say you have a lower pelvic pain. You're poked and prodded and questioned and every avenue is pursued. Your doctor says there is nothing wrong. But you're still in pain. Whaddayer mean there's nothing wrong? From a holistic perspective there may be no disease, but something *is* wrong—your pain indicates some form of disharmony.

This demonstrates another of the important differences between the old and new styles of health care. Medicine usually sees health as an absence of a disease, and illness as an observable or diagnosed disease. Holism sees health as a sense of positive wellness combined with the absence of disease. It makes a further distinction between being ill and having a disease.

A disease is a condition which can be defined by a technique such as blood tests or X-rays. Illness is a perceived sense of feeling sick or being unwell which may or may not be related to a disease. Functional disorders fall into this category. The organs may not be functioning correctly, but there are no signs of changes at a cellular level and routine tests remain within the normal range.

A muscle cramp is a good example of a functional disorder. The muscle is not diseased, even though there is excruciating pain. The muscle is behaving abnormally. The abnormal behaviour could be caused by many different things, and it might be a temporary pain which will never happen again. But the cramp is real and the body is indicating the presence of some sort of disharmony.

Many gynaecological conditions are classed as functional disorders, including most types of period pain and many conditions caused by hormone imbalance such as PMS. Many of the syndromes described by natural therapists are also functional disorders, for example, functional hypoglycaemia and adrenal exhaustion. It's impossible to diagnose these conditions with blood tests, but their response to traditional treatments is reproducible and predictable.

The traditions of natural therapy

Today, a good natural therapist will acknowledge the advances in scientific medicine, but base their knowledge on many of the earlier traditions of medicine, including Asian and European herbal and diagnostic methods.

Throughout the history of medicine a number of cultures have described remarkably similar systems for recognising health and disease. These include Greek, Roman, Arabic, Indian, Tibetan and Chinese territories. If you didn't know better you'd think all the ancient herbalists from different continents used to have mobile phone conferences and pinch each other's ideas.

The recurring themes had four major aspects: the belief in a 'vital force' as the living and generative energy in the body; the understanding that the universe is composed of a number of 'elements' which are found in varying concentrations in all life forms; the recognition of the potentially damaging influence of extreme weather changes; and the designation of 'constitutional' types to individuals in order to define a predictable framework for diagnosis and treatment.

Throughout the world, climate was respected as a health issue. Normal exposure generated life, but extremes caused death, disease, or at the very least, disruption in the supply of food. And in the case of, say floods, extreme grumpiness. Exposure to wind, cold, dry, damp or heat as a cause of disease was a handy explanation because the weather affected everybody and was easily understood.

Eventually, a classification of diseases according to 'quality' was adopted throughout much of the world. Any complaint accompanied by heat, fever, redness or itchiness, for example, was a Hot condition. Combinations of qualities were also found in each of the elements. Air, for example, was Hot and Moist; Fire was Hot and Dry.

Scientific medicine concerns itself with cellular changes, biochemical phenomena and dissection of the body into its parts. It developed the approach that, for example, the root of one medical problem was a diseased liver. The natural therapies approach is that an underlying disharmony in the whole body was causing the liver disease. In traditional philosophies, it is the lack of harmony and not the disease that is the starting point for treatment.

A good natural therapist will chuck out the information from the past that's no longer useful, and retain the stuff that is still working, for example, a tried and tested herbal remedy.

In the same way, scientific medicine has discarded one theory of the Middle Ages—that the womb wandered around the body—and recently revived another, the use of leeches to deal with certain bruising and strokes.

Types of natural therapy

Natural medicine is a generic term which covers any of the therapeutic disciplines that do not use drugs or invasive techniques (like surgery and tests). In Australia, the common practitioners are: naturopaths, herbalists, homoeopaths, acupuncturists, practitioners of traditional Chinese medicine (TCM), aromatherapists, all of the masseurs using various techniques, osteopaths and chiropractors.

Practitioners who use natural therapies may specialise or they may train in a variety of disciplines. A practitioner who uses the multidisciplinary approach has usually trained as a naturopath. Naturopathy is not made up of a specified group of disciplines and each of the colleges may train their students differently. If you're going to a naturopath, ask what disciplines they use before you make the appointment.

The quality of training is extremely varied and there are no regulations in Australia governing the practice of natural therapies. (A butcher could prescribe herbs and be within the law.) Many practitioners are not happy about this and most belong to professional associations as a way of ensuring their educational standing and to demonstrate their commitment to improving the status of their profession.

Here are the most popular disciplines:

Naturopathy. The use of any or all of the techniques listed below, usually with a holistic philosophy.

Herbal medicine. The prescription of herbs for the treatment of complaints. Prescriptions are usually based on the philosophical doctrine of medical herbalism, not as a straight substitute for drugs.

Homoeopathy. Based on the law of the minimum dose and 'like cures like', homoeopathy is the treatment of disease by minute doses of remedies that in healthy persons would produce symptoms like those of the disease.

Acupuncture. The insertion of specialised acupuncture needles to regulate and stimulate the body's energy flow, known as Qi (pronounced Chee).

Traditional Chinese medicine (TCM). The use of acupuncture, herbs, and the manipulation of the flow of Qi with massage and specific exercises.

Aromatherapy. The use of 'essential oils' as therapeutic agents. They are usually burned in an oil burner to scent the atmosphere or applied to the skin, appropriately diluted in oil, usually about 5 drops to 100 millilitres to be safe.

Massage. Massages may be relaxing or 'therapeutic'. A therapeutic massage involves deep tissue massage for the relief of injury, muscular spasm and tension. A relaxation massage is usually more gentle and is designed to relieve stress.

Chiropractic and osteopathy. The mobilisation and manipulation of the skeletal structures along with the strengthening and stretching of the muscular components of the body.

Not every natural therapist will adopt a holistic approach, nor will they always involve their clients in the decisions about treatments. A constant belief should be that the restoration of health is more important than treating a particular disease.

The liver

To say that natural therapists are into the liver is an understatement. It has always been considered important. These days, it has become such a scapegoat that while doctors vaguely say 'it's your hormones, dear', some natural therapists blame *everything* on the liver, and some people think a diet which 'cleanses' the liver will fix everything. Balderdash, poppycock, and furthermore, pish-tosh.

It *is*, however, the focus of heaps and heaps of disorders and illnesses investigated by natural therapists, and a healthy, working liver is known to be a great advantage for all women.

Back in the Middle Ages, the humoural theory described two personality types or temperaments related to bile and the liver—the choleric and the melancholic. The choleric person was hot-tempered and irascible. Even now, this filters through when we still describe a bad-tempered person as 'liverish'.

The symptoms of liver disharmony described by traditional Chinese medicine include irritability, depression, frustration, anger, and digestive upsets, and common gynaecological complaints such as PMS, irregular periods, light periods or no periods, infertility and period pain.

Many of the broader concepts of the humoural theory and liver dysfunction are incorporated into the herbalist's diagnosis and treatment today. Herbs and foods which improve liver function are used to treat conditions accompanied by emotional symptoms, such as PMS; and conditions caused by hormonal imbalance such as fibrocystic breast disease, endometriosis, fibroids, and some types of excessive bleeding.

Liver function is adversely affected by poor diet; overeating; excessive intake of fats, sugars, alcohol, and coffee; and the ever-increasing burden of environmental poisons.

As the major organ of detoxification in the body, the liver must be ready to process about 3000 chemicals which can be added to foods during processing, and another 12 000 or so chemicals which can be used in food packing materials. It must also neutralise and process the pesticides, fungicides and antibiotics which contaminate food and the environment; and any of the prescribed, recreational or social drugs. The liver never has a minute to itself.

It produces bile, stores vitamins and minerals, sugar, blood and plasma proteins. It makes energy and heat, and breaks down, recycles or excretes hormones.

To protect liver cells

- *Silybum marianum* (St Mary's thistle) seeds contain the most potent liver cell protective compounds known to exist.
- Anti-oxidants, such as vitamins A, E and C, betacarotene and selenium.

- Phosphatidyl choline, or lecithin, is a major component of healthy cell membranes. It protects liver cell membranes from damage from the continual attack of toxins and free radicals.

To improve bile flow

- Bitter foods and herbs increase the flow of bile which is the vehicle for removing the substances broken down by liver cells.

To improve detoxification

- Specific herbs can improve liver enzyme activity such as *Silybum marianum* (St Mary's thistle) and *Schizandra chinensis*. (More on these under Herbs, below.)
- Sulphur compounds found in cabbage family vegetables, garlic, and dandelion can induce enzyme reactions in the liver which assist with detoxification. Brussels sprouts and cabbage, for example, can improve the breakdown and removal of some drugs.
- An adequate protein intake is necessary to deal with some toxic materials.
- Carbohydrates assist with detoxification pathways. Low-kilojoule diets may not provide enough carbohydrate for the liver to function as an organ of detoxification.
- Minerals such as magnesium, calcium, zinc, copper and iron are essential components of many of the enzymes needed to drive detoxification pathways and are also involved in biochemical reactions which help to prevent free radical damage in liver cells. Information pages on magnesium, calcium, zinc and iron are in the Minerals section of the Self Care chapter. Magnesium is a particularly good mineral because it helps with the symptoms of hormonal imbalance.
- Eat foods which help the liver correctly process oestrogens, especially methionine found in beans, eggs, onions and garlic.

To help your liver function, eat some of these foods when you can: endive, chicory, silverbeet, radicchio, outer leaves of cos lettuce, mustard greens, dandelion leaf, dandelion root ('coffee'), grapefruit, and any other bitter-tasting, green leafy, vegie-typey thingies. In the herbal department, look for extracts from St Mary's thistle, gentian, barberry, centaury, hops and artichoke leaves.

Herbs

Presumably one day a cavewoman realised it made more sense to put soothing herbs on a cut rather than rub in some gravel. Good one, Og.

Evidence that plants may have been used as medicines as early as sixty thousand years ago came from the discovery of the pollens of common plant medicines at the burial site of a Neanderthal man. Marshmallow, grape hyacinth, yarrow, ephedra—all in use today—were placed beside him, maybe as decorative offerings, or perhaps for his journey to the afterlife. (It's also possible that he died because the naughty boy didn't take his herbs, and he was used ever after as an example. Cave-parents would say things like, 'Remember what happened to Urp? So eat up all your yarrow and hyacinth or there'll be no mammoth for dessert.')

Virtually all peoples throughout the world have used some form of plant medicine. Those who still use herbal remedies seem to share common traits. Almost all cultures have specialists—individuals entrusted with the knowledge of specific plants who will pass on the information only to selected initiates. Many made sure there were specialists: Australian Aboriginal groups and other cultures have different men's and women's knowledge and use of medicines.

Over centuries, careful observation revealed that there were optimum times to pick plants and administer medicines according to the phases of the moon, seasons or times of day; and that some parts of the plant were more effective than others. It soon became clear that some plants were more effective when administered in certain ways. Gradually the doctoring and supply of herbs developed into recognised professions: the physician became the early doctor and the apothecary became the pharmacist.

The remnants of writings from the Arabs, Greeks, Romans and Egyptians survived to give a good indication of the practice of herbal medicine by the scholarly and educated. But much of the early practice of women's medicine was continued as a verbal herbal gerbil tradition. Sorry. There were no gerbils. Information was either passed on from one initiate to another by the priestesses and 'wise women' to be used in strict accordance with the current law; or in the case of the common and everyday remedies, passed on from mother to daughter or between friends. The sisterhood has always been abuzz with contraceptive hints.

Science and medicine have remained sceptical of the effectiveness of plants for contraceptive purposes although some cultures still use them. Rue is still used in a number of cultures in Latin America, and the common pea is believed by some people to be responsible for the low birth rate in Tibet. The seeds of Queen Anne's lace (*Daucas carota*) have been investigated for their contraceptive qualities and found to stop implantation of the embryo as well as inhibit the production of progesterone.

Don't bother trying herbal contraception—what was once common knowledge and passed on through word of mouth is temporarily lost to today's herbalist. And eating a lot of peas would probably give the rhythm method a run for its money in the unreliability stakes. The other herbs could just make you sick, or even a bit dead.

Over the past 50 years, herbal medicine in the West has changed its focus from the individual patient to what individual herbs will do to an individual disease. Detailed information is now available on the effects of many herbal medicines and it is possible to prescribe precisely for a number of complaints. Many doctors and surgeons are now recommending their patients also try natural remedies if they are appropriate, where a few years ago they might have dismissed them as 'unscientific mumbo jumbo'. Doctors in Europe and Japan are increasingly likely to prescribe herbal remedies themselves.

So if doctors are prescribing herbs, what's the point of having herbalists? First, herbalists can offer something special if they retain their traditional understanding that underlying disharmony causes the problem. In this way, the whole person is treated, and not just symptoms. A real natural practitioner will still focus on the individual, on *why* there is disease rather than what disease, and consider

Some herbal concoctions taste weird

the vitality and constitutional type of the person along with the particular strain of bacteria or the results of a blood test.

And of course, professional herbalists are trained to know a lot more about the correct combinations, doses and species required for treatment. A doctor or naturopath untrained in herbs might well recommend a useless dose or another strain of a plant that isn't exactly right.

One of the fundamental beliefs of herbalism is that the body will want to repair itself. Herbs are ideal agents to support healing and the return of normal function because they are gentle and effective when properly prescribed. If the situation demands it, a combination of the two disciplines can lead to the best possible outcome.

How to take herbs

Many herbs are strong stuff, and their effects can be changed by the presence of other herbs or drugs you are taking. So it's very important to be aware of a few rules:

1. Do not self-prescribe herbs, or take a herb because it worked for a friend.
2. Find a trained herbalist with a specialty in your problem.
3. If you are on any other medication, tell both your herbalist and your doctor exactly what you are taking.
4. Follow the instructions carefully. This is just as important as when you are taking prescribed drugs.
5. Never assume a herb is harmless or can be taken whenever you feel like it because it is 'natural'. Some herbs are naturally poisonous, toxic, otherwise dangerous, or useless in some combinations or doses and in certain situations.
6. Any herb is unsafe in pregnancy in the wrong hands if taken at the wrong time, in the wrong dose or in the wrong combination.

Herb prescriptions are usually made up as mixtures in a bottle, looking somewhat like a cough mixture and tasting, in some cases, rather like eye of newt. Some herbalists will give you the roots, leaves and herbal extracts to boil up yourself on the stove. We recommend you don't have a hot date over on the same night, as the house is likely to smell somewhat startling. Some herbs and most supplements (like vitamins and minerals) are available in tablet form.

Herbs for women's trouble

There is a large range of the herbs used to treat 'women's' complaints—some of them have been used and modified for thousands of years. Others are providing new and contemporary possibilities. Modern science has more recently begun to support and extend the understandings of the uses of these herbs, through scientific testing and a more open mind.

None of these herbs may be prescribed by somebody without specialist training. Most of the herbs have lots and lots of other effects as well as gynaecological ones, and all these need to be taken into account when working out a prescription. For example, rue, an emmenagogue herb, has been used as an insecticide, a sedative, and a trial preparation with some promising results on multiple sclerosis symptoms.

The results of clinical trials on the herbs and their effects, doses, and information about how they must be prepared and prescribed by practitioners is outlined in Ruth's book, *Women, Hormones and the Menstrual Cycle*, published by Allen & Unwin.

The uterine tonics

The uterine tonics may be taken through the whole menstrual cycle and are usually prescribed as part of a formula if a complaint involves the uterus. These herbs are used to treat period pain because they are believed to regulate the muscular activity of the uterus and help kick-start contractions which are regular, rhythmic and more orderly. Uterine tonics are prescribed for uterine pain, for abnormal bleeding patterns, for prolapse, malposition or enlargement of the uterus, to help with some fertility problems and/or to regulate uterine tone until labour starts, help with a smooth delivery and regulate labour contractions.

All uterine tonics should be used with care in the first trimester of pregnancy because of a slight possibility of miscarriage. It's best not to use *any* medication during the first three months of pregnancy unless absolutely necessary and under expert supervision.

Rubus idaeus/strigosus (red raspberry leaf)

Traditionally, the herb was drunk as a tea for period pain and heavy periods, to prevent or relieve pregnancy-related nausea, to ease labour and to assist with breast milk production. The active constituents of raspberry leaves relax the uterine muscle and, surprisingly, also initiate contractions. It's not usually useful for period pain unless prescribed with specific other herbs. It's a good uterine tonic following surgery of the uterus, including removal of fibroids, termination of pregnancy or a curette.

Chamaelirium luteum (false unicorn root or helonias)

Helonias is used for no periods, heavy periods, irregular periods, period pain and to regulate the uterus. It is recommended to prevent miscarriage. Another traditional use is to regulate ovarian function and problems which originate 'in the first half of the cycle'. It's threatened in the wild because of the increasing demands for collection and so its use should be restricted. *Paeonia lactiflora* or *Aletris farinosa* can be good substitutes.

Aletris farinosa (true unicorn root)

This is one of the best uterine tonics for women with a sense of pelvic heaviness or congestion, especially beneficial for women in their forties and fifties. It's used traditionally, in combination with spasmolytic herbs, to prevent miscarriage. There are conflicting reports on its actions, and it needs to be used in combination with other herbs. Like all the uterine tonics, *Aletris farinosa* is recommended for light or absent periods, periods which are too heavy or too frequent, for period pain and infertility, and for symptoms that accompany retroverted uterus.

Angelica sinensis (Dang Gui)

Dang Gui, *Aletris farinosa* and *Chamaelirium luteum* can sometimes be used interchangeably. Dang Gui can also improve blood circulation through heart muscle and is a 'blood tonic'. It is prescribed for pallor, weakness, dizziness, and dry skin; late, irregular or absent periods; pale period blood; weakness after the period, after giving birth or while breastfeeding; and period pain. Dang Gui can increase uterine tone, strengthen and order contractions, and relax the uterine muscle. It shouldn't be used in the first trimester of pregnancy unless prescribed by a trained herbalist as part of a traditional formula. Dang Gui works best when combined with *Paeonia lactiflora* and *Ligusticum wallichii*. For period pain that's worse with cold and associated with a slow start to periods, it's prescribed with *Cinnamomum*.

Caulophyllum thalictroides (blue cohosh)

Historically blue cohosh was used to prepare the uterus for labour, for period pain and for various 'inflammations' of the uterus. It's ideal as a uterine tonic for the last six weeks of pregnancy to improve the normal function of the uterus during labour. On the other hand, it is recommended to prevent miscarriages. The trick for successful use during pregnancy is getting the right combination with other herbs.

Spasmolytics: the uterus relaxers

The spasmolytics or anti-spasmodic herbs have a relaxing effect on the smooth muscle and can slow or regulate the rate of contractions in the uterus and in the bowel. Spasmolytics reduce spasm and calm uterine activity; reduce period pain which is colicky, crampy or contraction-like; calm the uterus in pregnancy and help prevent miscarriage and early labour.

Anti-spasmodic herbs are used for crampy period pain and are more effective if given to stop the onset of spasm, rather than to treat pain that has already started. They should be started several days before the expected onset of the period. There's often no point taking anti-spasmodics through the whole cycle.

Viburnum opulus (cramp bark) and *V. prunifolium* (black haw)

These viburnums have similar therapeutic effects and are used to treat any condition associated with uterine spasm. *Viburnum prunifolium* has been extensively used to treat spasmodic period pain, prevent miscarriage, and to tone the uterus after fibroid removal.

The use of these herbs in pregnancy should be left strictly to trained herbalists. They are usually prescribed for period pain with other spasmolytics and are best combined with Warming herbs such as *Cinnamomum* or *Zingiber* to offset stomach upsets and to improve their effect.

***Ligusticum wallichii* (Cnidium or Chuan Xiong)**
Used to relax smooth muscle and against period pain and uterine overactivity. *Ligusticum wallichii* and *Angelica sinensis* are traditionally combined to treat period disorders. *Ligusticum wallichii* also shows promising results in preventing miscarriage and early labour.

The emmenagogues: the uterus stimulators

Emmenagogues are herbs which can increase the strength of uterine contractions, start the uterus contracting and start the period flow. They are usually prescribed when the period is slow or delayed. Traditionally, they have also been prescribed to bring on a late period due to pregnancy, but this is dangerous, illegal and often doesn't work anyway.

Emmenagogues are particularly indicated for dull and congestive period pain in periods which are slow to get going. This category of herbs especially should only be used by a properly trained herbalist: as Aunty Myrtle always said, never let an amateur near your uterus, dear.

Emmenagogues can also be prescribed for certain conditions characterised by symptoms of heavy period flow, with little or no pain and large clots. (First, you need a diagnosis and treatment of the causes.)

After a miscarriage, childbirth or a curette, a useful combination can be an emmenagogue with a uterine tonic to help removal of retained tissue and with healing and regeneration of the uterine lining. The combination of emmenagogues and bacteriostatic herbs for women who have refused to take antibiotics reduces the risk of a pelvic infection. Emmenagogues are difficult to prescribe, needing appropriate dosage, duration of use and combinations with other herbs; they can be very irritating and potentially dangerous in too high a dose.

Artemisia vulgaris (mugwort)

Used largely as a uterine stimulant to improve congestive period pain and to bring on a delayed period. It is discussed extensively in early writings as an abortifacient. (There is the justifiable concern that 'many emmenagogue herbs damage the foetus rather than completely terminating the pregnancy'.) *Artemisia vulgaris* is also used, with other herbs, to regulate the period and stop period pain.

Salvia officinalis (sage)

Sage is another of the abortifacient herbs and should be avoided in pregnancy. It is often used for delayed or scanty periods; or for congestive period pain. It is also useful after childbirth to help expel the placenta. Sage contains oestrogenic elements and is useful for menopausal problems, especially night sweats and hot flushes.

Mentha pulegium (pennyroyal)

Another abortifacient. The oil taken internally is highly toxic and has caused the death of women using the oil to try to induce an abortion. The whole herb is used for insufficient and painful periods, to strengthen uterine contractions, and for delayed periods (with *Tanacetum vulgare*).

Astringents: drying herbs

The uterine astringents are used to 'dry up' heavy periods and include *Trillium erectum, Equisetum arvense, Achillea millefolium, Tienchi ginseng, Capsella bursa-pastoris* and *Hydrastis canadensis*. The important astringents for heavy periods in adolescence are *Achillea millefolium* (yarrow), *Alchemilla vulgaris* (ladies mantle), *Capsella bursa-pastoris* (shepherd's purse) and *Geranium maculatum* (cranesbill).

The herbs are a large group of (usually) tannin-containing plants which reduce blood loss. This effect is seen on the stomach lining, the bowel wall, on the skin, and in the urinary, respiratory and reproductive tract. Long-term administration of tannin-rich plants can reduce the uptake of nutrients, and long-term, continuous use is not a good idea.

Achillea millefolium (yarrow)

Achillea millefolium is an important herb mostly used to reduce heavy periods. It can also help with stopped periods, or to relieve pain or act as a uterine stimulant to increase muscular tone and start a period. This is because it has a number of different effects on the uterine muscle, the sum total of which result in uterine stimulation without also causing spasm.

Alchemilla vulgaris (ladies mantle)

Used traditionally for heavy periods, as an emmenagogue and to promote contractions during labour. It can also be used to treat period pain and regulate the menstrual cycle. It is popular in Europe for teenage heavy periods. It's also recommended for heavy bleeding around menopause, and for urinary incontinence in post-menopausal women.

Hydrastis canadensis (golden seal)

Its main effect on excessive bleeding is believed to be due to its action on the capillaries. *Hydrastis canadensis* is commonly used with other herbs in a mix for heavy periods, particularly the uterine tonics as well as the tannin-containing herbs such as *Achillea millefolium* and *Geranium maculatum*. It must not be used in pregnancy.

Capsella bursa-pastoris (shepherd's purse)

Used for heavy periods of practically any origin (but an understanding of the cause must always come first). It combines well with *Trillium erectum* and *Hydrastis canadensis*, but this combination has a very strong taste and people hate it. Shepherd's purse should not be taken by anyone with hypothyroidism unless closely supervised.

Lamium album (white deadnettle)

Lamium album is popular for late or heavy periods caused by stress or nervous tension and is specifically used for a lack of uterine tone and bleeding between periods caused by hormonal irregularities. It's also useful for late, irregular and light periods related to weakness, nutritional deficiencies and overwork. As always, a diagnosis is a must before treatment is started.

Panax notoginseng (Tienchi ginseng)

Good for heavy bleeding caused by conditions such as fibroids, dysfunctional uterine bleeding and childbirth. It is usually prescribed only at the time of bleeding. Not to be used during pregnancy. Because it's so effective at stopping bleeding (but not treating the cause), it is absolutely essential that the reason for the heavy periods be identified before treatment or a serious condition may be masked. It's also useful for conditions with localised, congestive pain; and heavy and/or dark clotted menstrual blood, which may be accompanied by immobile abdominal masses. These can accompany complaints such as fibroids, endometriosis and period pain with congestive pain. For these types of conditions, Tienchi might either be prescribed all month or just when pain occurs.

Trillium erectum (beth root)

Trillium erectum is used as an aid to labour and to stop bleeding, to be used in and after the third stage of a birth. It's also used in any situation where abnormal bleeding is a feature of a gynaecological complaint.

It is the best herb for women 30 to 50 years old with heavy periods because it also seems to regulate ovulation. Long-term use—between three and six months—is usually needed.

Herbs affecting the hypothalamic-pituitary unit

A number of herbs are used for period problems related to a disturbance in the hypothalamic-pituitary department. These disorders can cause a wide range of complaints including heavy periods or no periods at all, irregular cycles and PMS.

Vitex agnus castus (chaste tree berries)

Vitex agnus castus is said to be a herb for the luteal phase (second half of the cycle) and can be useful for heaps of gynaecological complaints, especially ones which appear or get worse before the period. Many PMS symptoms, such as fluid retention and breast soreness improve with Vitex.

Latent hyperprolactinaemia (a result of changes in the activity of the hypothalamic-pituitary unit) causes problems such as PMS, disturbed menstrual cycle lengths, stopped ovulation and periods. Vitex seems capable of improving stopped periods, menstrual irregularities, and especially cyclic changes caused by latent hyperprolactinaemia.

Smaller doses of Vitex can also be used to promote breast milk especially in the first ten days after childbirth. Leading up to the menopause, it can be used to regulate the menstrual cycle by improving the regularity of ovulation.

Vitex must be prescribed by a trained practitioner familiar with its actions and contraindications. It should be started in the early part of the cycle, preferably before ovulation, and is usually given as a single dose in the morning. Dosage is important—too high or too low may make some conditions worse—and should be adjusted according to the problem treated, any additional symptoms, and your age.

Vitex should not be prescribed when hormonal preparations are used, including the Pill, HRT, or any of the common progestogen drugs such as Provera, Primulut, Duphaston and Danazol. It should be prescribed cautiously by a practitioner for women under 20, for whom the hypothalamic-pituitary-ovarian interplay is still fragile and easily disrupted. For full benefit, it is usually prescribed for between three and nine months.

Paeonia lactiflora (peony, Bai Shao)

In traditional Chinese medicine (TCM) three different types of peony are used—the white peony (*Paeonia lactiflora*), red peony (also usually from *Paeonia lactiflora*, but collected from wild plants and known as Chi Shao), and peony bark from *Paeonia suffruticosa* (Mu Dan Pi). 'Peony' indicates white peony/Bai Shao.

Paeonia lactiflora is effective in the treatment of PMS, polycystic ovarian disease (PCOD), hyperprolactinaemia, not ovulating, infertility, endometriosis and adenomyosis, androgen excess, breast soreness and menopausal symptoms. These conditions have at their core various hormonal irregularities which are influenced by peony, including elevated androgens, low progesterone, high or low oestrogen, and elevated prolactin.

Other peony-responsive conditions include period pain and uterine overactivity during pregnancy, low oestrogen levels and erratic ovulation and low progesterone levels. Peony-containing formulas can also be used to treat lowered rates of fertility due to androgen excess.

The two-herb formula, Liquorice and Peony Combination, reduces testosterone levels in women with PCOD and improves pregnancy rates. The luteinising hormone (LH) to follicle stimulating hormone (FSH) ratio is also normalised. The same formula is also useful for the treatment of hyperprolactinaemia.

Complaints linked to relative oestrogen excess also respond well to peony-containing formulations, including adenomyosis and endometriosis, uterine fibroids and breast soreness. Peony is also used in association with liquorice for abdominal pain caused by muscle spasm.

Cimicifuga racemosa (black cohosh)

Cimicifuga racemosa is used for hot flushes and arthritic complaints in menopause and for delayed teenage periods caused by hormonal imbalance, especially when associated with stress. It contains hormonally active substances, one of which suppresses luteinising hormone (LH) after long-term use, and two of which have weak oestrogen-like effects. During menopause, it helps to reduce symptoms of vaginal dryness and irritation over time, and trials show it to be as effective as synthetic oestrogen.

It is helpful for younger women with menopausal symptoms caused by removal of their ovaries. And *Cimicifuga racemosa* can be used instead of HRT, as well as HRT, or as a treatment to 'wean' you off HRT. To come off HRT you take both *Cimicifuga racemosa* and HRT together until the herb has taken effect (usually 6–8 weeks), then stop the HRT. It is usually combined with other herbs so see a practitioner for best results.

Warming herbs

Warming herbs improve the action of the anti-spasmodic herbs, especially when the period pain is aggravated by cold, relieved by heat (the trusty hot-water bottle), or you have a tendency to 'feel the cold' easily.

Zingiber officinale (ginger)

The Warming properties of *Zingiber officinale* make it useful for period pain that is improved by the application of heat or warm drinks, and it has analgesic effects. The prostaglandin-inhibiting actions probably are also useful. It is also useful for nausea and vomiting with a period.

Premenstrual and menstrual migraines can be helped by *Zingiber officinale*, but it may aggravate menopausal flushing.

Warming herbs are best if taken hot. To make ginger tea, grate 2–4 centimetres of fresh root ginger, place in a saucepan with 1–2 cups of water, cover and bring slowly to the boil. Keep covered and simmer for about ten minutes. Strain, add honey to taste and sip while still hot. If possible, also have a warm bath. Other herbs can be taken at the same time.

Cinnamomum zeylanicum (cinnamon)

It's good for 'cold' period pain or pain accompanied by other symptoms such as localised pain, dark clotted period blood and immobile masses. It is often combined with *Angelica sinensis, Ligusticum wallichii* and/or *Paeonia lactiflora*. *Cinnamomum zeylanicum* can also reduce heavy periods.

Anodynes: the painkillers

The best-known anodyne herb is the opium poppy, now pharmaceutically manufactured as morphine, codeine and pethidine. Much weaker anodynes still in use by herbalists play a secondary role when treating the cause of the pain.

Corydalis ambigua (corydalis)

One of the strongest anodynes used in herbal medicine, this herb has an analgesic effect estimated to be 1 per cent that of opium. It is rarely used alone, usually being combined with anti-spasmodic herbs for best effects.

Corydalis ambigua is used to treat congestive or crampy period pain. It can stop heavy periods and accompanying severe pain. Not to be used in pregnancy.

Piscidia erythrina (Jamaican dogwood)

This particularly useful herb has anti-spasmodic and sedative effects which reduce period pain. *Piscidia erythrina* has a very low toxicity, even at high doses, but mustn't be taken in pregnancy.

Anemone pulsatilla (pulsatilla)

Used in painful and spasmodic conditions of the uterus, such as spasmodic period pain, and inflamed conditions of the genito-urinary tract including the pain of pelvic inflammatory disease (PID) and some types of cystitis. *Anemone pulsatilla* can be used for stopped periods caused by nervousness or stress. For period pain it's often combined with *Viburnum opulus* or *V. prunifolium*.

The herb is an emmenagogue, and must not be taken in pregnancy. The fresh plant is poisonous and it must be taken as a precisely prescribed tincture.

Tanacetum parthenium (feverfew)

Can be used for women of all ages for period pain, recurrent premenstrual, mid-cycle or peri-menopausal migraines. It must be used all month as a preventative for best results. During labour, it's said to increase the frequency and regularity of contractions and relax a rigid cervix and is also traditionally used as an emmenagogue to bring on delayed periods. An oft-repeated caution that it causes mouth ulcers is only related to chewing the fresh leaf which may cause a type of contact dermatitis on sensitive skin—not usually a problem with tablets or tinctures.

Nervines

The nervine tonics can be used for either anxiety or depression and are seen to have a 'balancing effect'; the nervine sedatives are calming, and the nervine stimulants do what you'd expect—one of them is coffee. Nervines find a particular role in gynaecology in the treatment of premenstrual and peri-menopausal complaints, and as adjuncts to the treatment of period pain.

Hypericum perforatum (St John's wort)

Used for the treatment of mild to moderate anxiety and depression. It is especially useful during menopause and good for conditions where exhaustion and tension combine with hormonal problems. *Hypericum perforatum* extracts (infusions or fluid extracts) may produce photosensitisation if you're on a high dose or take the herb for a long time. Its use should be supervised.

Leonurus cardiaca (motherwort)

Its effects are gentle and progressive and long-term administration is usually advisable. A spasmolytic, sedative, and diuretic, it is also a mild emmenagogue and in large doses brings on the period. It's often used in the last weeks of pregnancy to facilitate labour, and after childbirth to minimise blood loss. For menopausal insomnia, night sweats and palpitations, *Leonurus cardiaca* is used with *Humulus lupulus* (hops) and *Cimicifuga racemosa* with excellent results.

Humulus lupulus (hops)

Hops is used for hot flushes, irregular periods with polycystic ovarian disease (PCOD), and flushing that accompanies stress, worry or insomnia. Hops, combined with *Cimicifuga racemosa*, is a useful treatment for PCOD perhaps because of their effect on luteinising hormone (LH) levels. It can also be used for spasmodic period pain.

Verbena officinalis (vervain)

Vervain can be used to treat spasmodic period pain and delayed periods, and to reduce the impact of menopausal symptoms.

Valeriana officinalis/edulis (valerian)

Herbal medicine's best-known sedative. It's used to boost the action of the spasmolytic herbs used in the treatment of period pain and is also good for sleeplessness.

***Zizyphus spinosa* (zizyphus)**
Traditionally for spontaneous sweating and night sweats, especially when accompanied by anxiety, irritability, palpitations and insomnia. These symptoms can occur during the peri-menopausal years, as well as being common symptoms of nervous exhaustion.

***Piper methysticum* (kava-kava)**
It reduces the anxiety depression symptoms sometimes seen in association with menopause, and can also be used for PMS anxiety. Used in the Pacific region as part of religious ceremonies and in kava bars, where it is used like wine. Kava abuse has been reported in the Pacific and northern Australia, but this is linked with intakes more than ten times the recommended therapeutic dose used by herbalists.

Adaptogens: the tonics

Adaptogens are prescribed like an old-fashioned tonic when stress is high, or during convalescence from surgery or illness. Tonics are often helpful following childbirth, during lactation, or around menopause. Adaptogens are often prescribed with extra herbs specific to other complaints.

***Eleuthrococcus senticosus* (Siberian ginseng)**
Useful for any type of stress or during convalescence. It can regulate stress-induced PMS symptoms; it is a useful general tonic after childbirth and following surgery; and it is one of the best adaptogens for the menopause, especially in combination with other herbs for low oestrogen symptoms. Excess coffee intake should be avoided when taking any kind of ginseng.

***Panax ginseng* (Korean ginseng)**
Panax ginseng is one of the most commonly used adaptogens for stress and depression. It is believed to be more 'stimulating' and tends to have an uplifting effect which is usually noticed fairly quickly. It should not be taken with herbs which contain large amounts of caffeine or by heavy coffee drinkers, or by anyone with high blood pressure, acute asthma, or acute infections including viral infections.

Panax ginseng can be useful around menopause or for convalescence and exhaustion. Long-term unsupervised use, however, is not a good idea. Two weeks on, two weeks off is a sensible course.

Codonopsis pilosula (codonopsis)

Codonopsis pilosula can be used if *Panax ginseng* is too stimulating, or if there's anxiety as well as fatigue.

Glycyrrhiza glabra (liquorice)

Glycyrrhiza glabra has very weak oestrogen-like effects and is sometimes self-prescribed for menopausal symptoms. This is a risky practice, except in the short term, because it can cause an elevation in blood pressure, fluid retention and potassium depletion with prolonged use. Those who self-administer are usually unaware of these cautions. Some have even taken the lolly liquorice under the mistaken impression that it has the same properties as the unrelated herb.

Glycyrrhiza glabra is commonly used for coughs and dry mucous membranes, gastric ulcers and other gastro-intestinal complaints and to improve tolerance to a herbal formula. It can lower androgen levels, especially with peony. Its use should be restricted to less than six weeks unless closely supervised.

The bitters: liver herbs

It is the taste of bitterness that gives these herbs many of their therapeutic effects. The bitter taste on the tongue triggers a series of impulses which are carried by the nervous system and culminate in physiological and biochemical changes. Bitters medicine has the ability to improve your overall state by improving digestion, assimilation and (do you mind) evacuation (that's what it says here).

Taraxacum officinale (dandelion root)

Taraxacum officinale root is used as a general liver tonic and diuretic after debilitating illness or surgery; to improve liver function generally, and especially in conditions related to relative oestrogen excess such as endometriosis; or to protect the liver from the effects of hormonal preparations, including the Pill. It can be used after childbirth as a laxative and to increase milk flow. It's advertised as dandelion root coffee. It tastes more like dirt than a café latté but it's good for you.

Berberis vulgaris (barberry)

A very useful liver herb for women with congestive period pain where the flow is slow to start, or where the pain is relieved when the flow commences. The flow is easier, redder and usually starts quickly and there's less heavy, dragging pain. Berberis is used for oestrogen-related conditions like endometriosis.

Silybum marianum (milk thistle or St Mary's thistle)

Silybum marianum is useful at any time that a liver dysfunction is a factor in a gynaecological problem. It is one of the best liver-protective agents known and is also a gentle laxative.

Bupleurum falcatum (bupleurum)

This is the most commonly used herb in Chinese medicine, used in four out of five traditional formulas. *Bupleurum falcatum* is prescribed for period problems accompanied by stress and worry, stopped periods, irregular periods, period pain and PMS. For these complaints, it is usually combined with *Paeonia lactiflora* and *Angelica sinensis*.

Diuretics

A diuretic is any substance that increases urine output. Some are only effective if the patient already has a diminished urine output, others can have effects which are comparable to drugs.

Herbal diuretics include celery juice, parsley, and dandelion leaf tea. You could try a vegetable juice with parsley and celery in it, or some herbal diuretic tablets, if your practitioner says it's a good idea.

Taraxacum officinale (dandelion leaf)

A very safe and effective diuretic that, unlike many diuretics, adds to the body's stores of potassium instead of depleting it. *Taraxacum officinale* leaf assists with the symptomatic relief of premenstrual fluid retention.

To make dandelion leaf tea, add one or two teaspoons a cup, twice daily. You can mix it with peppermint tea, because it does taste a bit like grass clippings. Drink it in the morning.

Juniperus communis (juniper berries)

Juniperus communis has a reputation as fertility control agent and an abortifacient. This herb should not be used in pregnancy by the untrained and should be used cautiously in very large doses for any complaint. The injudicious use of juniper oil has caused death and so the oil is unavailable.

The mild diuretic activity of *Juniperus communis* makes it a suitable premenstrual remedy especially in cases of urinary irritation or premenstrual low-grade urinary tract infections. The mild emmenagogic activity can also be useful to bring on a delayed period caused by hormonal irregularities, especially associated with discomfort and bloating. The cause of the hormone imbalance should always be treated.

Equisetum arvense (horsetail)

Equisetum arvense is a safe, gentle and well tolerated diuretic, even at high doses and during long-term use. For heavy periods, especially those accompanied by premenstrual fluid retention, it can be given throughout the cycle.

Herbs for infection control

Many herbs improve the body's resistance to infections and any antiseptic effect is seen as a bonus. Of course, some infections are so extreme that antibiotics are necessary to save lives or prevent serious complications. Many infections are trivial, while others are more a nuisance than actually scary. Included in this latter group are colds and flus, sinusitis, sore throats and low-grade vaginal infections.

Echinacea species

Echinacea is a useful herb for the prevention of those chronic recurrent infections which occur in the premenstrual phase, such as recurrent sinusitis, genital herpes, acne and colds. It also helps in the treatment of pelvic inflammatory disease and can help control some common vaginal infections, in conjunction with other treatments.

Hydrastis canadensis (golden seal)

Hydrastis canadensis is a useful topical application as a cream or vaginal suppository for many gynaecological infections, including candidiasis (thrush), trichomonas and gardnerella. It is endangered due to overharvesting of wild plants and its use should be restricted until commercial crops are established.

Calendula officinalis (marigold)

Calendula officinalis can be taken internally for the treatment of heavy periods and seems to play a role in bringing on late periods. It is also a circulatory stimulant and reduces pelvic congestion, effects which when combined with its antimicrobial properties make it ideal for pelvic infections and inflammation. It also has a reputation as a mild anti-spasmodic and is useful in the treatment of endometriosis.

Melaleuca alternifolia (tea tree oil)

Tea tree oil is extracted from a shrub native to northern New South Wales. The essential oil is a powerful antimicrobial which is active against many common bacteria and fungi, including *Staphylococcus aureus* (golden staph) and *Candida* (the organism that causes thrush). It is a superb first aid topical antiseptic, but needs to be diluted as the pure oil can be very irritating on broken skin. (Put undiluted tea tree oil on your private parts and you may be orbiting the earth, screeching, in seconds.) A cream or olive oil base is commonly used with the diluted oil. It can be included in vaginal suppositories for the treatment of thrush, trichomonas infections and gardnerella. It should not be swallowed.

Caring for yourself is not about self-diagnosis or treatment without proper guidance. It *does* involve learning to recognise signs and symptoms to prevent illness. If you learn more about your body it will help you to recognise early signs of any change that may need attention.

Here are some important things to remember about looking after yourself:

- Get tested. Breast exams and cervical screening (Pap tests) are available from local doctors, women's clinics and Family Planning centres. You should have an internal pelvic examination every year to detect any changes in the pelvic structures, particularly the ovaries. (These procedures are outlined under the Screening section of The Medical Approach chapter.)
- Learn to 'listen' to your body. This doesn't mean a hippy-drippy psychic version of the stethoscope, it means if you really feel like there's something wrong, there probably is. Don't ignore warning signs and symptoms.
- Take prescriptions from doctors and natural therapists exactly as recommended, and make sure that each of your health care providers knows what the other ones are doing.

- Don't self-diagnose, don't prescribe yourself drugs or herbs, and don't wear your underpants on your head. You'll look stupid.
- Be as well informed as possible about any condition or disease you are dealing with. Don't just read one book, or one theory, or listen to one piece of advice. It can be tempting to fasten onto one reason or theory to explain everything, because it's simple.
- Be willing to accept that self care can only go so far with some conditions, and further or more complex treatment may be necessary.
- Remember that even if you are doing all the right things with your diet and lifestyle, you may still need to manage an illness in other ways. Don't be mad at yourself, just think how much worse it would be if you had a packet of Peter Stuyvesants and a Coke for breakfast every day.

Food for health

About the closest most doctors get to asking about your diet is to say 'Are you eating well?' To which you can reply, 'Oooh yes, doctor', meaning that you skip breakfast, have eight Tim Tams for lunch and usually eat the weight of a small Torana each evening, mostly from the food groups entitled 'lard' and 'utter crap'.

Natural therapists are more likely to pry into your eating habits and suggest some specific changes. Let's be frank: eating properly doesn't mean you'll never get sick, but it will make you healthier and less likely to get sick. And it means you recover more quickly. Not that we're the type to say 'Oh, you've just had your leg amputated. Half a cup of dandelion tea a day and that'll grow right back in no time.'

There are also some specific foods and combinations of foods which can help with recognised conditions. So we've included a couple of therapeutic short-term diets. These are not like the short-term weight-loss diets and should be used under the supervision of your health practitioner.

Here's a 'top 20' of sensible suggestions for healthy eating. It's a general guide which you can use to introduce healthy changes to the way you eat. Don't try and change everything at once, don't regard the hints as a set of hard and fast rules and don't start faffing around the place weighing bits of food and stressing about whether you need another 76.4 grams of tofu before Thursday, or you'll bore yourself to death.

Remember that girls who haven't finished growing to their full height, and pregnant women, will need more of everything (well, you know, food, not bottles of gin) than the average adult woman.

20 diet hints

1. Eat varied and interesting food

We're not talking about sitting down to a bowl of chaff three times a day with half a mung bean for morning tea. Don't eat foods you hate just because 'they're good for you'. Lots of different kinds of food is the go. And relax. You're not going to explode if you have a chocolate bickie every now and then.

2. Drink plenty of fluids every day

Because otherwise you'll shrivel up like a dried apricot and blow away. Well, not quite. But you need at least 2 litres of water a day, and more when it's hot or you're exercising. By the time you have a dry mouth, dehydration has already started, so don't wait until you're really thirsty.

Fluids should be varied and should not come only from coffee, tea and fluffy duck cocktails. Two or three glasses of plain water, preferably filtered, throughout the day are essential. Fruit juices should be diluted because of their high sugar content.

3. Eat fresh and organic foods

Fresh is best—there are less preservatives, the food is less likely to be rancid, nutrient levels are higher and it tastes better. It's easier to see if fresh food has been spoiled or is old and past its 'use by' date.

The closer you can get to the original source of the food, the better. This doesn't mean you have to go out and pick everything yourself, it means make sure your best pal is not the can-opener. Where possible, buy organic foods to minimise exposure to chemicals.

4. 'Therapeutic' diets are temporary

A therapeutic diet is prescribed with a particular goal—say, lowering cholesterol, improving anaemia, getting rid of thrush, or calming an irritable bowel. Therapeutic diets should only be used until the result is achieved, and always under the supervision of a health practitioner. Many of them don't contain the required nutrients, kilojoules or balance for extended use. If you react badly, go off it: therapeutic diets are not appropriate for all conditions or people.

5. Eat 5 to 7 different vegies and 3 fruits a day

Vegies and fruit contain a good range of vitamins, minerals, trace elements, essential fatty acids, anti-oxidants and fibre. Particular foods can also help to target particular problems. Cabbages and tomatoes reduce cancer risk; legumes contain plant oestrogens; bitter components flush the gall bladder; fruit pectin lowers cholesterol; and celery lowers blood pressure and reduces acid build-up in joints.

The old habit of 'a huge hunk of meat and three vegies boiled to death' should be abandoned with a sense of wild glee. To retain the most nutrients, it's best to cook vegies by steaming, stir-frying or baking. Every day you should eat from two to three different orange, red or yellow vegetables, a minimum of two green vegetables, and at least one of the cabbage family such as broccoli or cabbage—and some garlic or onion for their cancer-preventing and blood vessel protecting properties.

Fruit should be limited to three pieces a day because it doesn't seem to have the same energy-improving qualities of vegies (this may be because fruits are generally lower in minerals and higher in sugars). Fruit should preferably be eaten whole and not juiced, because juicing reduces the fibre content.

6. Main energy foods should be complex carbohydrates

Carbohydrates are energy foods which are eaten as whole foods like complex carbohydrates (such as brown instead of white rice) or as the more fatty and less useful refined carbohydrate like white bread. The main part of the diet should be based on complex carbohydrates from grains and legumes, dried beans and peas, nuts and seeds, soya products and some of the root vegies like potato, carrots and sweet potato. Common good energy foods include breakfast cereals and muesli, bread, rice, beans, tofu, pasta and potato.

Complex carbohydrates are high in fibre and many also contain plant oestrogens. They can lower blood cholesterol, stabilise blood sugar, regulate the bowel, reduce the appetite and ensure a good supply of regular energy. The slow energy release leads to greater stamina and fewer energy slumps. This is important for anyone troubled by blood sugar symptoms, and you there with premenstrual sugar cravings.

Carbo combos

Complex carbohydrates contain some of the amino acids which make up proteins and can be combined in a meal so that they become a substitute for animal protein. Carbohydrate-combining should be used by vegetarians to make sure that they get enough protein every day. The common combinations are:

- grains with beans: tofu and rice (Asia), lentils and rice (India), tortilla and beans (Mexico)
- grains and nuts: peanuts and rice (Southern Asia), nut butters and bread (bread-eating countries), rice and cashews (Asia)
- beans and seeds: sesame seed paste and beans (Middle East).

Many people instinctively cook like this or follow traditional recipes which incorporate food combinations. Combining carbohydrates gives all of the energy benefits of protein, as well as the positive benefits of complex carbohydrates without a high animal fat intake.

7. Eat enough fibre

Eating more fibre can correct a blocked-up or farty bottom (known in the trade as bowel complaints), and reduce the incidence or severity of diabetes, gall stones and heart disease. A high-fibre diet lowers the risk rate of breast and colon cancer.

The best source of dietary fibre is from whole foods, but occasionally it may be necessary to use processed fibre products (like wheat bran, oat or rice bran), to effectively treat some diseases. Wheat bran, 'fibrous' vegetables (like celery and carrot), potato and other root vegies, tofu, legumes and linseed meal are all good sources of fibre.

Fibre is sometimes included in therapeutic diets to achieve a specific outcome such as lowering of blood fats (cholesterol) and oestrogens; to reduce the incidence of gall bladder disease and colon cancer; for weight loss; or to treat constipation. Fibre is specifically important for women because it reduces the risk of oestrogen-dependent cancers, including breast cancer.

The recommended daily intake for fibre is 30 grams for an adult from whole foods and not as fibre-only breakfast cereals. This could be achieved by eating the following in the one day: five serves of whole-grain or legume products (such as two slices of bread, a cup of cooked beans, a cup of brown rice, and a cup of breakfast cereal) and five serves of different vegetables and three pieces of fruit.

8. Eat less 'bad fats' and more 'good fats'

Fat is the devil! It causes heart disease! It turns you into a hideous gargoyle! You'll get cholesterol problems and your head will fall off! And now they've invented a synthetic oil with no absorbable fat which causes 'anal leakage'. So what! It hasn't got any fat! Hmmm. It's just an inkling, but maybe it's time to get a bit less hysterical.

The fact is that if you cut out all fats you'll have more problems than when you started. There's good ones and bad ones. We all need a reasonable level of fats in our diet. They are essential for the production of sex and adrenal hormones, for the health of our skin and mucous membranes. When the right fats are eaten, they protect against high cholesterol and heart disease, skin and period problems and a whole lot else.

Bad fats

- An overall reduction of all fats is good.
- Cut down on saturated fats—they're in animal products (pork, beef, dairy products and lamb) and in the tropical oils (coconut and palm oils). Excessive saturated fat intake is linked to heart disease, obesity and an increased risk of some cancers.
- Cut down on the Omega-6 polyunsaturated fats. High levels of Omega-6 polyunsaturated fats are found in cooking oils and margarine.
- Avoid trans-fatty acids. These are in oils which are processed to become solid, like margarine and vegetable shortening. The high temperature process changes the oil molecule, and destroys essential fatty acids ('good fats'). Trans-fatty acids interfere with the production of the useful group of prostaglandins which prevent PMS, period pain and a heap of inflammatory problems.
- Look for 'contains hydrogenated fats' on labels and avoid it.
- Overall, too many fats, sugars, alcohol or carbohydrates are converted into triglycerides which increase the risk of heart disease, kidney failure, high blood pressure and cancer.
- To reduce risk of heart disease, cholesterol-containing foods should be minimised, but the 'good fats' must be increased as well, to have the right effect. Cholesterol is used by the body to make hormones and other bits and pieces, so you shouldn't cut it out altogether. It is found in all animal fats but not vegetable fats. (The body makes its own cholesterol, partly from eating cholesterol, and partly as a response to eating other saturated fats.)

Good fats

To let the good fats do their work properly, you need to cut down on the bad fats, which can interfere with their work.

- Mono-unsaturated fats are the good vegetable oils to cook with and are more stable than polyunsaturated fats when they are exposed to heat, light or oxygen. Olive oil is the best-known mono-unsaturated oil and when used as a substitute for saturated fats, helps to lower cholesterol and reduce the risk of heart disease.
- Fatty acids are necessary for the normal function and development of most tissues including the kidney, liver, blood vessels, heart and brain. A deficiency leads to excessive scaliness of the skin, reduced growth rates and infertility in both males and females; and can also cause a greater susceptibility to infections, fragile red blood cells and difficulty in making prostaglandins.

Omega-3 fatty acids

The Omega-3 fatty acids are particular polyunsaturated fats. Suffice to say that we all need Omega-3 fatty acids, which are known as EPA (eicosapentaenoic acid), DHA (docosahexaenoic acid). ALA (alpha linolenic acid) is an *essential* fatty acid which the body cannot make itself from other fatty acids.

To keep your prostaglandins in balance, and to control imbalance-related conditions, like period pain, some kinds of infertility, wound healing—all sorts of things—you need to regularly eat foods rich in Omega-3 fatty acids.

To make the right prostaglandins, you need to include these Omega-3s in your diet:

- Linseeds or linseed (flax seed) oil. These are very rich sources of ALA. You can take 1 to 2 tablespoons of ground linseeds a day. To help digestion and absorption, linseeds should be ground in a coffee grinder used only for seeds, never coffee (or mortar and pestle if you're feeling rustic), and can be sprinkled on muesli or tossed in a smoothie. They must be refrigerated in airtight containers or scoffed immediately after grinding. (Don't bother buying the pre-ground linseeds in packets at health food shops.) Alternatively, you could take 2 teaspoons of linseed/flax seed oil a day to be stored the same way. When served as recommended, linseed oil has 60 per cent ALA.

- Other sources. Pumpkin seeds (15 per cent ALA); canola oil (10 per cent); mustard seed oil (10 per cent) soya bean oil (7 to 9 per cent). Walnut oil also has moderate levels; and dark green leafy vegetables have small amounts. These fatty acids tend to go off and must be refrigerated in opaque bottles. No ALA oils should be cooked.
- Oily fish. The best fish to eat are cold-water and oilier fish. Include some of these fish in at least four meals a week. 'Oily' fish are often deep sea fish, where they've needed a bit of protection from the cold.

  If you can't buy fresh fish, get it in cans, although the benefits will be less obvious. Choose from: gemfish, blue mackerel, sea mullet, blue warehou, silver warehou, yellowtail kingfish, King George whiting, redfish, tuna, sardines, herring, pilchards, Atlantic salmon, silver trevally, luderick, ocean trout, blue eye, golden perch, blue grenadier, and rainbow trout.

  Fish oil supplements are usually capsules which include 18 per cent EPA and 12 per cent DHA and are made from fish oils or fish liver oils. Cod liver and halibut liver oils, however, also contain vitamins A and D, which means that they are no good for the long term at large doses. (It's dangerous to take vitamin A supplements if you're pregnant.) Fish oils have a long list of therapeutic effects which includes reducing heart disease; reducing arthritic inflammation; and an improvement in allergy-related conditions such as asthma and eczema.

Omega-6 fatty acids

- Linoleic acid. Eat some of this when you can. There may be positive effects on infertility linked to endometriosis and in reducing heavy periods. Linoleic acid is found in seed and vegetable oils, as well as most nuts, and organ meats. Coconut oil and dairy products contain very low levels of linoleic acid. Although the levels are low compared to seeds, any dark green vegetable is a source of linoleic acid. Linoleic acid is an *essential* fatty acid. Essential, in this case, merely means that you must eat them because the body won't manufacture them by itself.

There's lots of linoleic acid in seed oils: safflower oil (75 per cent); sunflower oil (60 to 70 per cent); walnut oil (60 per cent); corn oil (55 per cent) soya bean oil (50 per cent); peanut oil (35 per cent) and olive oil (8 per cent).

Evening primrose oil, blackcurrant seed oil and borage seed oil are also rich sources of linoleic acid.

- Gamma-linolenic acid. Gamma-linolenic acid (GLA) is the building block from which the body makes the prostaglandins that reduce inflammation, stop pain and activate the immune system. GLA is found in the oils of evening primrose, blackcurrant, safflower, sunflower, hemp, soybean, pumpkin seed, borage seed and walnut. These seed oils have been shown to reduce sore breasts and the severity of other PMS symptoms.

  Evening primrose, star flower oil and blackcurrant seed oil are available as capsules which contain beneficial amounts of GLAs as well as linoleic acid.

Cooking and storing hints for oils

- Mono-unsaturated fats are the best oils for cooking. Pour them into a pan that's already hot to reduce heating time. Never re-use oils.
- Don't cook in other oils. Heating induces irreversible changes to many oils which leads to oxidation or free radical formation. Foods can be cooked in just a little water, or even 'dry fried' in a non-stick pan. Fish, eggs and vegetables can be poached in water, or a fruit or vegetable puree and fish and vegetables can be baked rather than roasted in oil.
- Add oils to food *after* cooking as salad dressings or sauces.
- Eat more cold-pressed oils of linseed, safflower and canola as tablespoon doses once or twice a day or added to a seed breakfast or muesli, used in salad dressings, poured onto cooked food or mixed with yoghurt in a ratio of about one part oil to five parts yoghurt.
- Make your own spreads with avocado, tahini, yoghurt, chickpeas, nut butters or vegetable-based dips instead of margarine or butter.
- Buy oils manufactured without damage to the goodies ('cold-pressed', 'unrefined' or 'mechanically extracted') and in

opaque glass bottles. All oils and oil-containing foods should be refrigerated. Otherwise they have a habit of going off.

9. Eat dairy products in moderation

Many people are sensitive to dairy products, or at least some aspects of them, and some natural therapists recommend that they not be eaten at all, while dietitians see the enormous potential for nutrients, especially calcium, and recommend a high intake. What's going on? Are they good for us or what? Well, they're okay, if you eat the low-fat varieties, unless you have a dairy intolerance, and even then, you probably can eat yoghurt.

Don't drink milk with lactose if you're intolerant. Here's a simple test: somebody comes up and asks you the time, do you strike them repeatedly with your handbag? That is very intolerant. (Seriously, any food intolerance or allergy should be appropriately diagnosed.)

Yoghurt is an important food. It is easily digestible, provides good bacteria which makes the gut work properly, has more calcium than milk, and may help to reduce the risk of breast and other oestrogen-dependent cancers. It is also well tolerated by those with a dairy or lactose intolerance.

Read the label to make sure a yoghurt has live cultures; many of the snack-type yoghurts don't, especially the flavoured and 'fruit yoghurts'. Get low-fat, no-sugar brands.

Don't forget bones need magnesium too, if calcium is to be properly retained, and dairy foods don't have much magnesium.

10. Eat plant oestrogens

Plant oestrogens, also known as phyto-oestrogens, are structurally similar to animal oestrogen and are found in a large number of common foods and medicinal plants. They are explained fully later in this section. Eating plant oestrogens is associated with a reduced incidence of oestrogen-related disease such as endometriosis, and breast and endometrial cancer.

11. Eat enough protein regularly

When people go on 'healthy' or 'weight-loss' diets, they often drastically reduce or stop most of their protein intake. Protein is found in animal products such as meat, eggs, fish, milk and cheese, and also in the vegetable proteins such as tofu. Neither type is better or worse, unless you're a vegetarian.

Vegetarians (lacto-ovo), for example, can obtain protein from eating vegetable proteins, dairy products and eggs; vegans get it from eating combinations of vegetables. It's harder to get iron, and for the vegan, to get vitamin B12 as well. The advantage of being a vegetarian is a lower intake of fat and less likelihood of developing many of the chronic degenerative diseases; the disadvantage is a tendency to anaemia and fatigue.

Meat-eaters have an advantage when it comes to iron intake. Iron in meat is easier to absorb and it is present in much greater quantities. Animal protein is also of a better quality and meat-eaters can have a more relaxed attitude to nutrient intake and still maintain energy levels. On the down side, eating meat increases the intake of saturated fats and the risk of a number of diseases, such as heart disease and cancer. Deep sea fish is better because it contains high levels of essential fatty acids as well as protein. This means you have to ask the fishmonger if the fish is from the deep sea. Or there's a list of oily fish under Bad Fats and Good Fats, number 8 in this list.

For those who do eat meat, protein can come from (preferably chemical-free) lean, red meat in small quantities, some free-range chicken without the skin, plenty of fish, no more than three eggs a week and low-fat dairy products. You should have animal proteins at only one meal a day. The protein in other meals should come from properly combined vegetable sources. How to combine them is explained in the hypoglycaemic diet, coming up in a few pages.

It's kind of complicated, but on average, women over 20 should eat about 45–55 grams of protein each day. If you're between the ages of 11 and 20 you need to add another 10–15 grams to that. Here are some levels of protein in food:

100 grams of meat	20–25 grams
100 grams of seafood	15–20 grams
1 cup beans/legumes	7.5–15 grams

1 cup whole grains	5–12 grams
1 cup milk or yoghurt	8 grams
1 egg	6 grams
30 grams of cheese	6–8 grams
1 cup vegies or fruit	2–4 grams

12. Know your minerals

The key ones for women are in the next section, astonishingly enough entitled 'Minerals'.

13. Eat foods in season

Apart from the ludicrous price of foods that are out of season or imported (Darling, how marvellous! These July raspberries are only $6000 a punnet!) there's another reason to buy what's locally available at the right time of year.

All fruits and vegetables can be assigned with certain qualities in the same way that medicinal herbs are. Summer foods are generally juicy and light, winter foods tend to be dense and compact with lots of carbohydrate and protein. In summer, moist, easily digested raw foods make sense, but in winter they don't provide enough carbohydrate to counterbalance the energy expenditure needed to stay warm.

Winter foods should be mainly beans, legumes and root vegetables; salads can be made from root vegetables and cabbage. These are Warming and comforting foods on a cold winter's day.

Most summer fruits and vegetables have Cooling properties—melons are particularly Cooling while bananas, which tend to be dense and compact, are Warming. Eat stuff that seems instinctively right for that time of the year.

14. Vary the flavours

There are five main flavours in the diet: bitter, sweet, sour, salty and spicy or pungent. Australians traditionally rely heavily on the sweet and salty flavours, but other cultures include all or most of the flavours in their cooking as a matter of course—Thai food, for example, is cooked with the addition of salty, sweet, spicy and sour flavours.

Each of the flavours has subtle effects on digestion and health.

Bitter

Bitter foods improve digestion and bowel function by stimulating the bile flow. Bitter green vegetables and radicchio, chicory, dandelion leaves and silverbeet are often included in the European diet to aid digestion. (Spinach is not a 'bitter' because it doesn't taste bitter.) Grapefruit is sour and bitter, and the old practice of having half a grapefruit before a fatty breakfast such as bacon and eggs makes a lot of sense. (Almost as much as not eating the fatty breakfast every morning.) Dandelion coffee is a gentle and effective bitter that is available as a beverage. (It is available as a beverage that tastes like bat wee, if you asked one of the authors of this book, but we shall draw a tactful veil over this fact.)

Spicy

Warming spices in the diet improve sluggish digestion and are particularly useful for complaints of the upper gastro-intestinal tract such as nausea, burping and indigestion. Ginger, cardamom, cumin and coriander are all useful—ginger tea is particularly helpful for nausea. (Cut two or three bits of fresh knobbly ginger root, about 2 centimetres long, throw them in a teapot, add boiling water and let it steep for a couple of minutes.) These spices can be brewed in ordinary black tea to assist with digestion. Warming spices are useful for those who feel cold, have difficulties with cold weather, or catch colds easily.

Sour

Sour foods are drying and can be used to stop snuffly noses. For some people, sweet foods cause phlegm or catarrh and sour foods can reverse the process. Many sour foods, such as citrus fruit, are useful to protect the mucous membranes from infections. Sour foods also aid digestion.

15. Don't stuff yourself silly

Overeating (to be perfectly obvious) is linked to obesity and a shorter life expectancy. The digestive tract is chronically overburdened and the incidence of gall bladder disease increases. The heart has to work harder and the risk of high blood pressure also increases.

16. Don't argue with your food

Eat foods which agree with you. Listen to your body and act accordingly. Some common diets cause obvious problems in some people, such as abdominal upsets, diarrhoea, or fatigue. And sometimes your body decides it used to like something but now it's gone right off it.

Raw food diets can be a problem, for example, because raw food is quite difficult to digest. Bloating, wind or even diarrhoea can lead to a depletion of nutrients and ill health. Trading one health problem (for example, shocking wind) for another (like being overweight) doesn't make sense.

17. Limit sugar and salt

Sugar

All types of sugar should be minimised, including brown and unrefined sugars; as well as the foods which are prepared with sugar and processed food with added sugar (this includes stuff like tinned beans, even).

Salt

Salt intake is associated with high blood pressure and increases the excretion of minerals in the urine. Most sodium (salt) enters the diet in most manufactured foods, not through adding salt during cooking or at the table. Salt should be limited to around 3–5 grams daily.

18. Limit caffeine

Caffeine-containing drinks contain highly active substances known as xanthines. (Xanthines, while sounding like a girlfriend of Xena, Warrior Princess, are actually alkaloids which have diverse effects in the body.) Caffeine is in coffee, tea, cocoa and chocolate.

Caffeine increases anxiety, aggravates insomnia, helps to waste minerals and increases blood pressure.

Excessive caffeine intake is also linked with a number of common gynaecological conditions including endometriosis, fibroids, PMS and benign breast disease. Caffeine has also been shown to lower fertility. Gynaecological problems have been associated with the equivalent of two cups of coffee or four cups of tea every day. 'Plunger' coffee has the least harmful effects. Boiled coffee should be completely avoided if there are problems with high cholesterol levels.

19. Cut down on alcohol

Women are more affected by alcohol for longer periods of time than men. Women have a lower body water content and so alcohol is less diluted. They also metabolise (break down) alcohol more slowly because they have a smaller liver cell mass than men.

This is why there are different government health warnings for women and men. Two standard alcoholic drinks in less than an hour will take a woman to the legal blood alcohol limit for driving, but this figure may be influenced by hormonal fluctuations of the menstrual cycle (around the period and ovulation, alcohol is thought to be metabolised more slowly), by cigarette smoking and by diet.

Excess alcohol consumption has been linked to cancers, hypertension, heart disease, foetal abnormalities, and liver disease. A host of other more subtle health problems are caused or aggravated by alcohol. Some are caused by depletion of minerals such as calcium, magnesium, potassium and zinc, and vitamins A, C and the B complex, especially B1. The National Health and Medical Research Council have made the following recommendations for women:

- Women should limit drinking to two standard drinks or 20 grams of absolute alcohol per day and have two or three alcohol-free days a week to give the liver some recovery time.
- More than two drinks a day or 14 drinks a week is officially considered dangerous. Any more than that and you're officially damaging yourself.
- Don't drink at all if you're pregnant.

Also, if you do get legless drunk, don't go for the 'hair of the dog' and start all over again. Give your body free time to get over it: about two days between drinks is recommended.

20. Eat more serenely

A common cause of digestive problems and poor nutrient uptake, is the practice of eating in the car, watching TV or on the run. Meal times need to be a little sacred; a time set aside to think about food, be with family, friends or self. Taking time to chew food thoroughly is an essential beginning to good digestion.

Avoid unnecessary argument or conflict and try not to eat when upset or in pain. If possible wait until you feel better. Most importantly, enjoy what you are eating. If you happen to eat some junk food, enjoy it, then get on with wholesome eating.

What to aim to eat every day

Vegies

A minimum of five different vegetables daily; from at least two green and two orange, yellow or red vegetables.

Fruit

Pieces from three different fresh, seasonal fruits.

Complex carbohydrates or whole grains and beans/legumes

Include four to five serves of grains such as wheat, rice, corn, hulled millet and/or beans such as chickpeas, lentils, red kidney beans, lima beans, soya beans and soya products. A serve is equivalent to a slice of bread, one cup of cooked grain or beans, or one medium-sized to large potato.

Yoghurt and cultured milks

Include at least one cup of low-fat yoghurt daily. If sensitive to cow's milk, include soya, goat's or sheep's yoghurt instead. Yoghurts should contain live cultures.

Fibre

Fibre should come from whole foods such as grains, nuts, seeds, fruit and vegetables and not from fibre-only bran-based, commercial breakfast cereals.

Fats and oils

Include three teaspoons of raw seed/oils in the diet daily, such as flax, canola, safflower or sunflower, but try to avoid margarine. To make 'better butter' mix equal quantities by weight of a good quality canola oil and butter. Keep refrigerated.

Seeds and nuts

- **Seeds.** linseeds, sesame seeds, sunflower seeds, pumpkin seeds.
- **Nuts.** almonds, hazelnuts, walnuts, pecans, cashews, pine nuts and peanuts.

Nuts and seeds have a high ratio of oils and should be kept to a maximum of half a cup a day. This should be substituted for one of the grain or bean servings, as well as one of the teaspoons of oil.

Protein

Protein is found in meat, fish, eggs, dairy products and properly combined vegetable proteins. Some protein should be taken with every meal.

Meal suggestions

Morning kick-start

Start the day with one of these:

- the juice of a lemon diluted in a glass of warm water
- half a grapefruit
- citrus juice
- a whole piece of fruit.

(We're not suggesting that's your whole breakfast, but have one of them before anything else. It will wake up your digestive process.)

Breakfast ideas

- Home-made muesli: raw oatmeal, rice flakes, puffed millet, sunflower seeds, linseeds, sultanas, chopped almonds or cashews, dried paw paw, coconut and chopped pumpkin seeds. Add low-fat cow's milk, yoghurt or soya milk, and chopped fresh fruit.
- Fresh fruit in season with yoghurt and seeds or chopped nuts.
- Wholegrain bread, toasted with nut butter, hommos, low-fat cheese, miso, alfalfa or other sprouts. You don't need butter with these spreads. Avoid honey and jams.
- Cooked cereal such as oatmeal, millet meal, brown rice or buckwheat, with added seeds or soya grits. Add milk of choice and fruit or a bit of honey.
- Energy drink: blend together low-fat yoghurt with either fresh fruit of your choice or fruit juice (about half and half), and add a teaspoon each of rice bran, ground linseeds, almond meal, wheatgerm, and sunflower seeds.

Lunch ideas

- Wholegrain bread sandwich with a mixture of salad vegies. Include a bit of protein such as tuna, salmon, egg, low-fat cheese, or hommos.
- Salad of mixed vegies such as lettuce salad, coleslaw, tabouli salad, grated beetroot, tomatoes, carrot or celery. Protein should be included either in the form of correctly combined vegetable proteins or animal proteins as above.
- Soup with the addition of beans and grains, a little yoghurt or parmesan cheese.
- Any of the dinner choices or the breakfast energy drink.

Dinner ideas

Dinner should contain at least five different vegies, cooked or raw depending on season and preference; some protein; and a serve of complex carbohydrate like rice, root vegies, beans, or pasta.

To keep animal protein to a minimum, combine meat with grain or bean dishes. Examples might be lamb and chickpea casserole, or similar combination, common in the Middle East and the south-eastern European countries; pasta and tomato sauce with tuna; stir-fry vegetables with a little meat, and served with rice, common in Asia. Or:

- Steamed vegetables with rice and tofu.
- Stir-fry beef and vegetables with rice.
- Steamed vegetables with lentils and rice.
- Grilled or baked fish with vegetables or salad.
- Minestrone soup with beans and parmesan cheese.

Fluids

- Limit caffeine-containing beverages to two cups of coffee or four cups of tea (and you know that doesn't mean you can have two mega-jolt triple caffeine-screaming long blacks).
- Drink at least 2 litres of water daily.

Food for healing

In the past decade, the belief that diet can improve health and reduce the risk of a number of serious diseases has become proven fact. In particular, a low-fat diet reduces the risk of cancer and heart disease. And a diet high in fibre and plant oestrogens is likely to reduce your risk of getting oestrogen-dependent cancers such as breast cancer.

Short-term therapeutic diets can be designed with a specific outcome in mind like getting rid of a complaint, or long-term diets might have a preventative focus. A diet might be designed around a specific life event such as breastfeeding, becoming menopausal or needing surgery.

Therapeutic diets

Be sure to get a professional diagnosis before trying any therapeutic diets designed for specific complaints. This is a serious business and you don't want to go faffing about with de-tox diets or the like without knowing exactly what you want to achieve and why. Stop when you get the required result.

Continuing functional hypoglycaemia diet

To be supervised by your health practitioner

When your symptoms have stopped, you can try coming off and following the 20 Diet Hints listed earlier in this chapter.

Functional hypoglycaemia is caused by fluctuations in the blood sugar levels. Symptoms include fatigue, lethargy, sleepiness, insomnia, weakness, headache, sugar cravings or unusual hunger. This syndrome is most likely to happen after stress, or the consumption of excess sugars and highly refined foods. Hypoglycaemia is discussed in more detail under The Usual Suspects in the When Things Go Wrong chapter.

General guidelines

- Eat small amounts of protein regularly at meals and with snacks.
- Eat small meals often.
- Avoid all sugar, honey and dried fruit.
- Consume only small quantities of unsweetened, diluted fruit juice.
- Avoid all stimulants such as tea, coffee, chocolate, and cola drinks.
- Avoid alcohol and cigarettes.
- Eat wholegrain foods; avoid white flour and refined cereals.
- *Always* eat breakfast.

Protein

All animal protein is 'complete', and therefore meals containing milk products, eggs, meat or fish provide first class protein. Incomplete (plant) protein foods, however, need to be combined with complementary foods and eaten at the same meal to provide the same quality protein as animal protein.

Eat beans with grains: tofu (from soya beans) and rice; lentils and rice; corn and beans; buckwheat and tempeh; muesli and soya milk; kidney beans and barley. Or eat beans with seeds: tahini and beans; tofu and sesame seeds.

Or eat grains with nuts: nut butters on bread; rice and cashews; rice and peanut sauce.

Suggested menus

Breakfast

Choose from:

- Fruit with yoghurt, seeds and ground almonds.
- Wholegrain bread toast with nut butters, hommos or egg.
- Home-made muesli: oats, rolled barley, rice flakes, rice bran, seeds, coconut, and crushed almonds or cashews. Add fresh fruit and soya milk, low-fat milk or yoghurt as desired.
- Cooked cereal: oats (porridge), rice or buckwheat, with a selection of seeds.

Morning, Afternoon or Supper Snack

Choose from:

- A small handful of mixed seeds and nuts.
- Half a banana and a small handful of almonds.
- A glass of soya milk with seeds and nuts.
- A small container of low-fat yoghurt.
- Two wholegrain dry biscuits with nut butters or hommos.
- Energy drink: Blend together half a cup of fresh fruit or juice, half a cup of low-fat yoghurt, and seeds with a small handful of almonds, and/or wheatgerm and lecithin.

Lunch

Choose from:

- Mixed vegetable salad with protein—either fish, cheese, hommos, meat or other appropriately combined vegetable proteins.
- Salad sandwich with protein as above.

- Vegetable soup with yoghurt, cheese, or a combination of beans and grains.
- One of the dinner choices.

Dinner
Choose from:

- Bean and grain dish: stir-fry vegies with rice and tofu; dhal with vegetables and rice; tortilla and beans; buckwheat noodles with vegetables and tempeh; vegetable soup with barley and red kidney beans.
- Grain and nut meal: steamed vegies with rice and peanut sauce; stir-fry vegies with cashew nuts; pasta and pesto sauce.
- Beans and seeds: many of the Middle Eastern vegetarian meals are based on the principle of combined vegie proteins, like felafel and hommos.
- Meat or fish with plenty of vegies.

Eat smaller meals than you usually do, but eat more often: six half-size meals should be substituted for three normal-size meals.

Continuing diet for irritable bowel syndrome

To be supervised by your health practitioner

When your symptoms have stopped, you can try coming off and following the 20 Diet Hints listed earlier in this chapter.

These dietary recommendations help to reduce the spasm, pain and bloating of irritable bowel syndrome, and to regulate bowel function.

Seed breakfast

The seed breakfast consists of a combination of seeds, pectin-containing fruit and yoghurt.

In summer

- Linseeds
- Almonds
- Pumpkin seeds
- Sesame seeds
- Sunflower seeds
- Rice bran.

The seeds are ground daily (ground to a consistency of coarsely ground coffee) and then combined with the bran in quantities equal by weight. Any left-overs must always be refrigerated. Mix about 2 tablespoons of seed and bran mix with the following ingredients.

Plus, fruit:

- Grated raw apple *or*
- Stewed apple, pear or plums.

Plus, yoghurt:

- Plain (unsweetened) low-fat yoghurt with live cultures. (Jalna, Lesna, Hakea and Hellenic are all good brands.)

Chuck it all in a bowl and dig in.

In winter

Cooked grains:

Add 2 tablespoons of the seed mix to porridge or rice and eat with warmed stewed fruit. Yoghurt can either be eaten with the fruit and grains or eaten as a side dish.

Herb tea

Melissa officinalis (lemon balm), *Matricaria recutita* (chamomile) and *Mentha piperita* (peppermint tea) in equal quantities are prepared as for ordinary tea (2 teaspoons per cup).

Dose: 1–2 cups between each meal.

Foods to avoid or reduce

- Stimulants such as tea, coffee and cola drinks.
- Cereals made from 100 per cent wheat bran.
- Fried food, pastry, cream and ice-cream.
- Breads and other foods with yeast.
- Refined sugar and foods containing refined sugars.
- Alcohol, especially beer and wine.

Minerals

It is better to get all minerals from food, but if this isn't possible (as opposed to just inconvenient) you can take supplements. Always check with your health practitioner for acceptable doses for you.

Zinc

Most women don't get enough zinc—especially during the teenage years.

Some possible symptoms of zinc deficiency

Slow growth; infertility/delayed sexual maturation; hair loss; skin conditions of various kinds; diarrhoea; immune deficiencies; behavioural and sleep disturbances; night blindness; impaired taste and smell; white spots on fingernails; delayed wound healing; post-op complications; dandruff; hair loss; impaired glucose tolerance; connective tissue disease; reduced appetite.

Zinc deficiency can be caused by:

Anorexia nervosa, fad diets, 'weight-loss' diets; exclusion diets for food allergies; a strict vegetarian diet; restricted protein diets; long-term intravenous therapy or tube feeding through the nose; alcoholism.

Zinc absorption may be hampered by:
High-fibre diets; iron tablets; coeliac disease (gluten intolerance); food allergies; low or absent gastric acid levels; alcoholic cirrhosis; a dicky pancreas.

You need extra zinc if you're:
- going through puberty or a growth spurt;
- pregnant or breastfeeding;
- taking diuretics;
- on the drug penicillamine, a detoxifying drug;
- suffering from psoriasis, exfoliative dermatitis, or excessive sweating;
- troubled by intestinal parasites or hookworm;
- drinking too much grog;
- suffering from liver disease including viral hepatitis;
- prone to chronic diarrhoea and ileostomy fluid loss;
- recovering from surgery or trauma;
- diagnosed with cancer.

Recommended daily allowance:
12–15 milligrams a day for women.

Good sources of zinc
This chart shows how many milligrams of zinc in 100 grams of food:

Food	mg	Food	mg
Fresh oysters (as if you'd be having those every day)	45.0–75.0	Peanuts	3.0
Wheat bran	16.0	Sardines	3.0
Wheat germ	13.0	Dark chicken meat	2.85
Dried ginger root	7.0	Walnuts	2.25
Brazil nuts	7.0	Wholewheat bread	1.65
Red meats	4.5–8.5	Prawns	1.15
Parmesan cheese	4.0	Whole egg	1.10
Dried peas	4.0	Non-fat cow milk	0.75
Hazelnuts	3.5	Porridge	0.5
		Raw carrots	0.5

Iron

Iron requirements for women are around 80 per cent higher than for men. It is estimated that iron deficiency is the most common nutritional disease worldwide and that more than half of all women consume less than the recommended amount of 10–15 milligrams a day.

Those at most risk of iron deficiency

Pregnant women; women with heavy periods; children; vegetarians; serial dieters; people on strict exclusion diets; people with low gastric acid levels, such as after stomach surgery and with ageing, people with malnutrition.

Iron deficiency or anaemia?

Iron is stored in the body in red blood cells, the liver, bone marrow, spleen, muscles and in the serum. A test for anaemia will determine only whether there is a depletion of iron stored in the red blood cells (the haemoglobin level), but not whether iron levels are high enough in the rest of the body.

The symptoms of iron deficiency can happen before the red blood cells become depleted of iron. Many people are iron deficient even though their haemoglobin is normal. For this reason, many doctors now order a blood test to check iron stores in the plasma as well as the haemoglobin levels.

Symptoms of anaemia

Red blood cells need iron to be able to carry oxygen around the body. When that isn't around, anaemia symptoms happen, including poor stamina; shortness of breath on exertion; unreasonable limb fatigue and dizziness.

Other symptoms seem to be related to the lack of iron in the serum, called iron deficiency.

Symptoms of iron deficiency

A red sore tongue and cracks in the corners of the mouth; excess hair loss; concave finger nails; reduced resistance to infection; poor

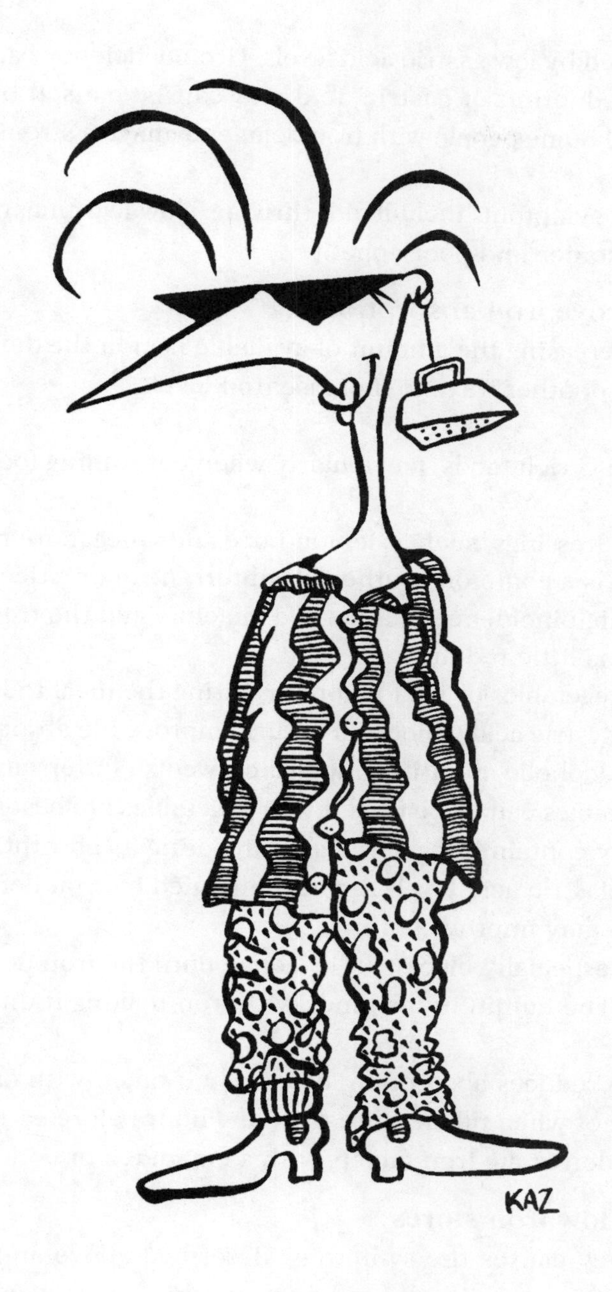

Iron is more important than ironing

digestion caused by low gastric acid levels. (Iron deficiency can cause decreased production of gastric acid and can be caused by it—a vicious circle.) Some people with iron deficiency have a strong desire to chew ice.

In children, symptoms include not thriving; slow learning; reduced infection resistance and poor appetite.

How to improve iron absorption

Apart from increasing the amount of available iron in the diet, there are a number of other ways to increase iron levels:

- Eat vitamin C rich foods, particularly when consuming foods high in iron.
- Add acidic dressings, such as lemon juice and vinegar, to iron-rich foods. This is a common southern Mediterranean practice, where there is a high incidence of inherited anaemia and the traditional diet contains little red meat.
- Eat bitter vegetables or fruit before or during the meal to increase the flow of gastric acid which will in turn improve the absorption of minerals. Alcoholic aperitifs, grapefruit, Swedish bitters and bitter green vegetables can all be used. Bitter vegetables are best because they usually contain iron as well as stimulating its absorption.
- When low gastric acid levels are accompanied by iron deficiency, taking iron may improve both.
- Avoid tea (especially black tea) or coffee until the iron deficiency improves. The tannin in tea binds with iron making it difficult to absorb.
- Coffee also reduces absorption, especially if taken with or after a meal, but not when taken more than one hour before eating.
- Definitely don't take iron tablets with a cup of tea or coffee.

Diagnosing low iron stores

Iron deficiency causes the symptoms described above and should respond to a low-dose iron supplement within a few weeks. Iron should not be taken unnecessarily as it will accumulate in the body and may become toxic. If symptoms do not respond, seek advice and ask for a blood test which evaluates serum iron levels.

Recommended daily allowance

10–15 milligrams a day for women.

Good sources of iron

This chart shows how many milligrams of iron in 100 grams of food:

Meat, fish and eggs

Mussels	7.7	Oysters	6.0
Lean beef	3.4	Lean lamb	2.7
Sardines	2.4	Eggs	2.0
Dark chicken meat	1.9	Lean pork	1.3
Light chicken meat	0.6	Cod	0.4

Grains

Special K™	20.0	Wheat bran	12.9
All Bran™	12.0	Wheat germ	10.0
Soya flour	9.1	Weetbix™	7.6
Raw oatmeal	4.1	Whole wheat flour	4.0
Rye biscuits	3.7	Whole wheat bread	2.5
White bread	1.7		

Legumes and vegetables

Raw parsley	8.0	Spinach	3.4
Silverbeet	3.0	Haricot beans	2.5
Lentils	2.4	Leeks	2.0
Spring onions	1.2	Peas	1.2
Broccoli	1.0	Raw mushrooms	1.0
Lettuce	0.9	Jacket potatoes	0.6

Fruits

Dried peaches	6.8	Dried figs	4.2
Dried apricots	4.1	Prunes	2.9
Sultanas	1.8	Currants	1.8
Raisins	1.6	Dates	1.6
Avocado	1.5	Stewed prunes	1.4
Raspberries	1.2	Fresh apricots	0.4

Other

Yeast	20.0	Almonds	4.2
Brazil nuts	2.8	Walnuts	2.4
Peanuts	2.0	Hazel nuts	1.1

Magnesium

Magnesium is vital for the maintenance of bone density, the prevention of heart attacks and the functioning of all muscles. Magnesium is a crucial female mineral, but never seems to get the sexy telly ads, probably because calcium has a dairy corporation behind it, and the beef industry likes to bang on about iron.

Bones

Magnesium is almost as important for bone health as calcium. It improves the absorption of calcium from food and increases its retention in the body. A high intake of calcium inhibits the absorption of magnesium. Foods traditionally thought of as being useful for bone density, such as dairy products, are also relatively low in magnesium (a cup of milk contains 290 milligrams of calcium, but only 35 milligrams of magnesium) which raises doubts about the suitability of large intakes of dairy products for bone health. Magnesium, either alone or with calcium, offsets the usual overnight bone mineral loss.

The heart

Magnesium protects the heart muscle from getting overexcited which can cause irregularities in the heart beat.

PMS

Magnesium and vitamin B6 can help alter the hormone levels and protect against PMS.

Signs and symptoms of magnesium deficiency

Weakness and/or tiredness; poor muscle co-ordination; premenstrual symptoms; apathy; insomnia, hyperactivity; susceptibility to toxic effects of the drug digoxin; abnormalities of the heart's rhythm, an abnormal reading on an electrocardiograph (ECG) which traces heart activity; muscle cramps; grimaces, tremors of the tongue, 'flickering' eyelids; loss of appetite, nausea, constipation; confusion, disorientation and memory impairment, learning disabilities; vertigo; difficulty swallowing or throat constriction.

Obviously these symptoms can have other serious causes, but when no obvious cause can be found, improved magnesium intake may help.

Recommended daily allowance

The recommended daily intake for magnesium is 400–800 milligrams for women.

Good sources of magnesium

This chart shows how many milligrams of magnesium in 100 grams of food:

Grains

Wheat bran*	520	Wheat germ	300
Whole wheat flour	140	Porridge	110
Muesli	100	Rye flour	92
White flour	36		

Seafood

Prawns	110

Vegetables

Beet tops	106	Silverbeet	65
Spinach	59	Raw parsley	52
Beans	35	Green peas	33
Broccoli	24	Beetroot	23

* Foods that are rich in magnesium, such as bran, may not provide the best source of minerals. Magnesium can become bound to the phytates in bran which reduce absorption. Whole foods from a wide variety of sources is the best way to attain a good intake of easily absorbed magnesium.

Beans and nuts

Brazil nuts	410	Soya flour	290
Almonds	260	Peanuts	180
Walnuts	130		

Fruits

Dried figs	92	Dried apricots	65
Avocado	30	Banana	20
Grapefruit juice	18		

Calcium

You can see below that the recommended daily allowance (RDA) varies depending on your age. If you are not getting enough calcium, you can either increase the number of calcium-rich foods, or take a supplement.

To maintain the bone density to prevent osteoporosis you need to keep up a high calcium intake before, during and after the menopause. Post-menopausal women should consume 4–5 serves of calcium-rich foods in order to obtain enough calcium, preferably from different sources. In other words, don't just eat a vat of yoghurt every day.

Recommended daily allowances

Babies: 350–550 milligrams
Kids aged 1 to 10: 800 milligrams
Teenagers: 1200 milligrams
Young women aged 20 to 35: 800–1000 milligrams
Pregnant/ breastfeeding women: 1500 milligrams
Women more than 35 years old: 1000 milligrams
After the menopause: 1500 milligrams.

Low-kilojoule calcium sources

Girls going through the growth spurt of their teenage years who are exercising regularly shouldn't worry about eating whole-fat dairy products. Others might like to consider these low-fat sources. All these low-kilojoule food sources have 300 milligrams of calcium:

1¼ cups of cooked spinach or other greens;
2 cups cooked broccoli;
1 cup Physical™ milk;
⅔ cup plain low-fat yoghurt;
¼ cup grated parmesan;
50 grams Swiss or cheddar cheese;
1½ cups whole milk;
1¼ cups plain yoghurt;
200 grams tofu;
1 can sardines;
300 grams tinned salmon;
2 cups low-fat cottage cheese.

Good sources of calcium

This chart shows how many milligrams of calcium in 100 grams of food:

Dairy products	
Skim milk powder (dry)	1190
Whole milk powder (dry)	900
Whey powder	645
Physical™ milk 100 millilitres	205
Yoghurt—cow's	180
REV™ milk 100 millilitres	150
Goat's milk	130
Skimmed cow's milk	123
Buttermilk	115
Cow's milk whole	115
Human milk	30

Cheese	
Parmesan	1091
Gruyère	1000

Seeds	
Unhulled sesame seeds	1160
Linseeds	271
Hulled sesame seeds	110
Sunflower seeds	98
Pumpkin seeds	52

Grains and cereals	
White SR flour	350
Muesli (depends on brand)	200
Wheat flour (white or brown)	150
Wheat bran	110
Bread (brown or white)	100
All Bran™	75
Rice bran	69
Wheat germ	69

Cheese (continued)

Mozzarella	817
Cheddar	810
Gouda	810
Edam (30% fat)	800
Edam (45% fat)	678
Gorgonzola	612
Camembert (30% fat)	600
Danish Blue	580
Blue (50% fat)	540
Camembert (60% fat)	400
Fetta	353
Ricotta	223
Cottage (low-fat)	77
Cottage	67

Eggs	56

Fish

Whitebait	860
Sardines (canned)	550
Scallops	120
Salmon (canned)	100

Soya products

Soya milk (dry)	330
Soya grits	255
Dried soya beans	225
Soya flour, full fat	210
Tofu	170
So Good™ soy milk	116
Vita Soy™ soy milk	32

Nuts

Almonds	250
Brazil	180

Grains and cereals (continued)

Wheat crispbread	60
Porridge	55
Rye crispbread	50
Brown rice	33
Weetbix™	33

Meat

All meat	10–20

Legumes (cooked)

Navy beans	95
Chickpeas	70
Kidney beans	70
Lentils	50
Black-eyed beans	40
Split peas	22

Sprouts

Alfalfa sprouts	28
Mung bean sprouts	20
Lentil sprouts	12

Vegetables

Parsley	260
Watercress	190
Dandelion greens	185
Spring onions	140
Onions	135
Spinach	135
Broccoli	125
Silverbeet	115

Fruits

Dried figs	260
Lemons	110

Nuts (continued)		Fruits (continued)	
Pistachio	136	Lemon juice (100 millilitres)	8
Pecan	75	Rhubarb (stewed)	93
Peanuts (fresh)	60	Orange juice (100 millilitres)	60
Walnuts	60	Blackberries	60
Macadamia	50	Other fruit except dried fruit	10–50
Hazelnuts	45		
Peanut butter	35	**Other**	
Cashews	30	Kelp	1095
		Crude molasses	654
		Torula yeast	425
		Carob powder	355
		Brewers' yeast	210

Plant oestrogens

What? Not more bloody oestrogens! The oestrogens made in our bodies are called endogenous oestrogens. Some plants naturally contain components that are structurally similar to oestrogen and can have similar effects on the body. These are called plant oestrogens. They are also known as phyto-oestrogens. (Pronounced fight-oh-east-roe-jens.)

Eating some phyto-oestrogens every day is a good idea. Basically, they're thought to be protective against cancer, and they may also reduce the incidence of oestrogen-responsive diseases such as endometriosis and fibroids. Extra amounts can help stop menopausal hot flushes.

Positive research results are relevant for just eating phyto-oestrogens as part of a normal diet—there is no evidence to support getting into complicated regimes of weighing foods and taking long-term supplements.

The simple message of this section is to whack into your diet some more phyto-oestrogens found in soya stuff, legumes, sprouty things and linseeds. Here's why.

What are phyto-oestrogens?

One of the first hints that hormones in plants could affect mammals came from the discovery that infertile sheep had been eating clover containing 'plant oestrogens'. Now, don't panic. This doesn't mean that if you eat clover-based honey you're infertile, or anything like that. If you've been going through a paddock or two of clover every week you might need to worry. (In more ways than one.)

Anyway, what we do now know, after researchers have ferreted around in laboratories, and a bit of trial and error, is that plant oestrogens are found in lots of growing things and that eating them can affect human health. In the way of scientists, they found a whizzbangery scientific term for plants containing oestrogenic components—the word is phyto-oestrogen, meaning a plant containing an oestrogen-like substance. *(Phyto* is Greek for plant.)

Phyto-oestrogens we eat that can affect our health include isoflavonoids, coumestans and lignans; the triterpenoid and steroidal saponins, the phytosterols and the resorcylic acid lactones, including zearalenone.

All of them are naturally occurring compounds found in a large range of whole foods including grains, seeds (linseeds have lots of phyto-oestrogens but linseed oil doesn't, for example), legumes, and medicinal plants, as well as other common foods.

Foods with plant oestrogens

Isoflavones: especially soya beans and all other legumes; whole grains.

Coumestans: especially soya sprouts; and all other sprouted beans or legumes, split peas, mung beans.

Lignans: especially linseeds; and whole rye, buckwheat, millet, sesame and sunflower seeds, legumes and beans, whole grains.

Resorcylic acid lactones: oats, barley, rye, sesame seeds, wheat, and peas.

Steroidal saponins: especially real liquorice, and potato.

The effects of phyto-oestrogens

The effects of plant oestrogens on our hormones are pretty complicated. They can cause periods to get lighter and less frequent, reduce the incidence of oestrogen-dependent cancers, and help with menopausal symptoms, especially hot flushes.

Asian women who eat a traditional diet excrete higher amounts of endogenous oestrogen than women who eat a 'Western' diet, which some researchers believe accounts for their lower risk of breast cancer. Soya products consumed regularly in Asian countries contain high levels of phyto-oestrogens, and are said to be responsible for these positive effects, along with genes.

The lignans and some of the isoflavones require normal levels of bowel bacteria to turn them into the right stuff, so if you've taken, or are taking antibiotics, you probably won't get the full benefit. Eating yoghurt seems to help maintain the right bacteria.

How they work

Phyto-oestrogens share many of the same biological roles with oestrogens produced in the body. This is probably because phyto-oestrogens and body-made oestrogens are structurally similar, and both have the ability to interact with oestrogen receptors.

We seem to need the phyto-oestrogens to balance our levels of oestrogens produced in the body throughout life.

According to lab tests, the oestrogenic effect of a phyto-oestrogen is estimated to range from around 160 to many thousands of times weaker than the body-made oestrogen oestradiol (pronounced eastro-die-al).

Before the menopause

Before menopause, the phyto-oestrogens we eat may help to protect against the 'proliferative effects' of too much oestrogen and reduce the incidence of related diseases like breast cancer, endometriosis and fibroids.

Some diseases and cancers may develop because of the over-stimulating effect of too much oestrogen, but it's possible for phyto-oestrogens to prevent many of the more stimulatory oestrogens from occupying receptor sites: this is called competitive inhibition. Competitive inhibition is believed to be one of the ways that diets rich in isoflavonoids and lignans reduce the risk of oestrogen-dependent cancers. Tamoxifen, a drug which is used to treat breast cancer, is structurally related to the phyto-oestrogens.

The phyto-oestrogens are also capable of slowing down the production of extra, non-ovarian oestrogen produced in the fat tissues.

As we've said, eating more soya products seems to lower the risk of breast cancer. This may be related to the phyto-oestrogens or be a result of many compounds acting together. There is evidence that eating phyto-oestrogens can help *prevent* cancer, but it isn't yet known whether eating phyto-oestrogens will help you if you already have an oestrogen-responsive breast cancer.

The isoflavonoids and lignans stimulate liver production of sex hormone binding globulin (SHBG). SHBG binds to the sex hormones, especially androgens and oestrogens, and acts as a carrier protein. When the major portion of these hormones are bound to SHBG in the blood, they are less available to bind to hormone-sensitive tissues. This is believed to be another way in which phyto-oestrogens lower the incidence of hormone-related diseases.

The symptoms of excess androgen production seen in polycystic ovarian disease and androgen disorders may be reduced by high levels of phyto-oestrogens because of the increase in SHBG. SHBG reduces the availability of androgens and may limit their masculinising effects.

Period regulation

Other more immediate benefits from phyto-oestrogens include lighter periods and longer menstrual cycles. They also reduce the risk of episodes of endometrial hyperplasia (too much cell production in the uterine lining).

Improved bone density?

A new area of research is the potential for phyto-oestrogens to improve bone density, although positive results about humans are in the preliminary stages of research.

After menopause

After menopause, the phyto-oestrogens have a mildly oestrogenic effect because they become more prevalent in a relatively oestrogen-poor environment. Recently Australian researchers found soya flour (high in phyto-oestrogens) decreased hot flushes by 40 per cent compared to 25 per cent in a wheat flour group (lower in phyto-oestrogens).

Getting your phyto-oestrogens

Increasing soya intake can be as easy as substituting low-fat soy milk for ordinary milk and using soya flour in cooking. Tofu is very useful, and even 100 grams a day can reduce hot flushes and vaginal dryness. Dried or 'fresh' soya beans (you can buy them frozen in Asian food shops) can be added to soups and bean dishes. As little as 25 grams or about 2 heaped dessertspoons of ground linseeds per day can help to reduce symptoms of low oestrogen levels, including vaginal dryness. Linseeds contain lignans and can be used in cooking or ground and added to muesli, porridge, or drinks, like a smoothie. (The easiest way to grind seeds is in a coffee grinder you don't use for coffee beans. It's best to grind and eat them immediately so there's no chance of rancidity.) Don't buy pre-ground linseeds.

USEFUL ORGANISATIONS

Use these contact points to find specific support groups for your illness, information and advice and for various contacts ranging from health problems to domestic violence shelters, sports and hobby groups in your area and lots more. These groups are almost always having their funding cut, so you can help out by ringing your local politicians to say we need them properly funded.

Women's information services

These groups will be able to point you in any direction you need. They're a clearing house for any requests for information.

Australian Capital Territory

Women's Information Referral Centre
Level 1, Block A
Callam Offices
Woden ACT 2606
Phone: 02 6205 1075, 02 6205 1076
Fax: 02 6205 1077

New South Wales

Women's Information and Referral Service
Department for Women
Level 11, 100 William Street
Woolloomooloo NSW 2011
Phone: 02 9334 1047, 1800 817 227,
TTY 1800 673 304
Fax: 02 9334 1023

Northern Territory

Darwin
Women's Information Network
PO Box 40596
Casuarina NT 0811
Phone: 08 8922 7276, 1800 813 631

Alice Springs
Women's Information Centre
Shopfront, corner Gregory and Bath Streets
Alice Springs NT 0870
PO Box 721, Alice Springs NT 0871
Phone: 08 8951 5880
Fax: 08 8951 5884

Queensland

Brisbane
Women's Information Link
56 Mary Street
Brisbane QLD 4000
PO Box 316, Brisbane QLD 4000
Phone: 07 3224 2211, 1800 177 577, TTY 07 3321 3343
Fax: 1800 656 122

Cairns
Women's Information and Referral Centre
230 Mulgrave Street

Cairns QLD 4870
Phone: 07 4051 9366

South Australia

Women's Information Service
122 Kintore Avenue
Adelaide SA 5000
Phone: 08 8207 7677, 1800 188 158, TTY 08 8232 1453
Fax: 08 8207 7676

Tasmania

Office of the Status of Women
Franklin Square
Corner Macquarie and Murray Streets
Hobart TAS 7000
Phone: 03 6233 2208, 1800 001 377
Fax: 03 6223 8807

Victoria

Women's Information and Referral Exchange
1st floor, 247 Flinders Lane
Melbourne VIC 3000
Phone: 03 9654 6844, 1800 136 570, TTY 03 9654 5124
Fax: 03 9654 6831
Email: wire@vicnet.net.au
Homepage: http://www.vicnet.net.au/-wire

Western Australia

Women's Information Service
Women's Policy Development Office
1st floor, West Australia Square
141 St George's Terrace
Perth WA 6000
Phone: 08 9264 1900, 1800 199 174, TTY 08 9264 1900
Fax: 08 9264 1925

Family Planning Clinics

For information on contraception, pregnancy termination, and other women's health and screening matters, you can't go past the Family Planning Clinics. Here are their head offices. Phone for a service nearer you.

Australian Capital Territory

Health Promotion Centre
Childers Street
Canberra ACT 2600
GPO Box 1317
Canberra City ACT 2601
Phone: 02 6247 3077
Fax: 02 6257 5710
Email: fpact@atrax.net.au

New South Wales

328–336 Liverpool Road
Ashfield NSW 2131
Phone: 02 9716 6099
Fax: 02 9716 6164

Northern Territory

Shop 11, Shopping Village
Rapid Creek NT 0810
Phone: 08 8948 1044,
1800 193 121
Fax: 08 8948 0626

Queensland

100 Alfred Street
Fortitude Valley QLD 4006
Phone: 07 3252 5151
Fax: 07 3854 1277

South Australia

17 Phillips Street
Kensington SA 5068
Phone: 08 8431 5177
Fax: 08 8364 2389

Tasmania

PO Box 77
North Hobart TAS 7002
Phone: 03 6234 7200, 1800 007 119

Victoria

901 Whitehorse Road
Box Hill VIC 3128
Phone: 03 9257 0100
Fax: 03 9257 0110

Western Australia

70 Roe Street
Northbridge WA 6865
Phone: 08 9227 6177, 1800 198 205
Fax: 08 9227 6871
Email: sexhelp@fpwa-health.org.au

Women's health care centres

For help in locating services and finding support groups and information about medical conditions. Call the relevant numbers to find local contacts in your suburb, district or town.

Australian Capital Territory

Women's Health Service
Corner Moore and Alinga Streets

Canberra City ACT 2601
Phone: 02 6205 1078
Fax: 02 6205 1394

New South Wales

Women's Medical Centre
Room 10, 2nd floor, 193 Macquarie Street
Sydney NSW 2000
Phone: 02 9231 2366
Fax: 02 9233 1020

Northern Territory

Darwin Hospital
Rockland Drive
Tiwi NT 0810
Phone: 08 8922 8888

Queensland

Women's Health Queensland Wide
165 Gregory Terrace
Springhill QLD 4000
Phone: 07 3839 9988, 1800 017 676, TTY 07 3831 5508
Fax: 07 3831 7214
Email: whcb@gil.com.au
Homepage: http://www.womhealth.org.au

South Australia

Women's Health Statewide
64 Pennington Terrace
North Adelaide SA 5006
Phone: 08 8267 5366, 1800 182 098
Fax: 08 8267 5597
Email: whs@peg.apc.org

Tasmania

Women's Health Centre
326 Elizabeth Street
North Hobart TAS 7000
Phone: 03 6231 3212
Fax: 03 6236 9449
Email: hwhc@trump.net.au
Homepage:http://www.tased.au/tasonline.hwhc/hwhc.htm

Victoria

Women's Health Victoria
Queen Victoria Women's Centre
2nd floor, 210 Lonsdale Street
Melbourne VIC 3000
GPO Box 1160K, Melbourne VIC 3001
Phone: 03 9662 3755
Fax: 03 9663 7955
Health information line: 03 9662 3742, 1800 133 321
Email: whv@peg.apc.org

Western Australia

Women's Healthcare House
100 Aberdeen Street
Northbridge WA 6003
Phone: 08 9227 8122, 1800 998 399
Fax: 08 9227 6615

Sporting bodies

Juice up your fitness and your immune system. Pick a sport, any sport and track down a local team through one of these organisations.

National

Women and Sport Unit
Australian Sports Commission

Levrerier Crescent
Belconnen ACT 2616
Phone: 02 6252 1522
Fax: 02 6252 1649

Australian Capital Territory

Womensport Australia
26 Brigalow St
O'Connor ACT 2602
Phone and fax: 02 6257 1402

New South Wales

Strategic Planning and Policy Unit
NSW Department of Sport, Recreation and Racing
MLC Building, 105–153 Miller Street
North Sydney NSW 2060
Phone: 02 9923 4300
Fax: 02 9923 4345

Northern Territory

Aussie Sport
Participation Branch, Department of Sport and Recreation
Sports House, Waratah Crescent
Fannie Bay NT 0820
Phone: 08 8982 2301
Fax: 08 8982 2320

Alice Springs
PO Box 1095
Alice Springs 0871
Phone: 08 8951 5326
Fax: 08 8951 5330

Queensland

Sport and Recreation Development Section
Office of Sport and Recreation
Department of Emergency Services
3rd floor, 85 George Street
Brisbane QLD 4000
GPO Box 354, Brisbane QLD 4000
Phone: 07 3237 9830
Fax: 07 3237 9879

South Australia

Women's Consultant
Department for Recreation and Sport
27 Valetta Road
Kidman Park SA 5025
Phone: 08 8416 6677
Fax: 08 8416 6753
Email: robertson.judith@saugov.sa.gov.au

Womensport and Recreation (SA) Inc.
1 Sturt Street
Adelaide SA 5000
Phone: 08 8410 1404
Fax: 08 8211 7115
Email: womsport@dove.net.au
Homepage: http://dove.net.au/~womsport

Tasmania

Office of Sport and Recreation Tasmania
13th floor, 110 Collins Street
Hobart TAS 7000
Phone: 03 6230 8325
Fax: 03 6230 8333

Sportswomen's Association of Australia (Tasmania)
GPO Box 773
Sandy Bay TAS 7005

Victoria

Women and Sport Consultant
Sport and Recreation Victoria
Level 3, 55 Collins Street
Melbourne VIC 3000
Phone: 03 9666 4358
Fax: 03 9666 4266

Women, Sport and Recreation Victoria
Level 3, 489 Elizabeth Street
Melbourne VIC 3000
Phone: 03 9329 4646
Fax: 03 9329 4647

Western Australia

Women's Sport Foundation of WA
Womensport West
Ministry of Sport and Recreation
Sir Thomas Meagher Pavilion, Meagher Drive
Floreat WA 6014
PO Box 66, Wembley WA 6014
Phone: 08 9387 9757
Fax: 08 9387 5641
Email: wswest@wamsr.ausport.gov.au

Cancer organisations

These mobs will have all the guff you need on breast checks, breast cancer, Pap tests, cervical cancer, ovarian cancer, support groups, and all other bits and pieces related to the Big Cs and the little cs.

Australian Capital Territory

ACT Cancer Society
15 Theodore Street
Curtin ACT 2605

PO Box 316, Curtin ACT 2605
Phone: 02 6285 3070
Fax: 02 6285 3221

Northern Territory

Cancer Council of the Northern Territory
Unit 3, 23 Vaderlin Drive
Casuarina NT 0810
Phone: 08 8927 4888
Fax: 08 8927 4990
Email: uvstop@cancernt.org.au

New South Wales

Cancer Information Service (CIS)
NSW State Cancer Council
153 Dowling Street
Woolloomooloo NSW 2011
Phone: 13 1120, 1800 422 760
Fax: 02 9357 2676

Queensland

Queensland Cancer Fund
553 Gregory Terrace
Fortitude Valley QLD 4006
Phone: 07 3258 2200
Fax: 07 3257 1306

South Australia

Anti-Cancer Foundation of the Universities of South Australia
202 Greenhill Road
Eastwood SA 5063
Phone: 08 8291 4111
Fax: 08 8291 4122
Homepage: http://www.acf.org.au

Tasmania

Cancer Council of Tasmania
13 Liverpool Street
Hobart TAS 7000
Phone: 03 6233 2030
Fax: 03 6233 2123
Email: ccth@info.tas.gov.au

Victoria

Cancer Information Service (CIS)
Anti-Cancer Council of Victoria
1 Rathdowne Street
Carlton South VIC 3053
Phone: 03 9279 1111, 13 1120
Fax: 03 9279 1270

Western Australia

Cancer Foundation of Western Australia
334 Rokeby Road
Subiaco WA 6008
Phone: 08 9381 4515
Fax: 08 9381 4523

NOTES

Chapter 1 Introduction

First period kills caterpillars: Bennett, J, 1991. *Lilies of the Hearth*. Camden House, Ontario, Canada. p 26. **Remedies of the Middle Ages:** Rowland, B, 1981. *Medieval Woman's Guide to Health: the first English gynecological handbook*. Kent State University Press, Kent, Ohio. **Harvard professor's theory:** Bullough, V, Voght, M, 1973. 'Women, menstruation and nineteenth-century medicine' *Bull Hist Med*. 47: pp 66–82. **1990s theory on:** Toufexis, A, 1993. 'A woman's best defense?' *Time*. Oct 4: pp 60–1. **Lunatic leopardskin period undies with red gusset available from Bloom:** telephone 1–800–068870.

Chapter 2 When things go right

Period symptoms diary: adapted from Abraham, GE, 1983. 'Nutritional Factors in the Etiology of the Premenstrual Tension Syndromes' *J Reprod Med.* 28: pp 446–64.

Chapter 3 It's your hormones, dear

Chemicals which affect oestrogen: Soto, AM, Chung, KL, Sonnerschein, C, 1994. 'The pesticides endosulphan, toxaphene, and dieldrin have estrogenic effects on human estrogen-sensitive cells' *Environ Health Perspect*. 102(4): pp 380–3; Robinson, AK, Schmidt, WA, Stancel, GM, 1985. 'Estrogenic activity of DDT: estrogen-receptor profiles and the responses of individual uterine cell types following o,p'-DDT administration' *J Toxicol Environ*

Health. 16(3–4): pp 493–508; Truelove, JF, Tanner, JR, Langlois, IA, et al, 1990. 'Effect of polychlorinated biphenyls on several endocrine reproductive parameters in the female rhesus monkey' *Arch Environ Contam Toxicol*. 19(6): pp 939–43; Soto, AM, Justicia, H, Wray, JW, et al, 1991. 'p-Nonyl-phenol: an estrogenic xenobiotic released from 'modified' polystyrene' *Environ Health Perspect*. 92: pp 167–73; Brotons, JA, Olea-Serrano, MF, Villalobos, M, et al, 1995. 'Xenoestrogens released from lacquer coatings in food cans' *Environ Health Perspect*. 103(6): pp 608–12. **Research on insecticides and cancer:** Adami, HO, Lipworth, L, Titus-Ernstoff, L, et al, 1995. 'Organochlorine compounds and estrogen-related cancers in women' *Cancer Causes Control*. 6(6): pp 551–66; Krieger, N, Wolff, MS, Hiatt, RA, et al, 1994. 'Breast cancer and serum organochlorines: a prospective study among white, black, and Asian women' *J Natl Cancer Inst*. 86(8): pp 589–99. **DDT in fibroid tissue:** Saxena, SP, Khare, C, Farooq, A, et al, 1987. 'DDT and its metabolites in leiomyomatous and normal human uterine tissue' *Arch Toxicol*. 59(6): pp 453–5; **Chemicals and male fertility:** Sharpe, RM, Skakkebaek, NE, 1993. 'Are oestrogens involved in falling sperm counts and disorders of the male reproductive tract?' *Lancet*. 341(8857): pp 1392–5. **Too much oestrogen—associated with endometriosis, fibroids:** Rzempoluch, J, Kaminski, BT, Wawryk, R, 1989. 'Serum levels of some fat metabolism parameters in women with uterine leiomyoma' *Zentralbl-Gynakol*. 111(12): pp 831–6. **with fibrocystic breast disease:** Parlati, E, Travaglini, A, Liberale, I, et al, 1988. 'Hormonal profile in benign breast disease. Endocrine status of cyclical mastalgia patients' *J Endocrinol Invest*. 11(9): pp 679–83. **With breast and endometrial cancer:** Cramer, DW, Wilson, E, Stillman, RJ, et al, 1986. 'The relation of endometriosis to menstrual characteristics, smoking, and exercise' *JAMA*. 255(14): pp 1904–8. **Eating fat and oestrogen levels:** Goldin, BR, Adlercreutz, H, Gorbach, SL, et al, 1986. 'The relationship between estrogen levels and diets of Caucasian American and Oriental immigrant women' *Am J Clin Nutr*. 44(6): pp 945–53. **Reducing fat and oestrogen levels:** Longcope, C, Gorbach, S, Goldin, B, et al, 1987. 'Effect of low fat diet on oestrogen metabolism' *J Clin Endocrinol Metab*. 64(6): pp 1246–9. **Fat and breast cancer:** Colditz, GA, 1993. 'Epidemiology of breast cancer. Findings from the nurses' health study' *Cancer*. 71(4 Suppl): pp 1480–9. **Fat and fibroids:** Ross, RK, Pike, MC, Vessey, MP, et al, 1986. 'Risk factors for uterine fibroids: reduced risk associated with oral contraceptives' *Br Med J Clin Res Ed*. 293(6543): pp 359–62. **Fat and endometriosis:** McCann, SE, Freudenheim, JL, Darrow, SL, et al, 1993. 'Endometriosis and body fat distribution' *Obstet Gynecol*. 82(4 Pt 1): pp 545–9. **Obesity and oestrogen-related disease:** Chu, SY, Lee, NC, Wingo, PA, et al, 1991. 'The relationship between body mass and breast cancer among women enrolled in the Cancer and Steroid Hormone Study' *J Clin Epidemiol*. 44(11): pp 1197–206; Austin, H, Austin, JM, Partridge, EE, et al, 1991. 'Endometrial cancer, obesity and body fat distribution' *Cancer Res*. 51(2): pp 568–72.

Cultured milk products and yoghurt associated with lower breast cancer risk: van't Veer, P, Dekker, JM, Lamers, JWJ, et al, 1989. 'Consumption of fermented milk products and breast cancer: a case-control study in the Netherlands' *Cancer Res*. 49: pp 4020–3. **Higher protein and liver metabolism of oestrogen:** Anderson, KE, Kappas, A, Conney, AH, et al, 1984. 'The influence of dietary protein on the principal oxidative biotransformations of estradiol in normal subjects' *J Clin Endocrinol Metab*. 59(1): pp 103–7. **Breast cancer and vitamin B6:** Bell, E, 1980. 'The excretion of a vitamin B6 metabolite and the probability of recurrence of early breast cancer' *Eur J Cancer*. 16: pp 297–8. **Alcohol and cancers:** Webster, LA, Weiss, NS, 1989. 'Alcoholic beverage consumption and the risk of endometrial cancer. Cancer and Steroid Hormone Study Group'. *Int J Epidemiol*. 18(4): pp 786–91; Byers, T, 1994. 'Nutritional risk factors for breast cancer'. *Cancer* (Suppl). 74(1): pp 288–95. **Low body weight and oestrogen:** Mishell, DR, Davajan, V, 1994. 'Differential diagnosis of secondary amenorrhea' *Management of Common Problems in Obstetrics and Gynecology*, eds DR Mishell, PF Brenner, Blackwell Scientific Publications, Boston. p 607. **Fibre and osteoporosis:** Feng, W, Marshall, R, Lewis-Barned, NJ, et al, 1993. 'Low follicular oestrogen levels in New Zealand women consuming high fibre diets: a risk factor for osteopenia?' *NZ Med J*. 106(965): pp 419–22. **Overexercise:** Snow-Harter, CM, 1994. 'Bone health and prevention of osteoporosis in active and athletic women' *Clin Sports Med*. 13(2): pp 389–404. **Smoking:** Baron, JA, La Vecchia, C, Levi, F, 1990. 'The antiestrogenic effect of cigarette smoking in women' *Am J Obstet Gynecol*. 162(2): pp 502–14. **Steroidal saponins:** Johnson, IT, Gee, JM, Price, KR, 1986. 'Influence of saponins on gut permeability and active nutritive transport in vitro' *J Nutr*. 116: pp 2270–7; Manilow, MR, 1984. 'Saponins and cholesterol metabolism' *Athersclerosis*. 50: pp 117–18. **Basal body temperature success rates:** Shoupe, D, Mishell, DR, LaCarra, M, 1989. 'Correlation of endometrial maturation with 4 methods of estimating day of ovulation' *Obstet Gynecol*. 73: pp 88–92. **Progesterone blood tests:** Filicori, M, Butler, JP, Crowley, WR, 1984. 'Neuroendocrine regulation of the corpus luteum in the human' *J Clin Invest*. 73: p 1638. **Wild yam creams did not produce progesterone boost:** Dr CM Dollbaum, MD, PhD, Medical Director of the Aeron LifeCycles Laboratory, California: 'we find no evidence that the Mexican Yam either directly or through conversion in the body provides progesterone, progestin activity or DHEA. If these products are clinically effective they must be working through other mechanisms.' Dollbaum, CM, 1996. 'Lab analyses of alivary DHEA and progesterone following ingestion of yam-containing products' *Townsend Letter For Doctors and Patients*, Oct. p 104. **Prostaglandins—Prostaglandin causes heavier blood loss:** Kelly, RW, Lumsden, MA, Abel, MH, et al, 1984. 'The relationship between menstrual blood loss and prostaglandin production in the human: evidence for increased availability of arachidonic acid in women suffering from menorrhagia' *Prost Leuk Med*. 16: pp 69–77. **Prostaglandins causing cramps:**

Kelly, RW, Lumsden, MA, et al, 1984. 'The relationship between menstrual blood loss and prostaglandin production in the human: evidence for increased availability of arachidonic acid in women suffering from menorrhagia' *Prost Leuk Med*. 16: pp 69–77. **Leukotrine levels and period pain:** Nigam, S, Benedetto, C, Zonca, M, 1991. 'Increased concentrations of eicosanoids and platelet-activating factor in menstrual blood from women with primary dysmenorrhoea' *Eicosanoids*. 4(3): pp 137–41. **Leukotrine, white cells and endometriosis:** Pungetti, D, Lenzi, M, Travisani, D, 1987. 'Prostanoids in peritoneal fluid of infertile women with pelvic endometriosis and PID' *Acta Eur Fertil*. 18(3): pp 189–92. **Leukotrine and breast cancer:** Abou-el-Ela, SH, Prasse, KW, Farrell, KW, et al, 1989. 'Effects of D,L–2-difluoromethylornitnine and indomethacin on mammary tumour promotion in rats fed high n–3 and/or n–6 fat diets' *Cancer Res*. 49(6): pp 1434–40.

Chapter 4 Starting out

Adolescence—body weight needed for periods to start and continue: Frisch, RE, 1990. 'The right weight: body fat, menarche and ovulation' *Baillieres Clin Obstet Gynaecol*. 4(3): pp 419–39.

Chapter 5 When things go wrong

The usual suspects—family attitudes and periods: Dramusic, V, Marjanovic, B, Erceg, J, 1974. 'Dysmenorrhea in adolescence caused by disturbed family relations' *The Family. Fourth International Congress of Psychosomatic Obstetrics and Gynecology*, ed SL Smith, Tel Aviv, Karger, Basel. pp 503–6. **Zinc and eating disorders:** Schauss, AG, Bryce-Smith, D, 1987. 'Evidence of zinc deficiency in anorexia nervosa and bulimia nervosa' *Nutrients and Brain Function*, ed WB Essman, Karger, Basel. pp 151–62. **Iron and vitamin B12, anaemia and heavy periods:** Taymor, ML, et al, 1964. 'The etiological role of chronic iron deficiency in production of menorrhagia' *JAMA*. 187: pp 323–7. **Exercise and period flow:** Harlow, SD, Campbell, BC, 1994. 'Host factors that influence the duration of menstrual bleeding' *Epidemiology*. May, 5(3): pp 352–5. **and endometriosis:** Barbieri, RL, 1990. 'Etiology and epidemiology of endometriosis' *Am J Obstet Gynecol*. Feb, 162(2): pp 565–7. **and breasts:** Wetzig, NR, 1994. 'Mastalgia: A 3 year Australian study' *Aust NZ J Surg*. 64: pp 329–31. **and timing:** Krolner, B, Toft, B, Nielson, S, et al, 1983. 'Physical exercise as prophylaxis against involutional vertebral bone loss: A controlled trial' *Clin Sci*. 64: pp 541–6; Chow, RK, Harrison, JE, Notarius, C, 1987. 'Effect of two randomised exercise programmes on bone mass of healthy postmenopausal women' *Br Med J*. 292: pp 607–10. **and book by Debbie Flintoff-King,** 1995. *Instant Vitality*. Published by Anne O'Donovan, Melbourne. **and bones:** Constantini, NW, Warren, MP, 1994. 'Special problems of the female athlete' *Baillieres Clin Rheumatol*. 8(1): pp 199–219. **and retrograde period flow:** Han, M, Pan, L, Wu, B, et al, 1994. 'A case-control epidemiologic study of endometriosis' *Chin Med Sci J*. Jun, 9(2): pp 114–18; Pan, LY, 1993. 'Menstrual status as risk factors of endometriosis: a case controlled study' *Chung Hua Fa Chan Ko Tsa Chih*. Mar, 28(3): pp 147–9, 188. **Over-exercise and stopped periods:** Elias, AN, Wilson, AF, 1993. 'Exercise and gonadal function' *Hum Reprod*. 8(10): pp 1747–61; Mira, M, Abraham, S, 1985. 'Amenorrhoea in female runners. What are the problems?' *Patient Management*. Sept, pp 25–31. **Athlete nutritional needs:** Hetland, ML, Haarbo, J, Christiansen, C, et al, 1994. 'Bone metabolism in female runners. Menstruation disorders are frequent among long-distance runners, but the bone mass is not influenced, with the exception of runners with amenorrhea' *Ugeskr-Laeger*. Nov 28, 156(48): pp 7219–23. **Coffee and infertility:** Grodstein, F, Goldman, MB, Ryan, L, 1993. 'Relation of female infertility to consumption of caffeinated beverages' *Am J Epidemiol*. Jun, 137(12): pp 1353–60. **Alcohol and infertility:** Grodstein, F, Goldman, MB, Cramer, DW, 1994. 'Infertility in women and moderate alcohol use' *Am J Public Health*. Sep, 84(9): pp 1429–32. **and early menopause:** Grodstein, F, Goldman, MB, Cramer, DW, 1994. 'Infertility in women and moderate alcohol use' *Am J Public Health*. Sep, 84(9): pp 1429–32. **and prolactin:** Alfonso, M, Marco, J, Balvis, IA, 1991. 'Direct action of ethanol on pituitary prolactin secretion in vitro' *Rev Esp Fisiol*. Sep, 47(3): pp 133–40. **Smoking and periods:** Baron, JA, La Vecchia, C, Levi, F, 1990. 'The antiestrogenic effect of cigarette smoking in women' *Am J Obstet Gynecol*. 162: pp 502–14. **Cocaine:** Kranzler, HR, Wallington, DJ, 1992. 'Serum prolactin level, craving, and early discharge from treatment in cocaine-dependent patients' *Am J Drug Alcohol Abuse*. 18(2), pp 187–95. **Methadone and periods:** Goodman, Gilman, A, Rall, TW, Nies, AS, et al, eds, 1992. *Goodman & Gilman's: The Pharmacological Basis of Therapeutics,* Eighth Edition. Published by McGraw-Hill International Editions, Singapore, p 533. **Functional hypoglycaemia—refined carbohydrates and sugars:** Sanders, LR, Hofeldt, FD, Kirk, MC, et al, 1982. 'Refined carbohydrate as a contributing factor in reactive hypoglycemia' *South Med J*. 75(9): pp 1072–5. **Alcohol:** O'Keefe, S, Marks, V, 1977. 'Lunchtime gin and tonic as a cause of reactive hypoglycemia' *Lancet*. 1(8025): pp 1286–8. **Blood sugar level drops:** Marsoobian, V, Grosvenor, M, Jacob, M, et al, 1995. 'Very-low-energy diets alter the counterregulatory response to falling plasma glucose concentrations' *Am J Clin Nutr*. Feb, 61(2): pp 373–8. **Chromium:** Anderson, RA, Polansky, MM, Bryden, NA, et al, 1987. 'Effects of supplemental chromium on patients with symptoms of reactive hypoglycemia' *Metabolism*. Apr, 36(4): pp 351–5. **Niacinamide:** Shansky, A, 1981. 'Vitamin B3 in the alleviation of hypoglycemia' *Drug and Cosmetic Industry*. 129(4): p 68. **Magnesium:** 1982. *Magnesium Bulletin*. 4(2). **PMS—five sub-groups of PMS:** Abraham, G, 1983. 'Nutritional factors in the etiology of the premenstrual tension syndromes' *J Reprod Med*. 28(7): pp 446–64. **Oestrogen excess theory:** Hammerback, S, Damer, JE, Backstrom, T, 1989. 'Relationship between symptom severity and hormone changes in women with premenstrual syndrome' *J Clin Endocr Metab*. 68: pp 125–30. **Fluid retention in PMS:** 'Backstrom, T, Carstensen, H, 1974. 'Estrogen and progesterone in plasma in relation to premenstrual tension' *J Ster Biochem*. 5: pp 257–60; Munday, MR, Brush, MG, Taylor, RW, 1981. 'Correlations between progesterone, estradiol, and aldosterone levels in the premenstrual syndrome' *Clin Endocrinol*. 14: pp 1–9; Rubinow, DR, Hoban, MC, Grover, GN, 1988. 'Changes in plasma hormones across the menstrual cycle in patients with menstrually related mood disorder and in control subjects' *Am J Obstet Gynecol*. 158: pp 5–11. **Faulty progesterone receptors:** Dalton, K, 1990. 'The aetiology of premenstrual syndrome is with the progesterone receptors'. *Med Hypotheses*. 31: pp 323–7; Merraim, GR, Brody, SA, Almedia, OF, 1983. 'Endocrinology of the menstrual cycle: Implication for premenstrual syndrome' *Proceedings of the National Institute of Mental Health Premenstrual Syndrome Workshop*, National Institute of Mental Health, Bethesda, MD; Nock, B, 1986. 'Noradrenergic regulation of progestin receptors: New findings' *Reproduction: A Behavioural and Neuroendocrine Perspective*, eds BR Komusaruk, et al, Annals New York Acad Sci, New York, pp 415–22. **Prostaglandins:** Lurie, S, Borenstein, R. 1990. 'The premenstrual syndrome' *Obst Gyn Surv*. 45(4): pp 220–8; Puolakka, J, Makarainen, L, Viinikka, L, et al, 1985. 'Biochemical and clinical effects of treating the premenstrual syndrome with prostaglandin synthesis precursors' *J Reprod Med*. 30(3): pp 149–53; Mira, M, McNell, D, Fransen, IS, et al, 1986. 'Mefenamic acid in the treatment of premenstrual syndrome' *Obstet Gynecol*. 68: pp 395–8. **Nutrients:** van den Berg, H, Louwerse, ES, Bruinse, HW, et al, 1986. 'Vitamin B6 status of women suffering from premenstrual syndrome' *Hum Nutr Clin Nutr*. 40C: pp 441–50. **Vitamin B6 40–200 milligrams a day:** Williams, MJ, Harris, RI, Dean, BC, 1985. 'Controlled trial of pyridoxine in the premenstrual syndrome' *J Int Med Res*. 13: pp 174–9; Brush, MG, Bennet, T, Hansen, K, 1988. 'Pyridoxine in the treatment of premenstrual syndrome: a retrospective survey of 630 patients' *Br J Clin Prac*. 42(11): pp 448–52. **Vitamin B6 300 mg a day with diet:** Fuchs, N, Hakim, M, Abraham, GE, 1985. 'The effect of a nutritional supplement, Optivite for women, on pre-menstrual tension syndromes: 1. Effect on blood chemistry and serum steroid levels during the mid luteal phase' *J Appl Nutr*. 37: pp 1–11. **Vitamin B6 doses and nerve damage absence:** Parry, GJ, Bredesen, DE, 1985. 'Sensory neuropathy with low-dose pyridoxine' *Neurology*. 35: pp 1466–8. **Vitamin E:** Chuong, JC, Dawson, EB, Smith, ER, et al, 1990. 'Vitamin E levels in premenstrual syndrome' *Am J Obstet Gynecol*. 163: pp 1591–5. **Vitamin A:** Chuong, JC, Dawson, EB, Smith, ER, 1990. 'Vitamin A levels in premenstrual syndrome' *Fertil Steril*. 54(4): pp 643–7. **Magnesium levels:** Abraham, GE, Lubran, MM, 1981. 'Serum and red cell magnesium levels in patients with PMT' *Am J Clin Nut*. 34: pp 2364–6; Sherwood, RA, Rocks, BF, Stewart, A, et al, 1986. 'Magnesium and the premenstrual syndrome' *Ann Clin Biochem*. 23: pp 667–70; Facchinetti, F, Borella, P, Valentini, M, et al, 1988. 'Premenstrual increase of intracellular magnesium levels in women with ovulatory, asymptomatic menstrual cycles' *Gynecol Endocrinol*. 2: pp 249–56. **Magnesium and specific symptom relief:** Facchinetti, F, Borella, P, Sances, G, et al, 1991. 'Oral magnesium successfully relieves premenstrual mood changes' *Obstet Gynecol*. 78: pp 177–81. **Vitamin E and breasts:** London, RS, Sundaram, GS, Murphy, L, 1983. 'Evaluation and treatment of breast symptoms in patients with the premenstrual syndrome' *J Reprod Med*. 28: pp 503–8. **and other symptoms:** London, RS, Sundaram, GS, Murphy, L, et al, 1982. 'The effect of alpha tocopherol on premenstrual symptomatology: a double-blind trial' *J Am Coll Nutr*. 2: pp 115–22; London, RS, Murphy, L, Kitlowski, K, et al, 1987. 'Efficacy of alpha-tocopherol in the treatment of premenstrual syndrome' *J Reprod Med*: 32: pp 400–4. **Vitamin B6 2–6 grams a day:** Parry, GJ, Bredesen, DE, 1985. 'Sensory neuropathy with low-dose pyridoxine' *Neurology*. 35: pp 1466–8. **Five subcategories of PMS:** Abraham, GE, 1983. 'Nutritional factors in the etiology of premenstrual tension syndrome' *J Reprod Med*. 28(7): pp 446–64. **Evening primrose oil with linolenic and gamma linolenic acid:** Puolakka, J, Makarainen, L, Viinikka, L, et al, 1985. 'Biochemical and clinical effects of treating the premenstrual syndrome with prostaglandin synthesis precursors' *J Reprod Med*. 30(3): pp 149–53. **Magnesium:** Abraham, G, 1983. 'Nutritional factors in the etiology of the premenstrual tension syndromes' *J Reprod Med*. 28(7): pp 446–64. **Pelvic congestion syndrome and stress:** Merzow, G, 1994. 'Dysmenorrhoea' *Management of Common Problems in Obstetrics and Gynecology*, eds DR Mishell, PF Brenner, Blackwell Scientific Publications, Boston. p 425. **and bioflavonoids:** Werbach, MR, Murray, MT, 1994. *Botanical Influences on Illness*. Third Line Press, California. p 307. **Heavy periods—prostaglandins:** Smith, SK, Abel, MH, Kelly, RW, et al, 1981. 'A role for prostacyclin (PGI2) in excessive menstrual bleeding' *Lancet*. 1: pp 522–5. **Prostaglandins-inhibiting drugs:** Mezrow, G, 1994. 'Treatment of dysfunctional uterine bleeding' *Management of Common Problems in Obstetrics and Gynecology*, eds DR Mishell, PF Brenner, Blackwell Scientific Publ., Boston. p 444. **Prescribed progestogens:** Smith, SK, Abel, MH, Kelly, RW, et al, 1981. 'A role for prostacyclin (PGI2) in excessive menstrual bleeding' *Lancet*. 1: pp 522–5. **Iron deficiency or anaemia:** Taymor, ML, Sturgis, SH, Yahia, C, 1964. 'The role of chronic iron deficiency in production of menorrhagia' *JAMA*. 187(5): pp 323–7. **Vitamin A:** Siddiqui, NA, Loughney, A, Thomas, EJ, et al, 1994. 'Cellular retinoid binding proteins and nuclear retinoic acid receptors in endometrial cells' *Hum Reprod*. 9(8): pp 1410–6; Lithgow, DM, Politzer, WM, 1977. 'Vitamin A in the treatment of menorrhagia' *S Afr Med J*. 51(7): pp 191–3. **Vitamin K:** Pizzorno, JE, Murray, MT, 1985. 'Menorrhagia' *A Textbook of Natural Medicine*. John Bastyr College Publications, Seattle Washington. pp VI:Menorr, 1–4; Gubner, R, Ungerleider, HE, 1944. 'Vitamin K therapy in menorrhagia' *South Med J*. 36(10): pp 556–8. **Vitamin K and antibiotics:** Cohen, H, Scott, SD, Mackie, IJ, et al, 1988. 'The development of hypoprothrombinaemia following antibiotic therapy in malnourished patients with low serum vitamin K1 levels' *Br J Haematol*. Jan, 68(1): pp 63–6; Schentag, JJ, Welage, LS, Grasela, TH, et al, 1987. 'Determinants of antibiotic-associated hyprothrombinaemia' *Pharmocotherapy*. 7(3): pp 80–6. **Flavonoids in herbs:** Havsteen, B, 1983. 'Flavonoids, a class of natural products of high pharmacological potency' *Bioch Pharm*. 32(7): pp 1141–8. **and oestrogen:** Markaverich, BM, Roberts, RR, Aleindro, MA, et al, 1988. 'Bioflavonoid interaction with rat uterine type II binding sites and cell growth inhibition' *J Steroid Biochem*. 30(1–6): pp 71–8; Ibrahim, AR, Abul-Hajj, YJ, 1990. 'Aromatase inhibition by flavonoids' *J Steroid Biochem Mol Biol*. 37(2): pp 257–60. **Plant oestrogens and periods:** Cassidy, A, Bingham, S, Setchell, KDR, 1994. 'Biological effects of a diet of soy protein rich in isoflavones on the menstrual cycle of premenopausal women' *Am J Clin Nutr*. 60: pp 333–40. **Uterine fibroids—women over 35:** March, CM, 1994. 'Uterine leiomyomas' *Management of Common Problems in Obstetrics and Gynecology*, eds DR Mishell, PF Brenner. Blackwell Scientific Publications, Boston. p 467. **Excess oestrogen:** Christiansen, JK, 1993. 'The facts about fibroids' *Postgrad Med*. 94(3): pp 129–37. **DDT:** Saxena, SP, Khare, C, Farooq, A, et al, 1987. 'DDT and its metabolites in leiomyomatous and normal human uterine tissue' *Arch Toxicol*. 59(6): pp 453–5. **Pregnancy:** Ross, RK, Pike, MC, Vessey, MP, et al, 1986. 'Risk factors for uterine fibroids: reduced risk associated with oral contraceptives' *Br Med J Clin Res Ed*. 293(6543): pp 359–62. **Coffee:** Stalder, R, Bexter, A, Wurzner, HP, et al, 1990. 'A carcinogenicity study of instant coffee in Swiss mice' *Food Chem Toxicol*. 28(12): pp 829–37. **The Pill:** Drife, J, 1990. 'Benefits and risks of oral contraceptives' *Adv Contracept*. 6 Suppl: pp 15–25; Parazzini, F, La Vecchia, C, Negri, E, et al, 1988. 'Epidemiologic characteristics of women with uterine fibroids: a case-control study' *Obstet Gynecol*. 72(6): pp 853–7; Parrazini, F, Negri, E, La Vecchia, et al, 1992. 'Oral contraceptive use and risk of uterine fibroids' *Obstet Gynecol*. 79(3): pp 430–3; Schesselman, JJ, 1991. 'Oral contraceptives and neoplasia of the uterine corpus' *Contraception*. 43(6): pp 557–79. **Herbal regulation of oestrogen excess:** Sakamoto, S, Yoshino, H, Shirahata, Y, et al, 1992. 'Pharmacotherapeutic effects of Kuei-chih-fu-ling-wan (Keishi-bukuryo-gan) on human uterine myomas' *Am J Chin Med*. 20(3–4): pp 313–17. **Dysfunctional uterine bleeding—Vitex agnus castus use and ovulation:** Cahill, DJ, Fox, R, Wardle, PG, et al, 1994. 'Multiple follicular development associated with herbal medicine' *Hum Reprod*. (United Kingdom). 9(8): pp 1469–70. **and the luteal phase:** Kayser, HW, Istanbulluoglu, S, 1954. 'Eine Behandlung von Menstruations-storungen ohne Hormone' *Hippokrates*. 25: pp 717–18; Probst, V, Roth, OA, 1954. 'Uber einen Pflanzenextrakt mit hormonartiger Wirkung' *Dtsch Med Wschr*. 79: pp 1271–6. **Endometrial hyperplasia— endometrial cancer:** Rivlin, ME, 1994. 'Endometrial hyperplasia' *Manual of Clinical Problems in Obstetrics and Gynecology*, eds ME Rivlin, RW Martin, Little, Brown and Company, Boston. pp 433–7. **SHBG levels reduced:** Lobo, RA, Kletzky, OA, 1982. 'Normalisation of androgen and sex hormone binding globulin levels after treatment of hyperprolactinaemia' *J Clin Endocrinol Metab*. 56: p 562. **Hyperprolactinaemia—adrenal elevation without hairiness:** Lobo, RA, Kletzky, OA, 1982. 'Normalisation of androgen and sex hormone binding globulin levels after treatment of hyperprolactinaemia' *J Clin Endocrinol Metab*. 56: p 562. **Low bone density regardless of oestrogen:** Schlechte, JA, Sherman, B, Martin, R, 1983. 'Bone density in amenorrheic women with and without hyperprolactinaemia' *J Clin Endocrinol Metab*. 56: p 1120. **Rehmannia Eight Combination and pregnancy:** Usuki, S, Usuki, Y, 1989. 'Hachimijiogan treatment is effective in the management of infertile women with hyperprolactinaemia or bromocriptine-resistant hyperprolactinaemia' *Am J Chin Med*. XVII(3–4): pp 225–41. **and dopamine, oestrogen:** Ota, H, Fukushima, M, 'Stimulation by Kanpo prescriptions of aromatase activity in rat follicle cell cultures' *Recent Advances in the Practice of Kanpo (Japanese Herbal) Medicines*, eds E Hosoya, Y Yamamura, Exerpta Medica, Amsterdam. pp 158–62. **Vitex agnus castus and prolactin:** Sluitz, G, Speiser, P, Schultz, AM, et al, 1993. 'Agnus castus extracts inhibit prolactin secretion of rat pituitary cells' *Horm Metab Res*. 25: pp 253–5; Milewicz, A, Gejdel, E, Sworen, H, et al, 1993. '*Vitex agnus castus* in the treatment of luteal phase defects due to latent hyperprolactinaemia: Results of a randomised placebo-controlled double blind study' *Arzneim Forsch Drug Res*. 43(II): pp 752–6. **Bleeding too lightly—chlorosis:** Kellogg, JH, 1902. *The Home Hand-Book of Domestic Hygiene and Rational Medicine*. Echo Publishing Company, Melbourne. **Polycystic ovarian disease—the thyroid:** Insler, V, Lunenfeld, B, 1991. 'Pathophysiology of polycystic ovarian disease: new insights' *Hum Reprod*. 6(8): pp 1025–9. **Weight gain and oestrogen:** Insler, V, Shoman, Z, Barash, A, et al, 1993. 'Polycystic ovaries in non-obese and obese patients: possible pathophysiological mechanisms based on new interpretation of facts and findings' *Hum Reprod*. 8(3): pp 379–84; Anttila, L, Ding, YQ, Ruutianen, K, et al, 1991. 'Clinical features and circulating gonadotrophin, insulin, and androgen interactions in women with polycystic ovarian disease' *Fertil Steril*. 55(6): pp 1057–61. **Body Mass Index and normal cycles:** Eden, Dr JA, 1991. *Women's hormone problems*. Booklet published in conjunction with Royal Hospital for Women, Paddington, NSW: pp 12–13. **Androgen excess—the Pill and blood clot formation:** Thomas, J, ed, 1995. *Australian Prescription Products Guide*. Australian Pharmaceutical Publishing Company Limited, Hawthorn, Australia. **Post-menopause vegetarians:** Armstrong, BK, Brown, JB, Clarke, HT, et al, 1981. 'Diet and reproductive hormones: a study of vegetarian and nonvegetarian postmenopausal women' *J Natl Cancer Inst*. 67: pp 761–7. **and plant oestrogens:** Mousavi, Y, Adleurcreutz, H, 1993. 'Genistein is an effective stimulator of sex hormone-binding globulin production in hepatocarcinoma human liver cells and suppresses proliferation of these cells in culture' *Steroids*. Jul, 58: pp 301–4. **Peony and liquorice combination:** Sakamoto, K, Watanabe, M, Aburada, M, 1988.

'Effect of Shakuyaku-kanzo-to (TJ68) and glycyrrhetinic acid on hyperandrogenism' *Recent Advances in the Practice of Kanpo (Japanese Herbal) Medicines*, eds E Hosoya, Y Yamamura, Exerpta Medica, Amsterdam, pp 163–70. **Endometriosis and adenomyosis—endo returns:** Wardle, PG, Hull, MG, 1993. 'Is endometriosis a disease?' *Baillieres Clin Obstet Gynaecol*. 7(4): pp 673–85. **Family traits:** Moen, MH, Magnus, P, 1993. 'The familial risk of endometriosis' *Acta Obstet Gynecol Scand*. 72(7): pp 560–4. **Long, heavy periods associated with endo; long and irregular cycles associated with lower risk of endo:** Han, M, Pan, L, Wu, B, et al, 1994. 'A case-control epidemiologic study of endometriosis' *Chin Med Sci J*. 9(2): pp 114–8; Parazzini, F, Ferraroni, M, Fedele, L, et al, 1995. 'Pelvic endometriosis: reproductive and menstrual risk factors at different stages in Lombardy, northern Italy' *J Epidemiol Community Health*. 49(1): pp 61–4; Pan, LY, 1993. 'Menstrual status as risk factors of endometriosis: a case controlled study' *Chung Hua Fa Chan Ko Tsa Chih*. 28(3): pp 147–9, 188; Candiani, GB, Danesino, V, Gastaldi, A, et al, 1991. 'Reproductive and menstrual factors and risk of peritoneal and ovarian endometriosis' *Fertil Steril*. 56(2): pp 230–4. **15 to 20% have endo, some have no symptoms:** Moen, MH, Muus, KM, 1991. 'Endometriosis in pregnant and non-pregnant women at tubal sterilization' *Hum Reprod*. 6(5): pp 699–702; Vercellini, P, Crosignani, PG, 1993. 'Minimal and mild endometriosis. Is there anything new under the sun?' *J Reprod Med*. 38(1): pp 49–52. **Only some get pain and infertility:** Evers, JL, 1994. 'Endometriosis does not exist; all women have endometriosis' *Hum Reprod*. 9(12): pp 2206–9. **Endo, prostaglandins and pain:** Koike, H, Egawa, H, Ohtsuka, T, et al, 1992. 'Correlation between dysmenorrheic severity and prostaglandin production in women with endometriosis' *Prost Leukot EFAs*. 46(2): pp 133–7. **Laparoscopy and pain relief:** Sutton, CJ, Ewen, SP, Whitelaw, N, et al, 1994. 'Prospective, randomised, double-blind, controlled trial of laser laparoscopy in the treatment of pelvic pain associated with minimal, mild, and moderate endometriosis' *Fertil Steril*. Oct, 62(4): pp 696–700. **Laser versus laparotomy and diathermy:** Israel, R, 1994. 'Endometriosis: Treatment' *Management of Common Problems in Obstetrics and Gynecology*. eds DR Mishell, PF Brenner, Blackwell Scientific Publications, Boston. **Infertility:** Mahmood, TA, Templeton, A, 1990. 'Pathophysiology of mild endometriosis: review of literature' *Hum Reprod*. 5(7): pp 765–84; Booker, MW, 1988. 'Endometriosis' *Br J Hosp Med*. 39(5): pp 440–5. **Ovulation problems: luteinised unruptured follicle syndrome:** Mio, Y, Toda, T, Harada, T, et al, 1992. 'Luteinized unruptured follicle in the early stages of endometriosis as a cause of unexplained infertility' *Am J Obstet Gynecol*. 167(1): pp 271–3; Holtz, G, Williamson, HO, Mathur, RS, et al, 1985. 'Luteinized unruptured follicle syndrome in mild endometriosis. Assessment with biochemical parameters' *J Reprod Med*. 30(9): pp 643–5. **Vitex agnus castus and overstimulation of follicles:** Cahill, DJ, Fox, R, Wardle, PG, et al, 1994. 'Multiple follicular development associated with herbal medicine' *Hum Reprod*. 9(8):

pp 1469–70. **Vitamin E reduces adhesions:** Kalfarentzos, F, Spiliotis, J, Kaklamanis, L, et al, 1987. 'Prevention of peritoneal adhesion formation in mice by vitamin E' *J R Coll Surg Edinb*. 32(5): pp 288–90; Hemadeh, O, Chilukuri, S, Bonet, V, et al, 1993. 'Prevention of adhesions by administration of sodium carboxymethyl cellulose and vitamin E' *Surgery*. 114(5): pp 907–10; Kagoma, P, Burger, SN, Seifter, E, et al, 1985. 'The effect of vitamin E on experimentally induced peritoneal adhesions in mice' *Arch Surg*. 120(8): pp 949–51; Sakamoto, W, Fujie, K, Nishihira, J, et al, 1991. 'Inhibition of PGE2 production in macrophages from vitamin E-treated rats' *Prostaglandins Leukot Essent Fatty Acids*. 44(2): pp 89–92; Tengerdy, RP, 1990. 'The role of vitamin E in immune response and disease resistance' *Ann NY Acad Sci*. 587: pp 24–33. **Exercise and retrograde flow:** Han, M, Pan, L, Wu, B, et al, 1994. 'A case-control epidemiologic study of endometriosis' *Chin Med Sci J*. 9(2): pp 114–8; Pan, LY, 1993. 'Menstrual status as risk factors of endometriosis: a case controlled study' *Chung Hua Fa Chan Ko Tsa Chih*. 28(3): pp 147–9, 188. **and oestrogen:** Barbieri, RL, 1990. 'Etiology and epidemiology of endometriosis' *Am J Obstet Gynecol*. 162(2): pp 565–7. **Caffeine:** Grodstein, F, Goldman, MB, Ryan, L, et al, 1993. 'Relation of female infertility to consumption of caffeinated beverages' *Am J Epidemiol*. 137(12): pp 1353–60. **Alcohol:** Perper, MM, Breitkopf, LJ, Breitstein, R, et al, 1993. 'MAST scores, alcohol consumption, and gynecological symptoms in endometriosis patients' *Alcohol Clin Exp Res*. 17(2): pp 272–8. **and fertility:** Grodstein, F, Goldman, MB, Cramer, DW, 1994. 'Infertility in women and moderate alcohol use' *Am J Public Health*. 84(9): pp 1429–32. **Essential fatty acids:** Yano, Y, 1992. 'Effect of dietary supplementation with eicosapentaenoic acid on surgically induced endometriosis in the rabbit' *Nippon Sanka Fujinka Gakkai Zasshi*. 44(3): pp 282–8; Covens, AL, Christopher, P, Casper, RF, 1988. 'The effect of dietary supplementation with fish oil fatty acids on surgically induced endometriosis in the rabbit' *Fertil Steril*. 49(4): pp 698–703; Ziboh, VA, Fletcher, MP, 1992. 'Dose-response effects of dietary gamma-linolenic acid-enriched oils on human polymorphonuclear-neutrophil biosynthesis of leukotriene B4' *Am J Clin Nutr*. 55(1): pp 39–45; Fletcher, MP, Ziboh, VA, 1990. 'Effects of dietary supplementation with eicosapentanoic acid and gamma-linolenic acid on neutrophil phospholipid fatty acid composition and activation responses' *Inflammation*. 14(5): pp 585–97; Fan, YY, Chapkin, RS, 1992. 'Mouse peritoneal macrophage prostaglandin E1 synthesis is altered by dietary gamma-linolenic acid' *J Nutr*. 122(8): pp 1600–6. **Pregnancy and risk:** Parazzini, F, Ferraroni, M, Fedele, L, et al, 1995. 'Pelvic endometriosis: reproductive and menstrual risk factors at different stages in Lombardy, northern Italy' *J Epidemiol Community Health*. 49(1): pp 61–4; Candiani, GB, Danesino, V, Gastaldi, A, et al, 1991. 'Reproductive and menstrual factors and risk of peritoneal and ovarian endometriosis' *Fertil Steril*. 56(2): pp 230–4. **IUDs and retrograde flow:** Kirshon, B, Poindexter, AN, et al, 1988. 'Contraception: a risk factor for endometriosis' *Obstet Gynecol*. 71(6 Pt 1): pp 829–31. **IUDs and prostaglandins:** Tang, DC, Wu, XR, 1991. 'Dynamic changes of myometrial activity, levels of PGF2 alpha and E2 in rabbits after insertion of four types of IUDs' *Adv Contracept*. 7(1): pp 29–38. **Mixed results on contraception:** Vercellini, P, Ragni, G, Trespidi, L, et al, 1993. 'Does contraception modify the risk of endometriosis?' *Hum Reprod*. 8(4): pp 547–51. **The Pill:** Vessey, MP, Villard-Mackintosh, L, Painter, R, 1993. 'Epidemiology of endometriosis in women attending family planning clinics' *BMJ*. 306(6871): pp 182–4.

Chapter 6 Finishing up

Menopause—herb to protect ovary from irradiation: Mei, QB, Tao, JY, Cui, B, 1991. 'Advances in the pharmacological studies of radix Angelica sinensis (Oliv) Diels (Chinese Dang gui)' *Ch Med J*. 104(9): pp 776–81. **Cancer drugs causing symptoms:** Otto, S, 1994. *Oncology Nursing*, 2nd ed. Mosby. p 503. **Women who retain ovaries with symptoms:** Coney, S, 1991. *The Menopause Industry. A Guide to Medicine's 'Discovery' of the Mid-Life Woman*. Penguin Books Ltd, Auckland, New Zealand. p 132. **Hysterectomy causing symptoms:** Siddle, N, Sarrel, P, Whitehead, M, 1987. 'The effect of hysterectomy on the age of ovarian failure: Identification of a subgroup of women with premature loss of ovarian function and literature review' *Fert Sterility*. 47(1): pp 94–100. **Tubal ligation causing symptoms:** Turney, L, 1993. 'Risk and contraception. What women are not told about tubal ligation' *Women's Studies Int Forum*. 16(5): pp 471–86. **Miriam Stoppard's quote** from her book, 1994. *Menopause*. Viking, Penguin, Australia. p 32. **Lifestyle and attitude has biggest effect on symptoms:** Dennerstein, L, Smith, AMA, Morse, C, 1993. 'Menopausal symptoms in Australian women' *Med J Aust*. 159: pp 232–6. **Offsetting testosterone with diet:** Armstrong, BK, Brown, JB, Clarke, HT, et al, 1981. 'Diet and reproductive hormones: a study of vegetarian and nonvegetarian postmenopausal women' *J Natl Cancer Inst*. 67: pp 761–7; Mousavi, Y, Adleurcreutz, H, 1993. 'Genistein is an effective stimulator of sex hormone-binding globulin production in hepatocarcinoma human liver cells and suppresses proliferation of these cells in culture' *Steroids*. 58: pp 301–4. **Three-quarters of menopausal women report flushes**: Khan, SA, Pace, JE, Cox, ML, et al, 1994. 'Climacteric symptoms in healthy middle-aged women' *Br J Clin Pract*. 48(5): pp 240–2. **Reports of troubling flushes:** Dennerstein, L, Smith, AMA, Morse, C, et al, 1993. 'Menopausal symptoms in Australian women' *Med J Aust*. 159: pp 232–6. **Plant oestrogens weaker than body ones:** Bradbury, RB, White, DE, 1954. 'Estrogens and related substances in plants' *Vitams Horm*. 12: pp 207–33; Cheng, EW, et al, 1954. 'Estrogenic activity of some isoflavone derivatives' *Science*. 120: p 575. **Vitamin E doses:** Werbach, MR, 1988. *Nutritional Influences on Illness*. Thorson's Publishing Group, London. p 297. **Hesperedin and flushes:** Werbach, MR, 1988. *Nutritional Influences on Illness*. Thorson's Publishing Group, London. p 297. **Evening primrose oil no better than placebo:** Chenoy, R, Hussain, S, Tayob, Y, et al, 1994. 'Effect of oral gamolenic acid from evening primrose oil on menopausal flushing' *BMJ*. 308(6927): pp 501–3. **Vaginal dryness and plant oestrogens:** Wilcox, G, Wahlqvist, ML, Burger, HG, et al, 1990. 'Oestrogenic effects of plant foods in postmenopausal women' *BMJ*. 301: pp 905–6. **Fenugreek vaginal poultice:** Willard, T, 1991. *The Wild Rose Scientific Herbal*. Wild Rose College of Natural Healing, Canada. p 123. **PMS or menopause?** Khan, SA, Pace, JE, Cox, ML, et al, 1994. 'Climacteric symptoms in healthy middle-aged women' *Br J Clin Pract*. 48(5): pp 240–2. **Evening primrose oil better for PMS than menopause:** Chenoy, R, Hussain, S, Tayob, Y, et al, 1994. 'Effect of oral gamolenic acid from evening primrose oil on menopausal flushing' *BMJ*. 308(6927): pp 501–3. **Research on moodiness:** Morse, CA, 1989. 'Menopausal mood disorders' *Comprehensive Therapy*. 15(3): pp 22–7. **I don't want to go through menopause theory:** Dennerstein, L, Smith, AMA, Morse, C, 1994. 'Psychological well-being, mid-life and the menopause' *Maturitas*. 20: pp 1–11; Morse, CA, 1989. 'Menopausal mood disorders' *Comprehensive Therapy*. 15(3): pp 22–7. **Hormone theory: stress and oestrogen:** Ballinger, S, 1990. 'Stress as a factor in lowered oestrogen levels in early postmenopause' *Ann NY Acad Sci*. 592: pp 95–113, discussion pp 123–33. **Oestrogen up as depression lifts:** Ballinger, S, Cobbin, D, Krivanek, J, et al, 1979. 'Life stresses and depression in the menopause' *Maturitas*. 1(3): pp 191–9. **HRT improves flushing and dry vagina:** Hunter, MS, 1990. 'Emotional well-being, sexual behaviour and hormone replacement therapy' *Maturitas*. 12(3): pp 299–314. **Australian high use of HRT:** Brenner, PF, 1988. 'The menopausal syndrome' *Obstet Gynecol*. 72(5 Suppl): pp 6S–11S. **Breast cancer and HRT links: US evaluation of 1.2 increased risk:** Hulka, B, 1994. 'Links between hormone replacement therapy and neoplasia' *Fertil Steril*. 62(6 Suppl 2): pp 168S–175S. **European study shows increased risk of 1.5:** Breckwoldt, M, Keck, C, Karck, U, 1995. 'Benefits and risks of hormone replacement therapy (HRT)' *J Steroid Molec Biol*. 53(1–6): pp 205–8. **European study shows increased risk of 1.7:** Adami, HO, 1992. 'Long-term consequences of estrogen and estrogen-progestin replacement' *Cancer Causes Control*. 3(1): pp 83–90. **Initial view of progesterone:** Gambrell, RD, 1987. 'Hormone replacement therapy and breast cancer' *Maturitas*. 9(2): pp 123–33. **Researchers suggest increased risk with oestrogen and progesterone given together:** van-Leeuwen, FE, 1991. 'Epidemiological aspects of exogenous progestagens in relation to their role in pathogenesis of human breast cancer' *Acta Endocrinol Copenh*. 125 (Suppl 1): pp 13–26. **Ten-year wait for long-term knowledge of combined approach:** Hulka, B, 1994. 'Links between hormone replacement therapy and neoplasia' *Fertil Steril*. 62(6 Suppl 2): pp 168S–175S. **Melbourne doctors prescribed oestrogen only:** Shelley, JM, Smith, AMA, Dudley, E, 1995. 'Use of hormone replacement therapy by Melbourne women' *Aust J Public Health*. 19: pp 387–92. **The Pill and bone density:** Recker, RR, Davies, KM, Hinders, SM, et al, 1992. 'Bone gain in young adult women' *JAMA*. 268(17): pp 2403–8. **HRT effect on bones lost after drug stopped:** Law, MR, Wald, NJ, et al, 1991. 'Strategies for prevention of osteoporosis and hip fracture' *BMJ*. 303: pp 453–9. **HRT reduces heart disease:** Ravn, SH, Rosenberg, J, Bostofte, E,

1994. 'Postmenopausal hormone replacement therapy—clinical implications' *Eur J Obstet Gynecol Reprod Biol*. 53(2): pp 81–93. **HRT may not reduce heart disease:** Posthuma, WF, Westendorp, RG, Vandenbroucke, JP, 1994. 'Cardioprotective effect of hormone replacement therapy in postmenopausal women: is the evidence biased?' *BMJ*. 308(6939): pp 1268–9; Kafonek, SD, 1994. 'Postmenopausal hormone replacement therapy and cardiovascular risk reduction. A review' *Drugs*. 47(Suppl 2): pp 16–24.

Chapter 7 The medical approach

Drugs—the Pill and side effects: Drife, J, 1990. 'Benefits and risks of oral contraceptives' *Adv Contracept*. Dec, 6 Suppl: pp 15–25. **and progestogen side effects:** Kaunitz, AM, 1993. 'Combined oral contraception with desogestrel/ethinyl estradiol: tolerability profile' *Am J Obstet Gynecol*. 168(3 Pt 2): pp 1028–33. **and getting periods back afterwards:** Long, CA, 1994, 'Amenorrhoea' *Manual of Clinical Problems in Obstetrics and Gynecology*, eds ME Rivlin, RW Martin, Little, Brown and Company, Boston, pp 385–8. **and fibroids, blood iron, and period flow:** Friedman, AJ, Thomas, PP, 1995. 'Does low-dose combination oral contraceptive use affect uterine size or menstrual flow in premenopausal woman with leiomyomas?' *Obstet Gynecol*. 85(4): pp 631–5. **and endo:** Vessey, MP, Villard-Mackintosh, L, Painter, R, 1993. 'Epidemiology of endometriosis in women attending family planning clinics' *BMJ*. 306(6871): pp 182–4; Barbieri, RL, 1990. 'Endometriosis 1990' *Drugs*. 39(4): pp 502–10; Vercellini, P, Trespidi, L, Colombo, A, 1993. 'A gonadotrophin-releasing hormone agonist versus a low-dose oral contraceptive for pelvic pain associated with endometriosis' *Fertil Steril*. 60(1): pp 75–9. **and return of endo after use:** Vercellini, P, Trespidi, L, Colombo, A, 1993. 'A gonadotrophin-releasing hormone agonist versus a low-dose oral contraceptive for pelvic pain associated with endometriosis' *Fertil Steril*. 60(1): pp 75–9. **and pregnancy rate after use in women with endo:** Israel, R, 1994. 'Endometriosis: treatment' *Management of Common Problems in Obstetrics and Gynecology*. eds DR Mishell, PF Brenner, Blackwell Scientific Publications, Boston. p 750. **and anti-depressants:** Thomas, J, ed, 1995. *Australian Prescription Products Guide*. Australian Pharmaceutical Publishing Company Limited, Hawthorn, Victoria. **Progestogens and heavy periods:** Smith, SK, Abel, MH, Kelly, RW, et al, 1981. 'A role for prostacyclin (PGI2) in excessive menstrual bleeding' *Lancet*. 1: pp 522–5. **Danazol and immune abnormalities:** Ota, H, Maki, M, Shidara, Y, et al, 1992. 'Effects of danazol at the immunologic level in patients with adenomyosis, with special reference to autoantibodies: a multi-center cooperative study' *Am J Obstet Gynecol*. 167(2): pp 481–6. **and used for PMS:** Watts, JF, Butt, WR, Logan Edwards, R, 1987. 'A clinical trial using danazol for the treatment of premenstrual tension' *Br J Obs Gynaecol*. 94: pp 30–4. **and hepatitis:** Thomas, J, ed, 1995. *Australian Prescription Products Guide*. Australian Pharmaceutical Publishing

Company Limited, Hawthorn, Victoria. **Supporters of progesterone for PMS, breast soreness:** Kenton, L, 1995. *Passage to Power*. Ebury Press, London; Lee, JR, 1993. *Natural Progesterone: The Multiple Roles of a Remarkable Hormone*. BLL Publishing, Sebastapol, USA; Dalton, K, *PMS: The Essential Guide to Treatment Options*. Thorson's Publishing Group, London. **Progesterone for PMS no better than placebo:** Freeman, E, Rickels, K, Sondheimer, SJ, et al, 1990. 'Ineffectiveness of progesterone suppository treatment for premenstrual syndrome' *JAMA*. 264: pp 349–53; Van der Meer, YG, Benedek-Jaszmann, LJ, Van Loenen, AC, 1983. 'Effect of high dose progesterone on the premenstrual syndrome: a double-blind crossover trial' *J Psychomat Obstet Gynaec*. 2–4: pp 220–1. **GnRH agonists and endo:** Rock, JA, Truglia, JA, Caplan, RJ, et al, 1993. 'Zoladex (goserelin acetate implant) in the treatment of endometriosis: a randomised comparison with danazol' *Obstet Gynecol*. 82(2): pp 198–205; Trabant, H, Widdra, W, de Looze, S, 1990. 'Efficacy and safety of intranasal buserelin acetate in the treatment of endometriosis: a review of six clinical trials and comparison with danazol' *Prog Clin Biol Res*. 323: pp 357–82. **and cyst size:** Donnez, J, Nisolle, M, Grandjean, P, et al, 1993. 'The role of GnRH agonists in the endoscopic treatment of endometriosis and fibromyomas' *Contracept Fertil Sex*. 21(1): pp 59–62. **and fertility:** Kauppila, A, 1993. 'Changing concepts of medical treatment of endometriosis' *Acta Obstet Gynecol Scand*. 72(5): pp 324–6. **and PMS:** Mortolla, JF, Girton, L, Fischer, U, 1991. 'Successful treatment of severe premenstrual syndrome by combined use of gonadotrophin releasing hormone agonist and estrogen/progestin' *J Clin Endocrinol Metab*. 72(2): pp 252A–F. **and ovulation return:** Van-Leusden, HA, 1994. 'Impact of different GnRH analogs in benign gynecological disorders related to their chemical structure, delivery systems and dose' *Gynecol Endocrinol*. 8(3): pp 215–22. **and bone loss:** Dawood, MY, 1994. 'Hormonal therapies for endometriosis: implications for bone metabolism' *Acta Obstet Gynecol Scand Suppl*. 159: pp 22–34. **and spine density:** Waibel-Treber, S, Minne, HW, Scharla, SH, et al, 1989. 'Reversible bone loss in women treated with GnRH-agonists for endometriosis and uterine leiomyoma' *Hum Reprod*. 4(4): pp 384–8. **Bromocriptine and PMS:** Andersch, B, Hahn, L, Wenderstam, C, et al, 1978. 'Treatment of premenstrual syndrome with bromocriptine' *Acta Endocrinol*. 88(S 216): pp 165–74. **and side effects:** Steinberg, S, 1991. 'The treatment of late luteal phase dysphoric disorder' *Life Sci*. 49: pp 767–802. **Prostaglandins-inhibiting drugs and period pain:** Kauppila, A, Ronnberg, L, 1985. 'Naproxen sodium in dysmenorrhea secondary to endometriosis' *Obstet Gynecol*. 65(3): pp 379–83. **and when taken before period starts:** Rees, MCP, 1990. 'Human menstruation and eicosanoids' *Reprod Fertil Dev*. 2: pp 467–76. **and the Pill or progesterone:** Mezrow, G, 1994. 'Treatment of dysfunctional uterine bleeding' *Management of Common Problems in Obstetrics and Gynecology*, eds DR Mishell, PF Brenner, Blackwell Scientific Publ., Boston. p 444. **and Ponstan uses:** Mira, M, McNeil, D, Fraser, IS, et al, 1986. 'Mefanamic acid in the treatment of premenstrual syndrome' *Obstet Gynecol*. 68(3): pp 395–8. **and seven-day limit:** Thomas, J, ed, 1995. *Australian Prescription Products Guide*. Australian Pharmaceutical Publishing Company Limited, Hawthorn, Victoria. **and side effects:** Thomas, J, ed, 1995. *Australian Products Prescription Guide*. Australian Pharmaceutical Publishing Company Limited, Hawthorn, Victoria. **Diuretics and misuse:** Steinberg, S, 1991. 'The treatment of late luteal phase dysphoric disorder' *Life Sci*. 49: pp 767–802. **Anti-depressants and hormonal changes:** Pariser, SF, Stern, SL, Shank, ML, et al, 1985. 'Premenstrual syndrome: concerns, controversies, and treatment' *Am J Obstet Gynecol*. 153(6): pp 599–604. **Surgery—myomectomy and size versus symptoms of fibroid:** Friedman, AJ, Haas, ST, 1993. 'Should uterine size be an indication for surgical intervention in women with myomas?' *Am J Obstet Gynecol*. 168(3 Pt 1): pp 751–5. **and caesareans, fertility:** Vergani, P, Ghidini, A, Strobelt, N, et al, 1994. 'Do uterine leiomyomas influence pregnancy outcome?' *Am J Perinatol*. 11(5): pp 356–8. **and lasers to help fertility:** Starks, GC, 1988. 'CO2 laser myomectomy in an infertile population' *J Reprod Med*. 33(2): pp 184–6. **Before and after surgery—nausea relieved by ginger:** Phillips, S, Ruggier, R, Hutchison, SE, 1993. '*Zingiber officinale* (ginger)—an antiemetic for day case surgery' *Anaesthesia*. 48(8): pp 715–7; Bone, ME, Wilkinson, DJ, Young, JR, et al, 1990. 'Ginger root—a new antiemetic. The effect of ginger root on postoperative nausea and vomiting after major gynaecological surgery' *Anaesthesia*. 45(8): pp 669–71. **Vitamin C and healing time:** Werbach, M, 1987. *Nutritional Influences on Illness,* Thorson's Publishing Group, London. p 447.

Chapter 8 Natural therapies

Symptoms of liver disharmony: Ross, Jeremy, 1985. *Zang Fu, The Organ Systems of Traditional Chinese Medicine*. Churchill Livingstone, Edinburgh. p 101; Hikino, H, Kiso, Y, Wagner, H, et al, 1984. 'Antihepatotoxic actions of flavonolignans from *Silybum marianum* fruits' *Planta Med*. 50(3): pp 248–50. **World-wide use of herbs:** Griggs, B, 1981. *Green Pharmacy*. Hale, London. p 5. **Raspberry leaf**: Wren, RC, 1907. rewritten Williamson, EM, Evans, FJ, 1988. *Potters New Cyclopaedia of Botanical Drugs and Preparations*. The CW Daniel Co Ltd, Saffron Waldron, Essex, UK. p 232; Scientific Committee, British Herbal Medicine Association, 1983. *British Herbal Pharmacopoeia*. British Herbal Medicine Association, West Yorks, UK. pp 59-60; Mills, S, 1985. *The Dictionary of Modern Herbalism*. Lothian Publishing Company Pty Ltd, Melbourne. **Dang Gui:** Bensky, D, Gamble, A, 1986. *Chinese Herbal Medicine Materia Medica*. Eastland Press, Seattle. p 474; Wang, H, Peng, RX, 1994. 'Sodium ferulate alleviated paracetamol-induced liver toxicity in mice' *Chung Kuo Yao Li Hsueh Pao*. 15(1): pp 81–3; Yan, RQ, 1986. 'Effect of bifendati and three Chinese traditional medicinal herbs on aflatoxin B1 (AFB1)-induced hepatocarcinogenesis in rats' *Am J Cancer*. 5(2): p 141; Harada, M, Suzuki, M, Ozaki, Y, 1984. 'Effect of Japanese angelica root and peony root on uterine contraction in the rabbit in situ' *J Pharm Dyn*. 7: pp 304–11; Ozaki, Y, Ma, JP, 1990. 'Inhibitory effects of tetramethylpyrazine and ferulic acid on spontaneous movement of rat uterus' *Chem Pharm Bull*. 38(6): pp 1620–3. **Blue cohosh:** Scientific Committee, British Herbal Medicine Association, 1983. *British Herbal Pharmacopoeia*. British Herbal Medicine Association, West Yorks, UK. p 245. **Cramp bark and black haw:** Woodbury, RA, 1951. 'The Viburnums' *Drug Standards*. 19(7–8): pp 143–52; Youngken, HW, 1932. 'The pharmacognosy, chemistry and pharmacology of Viburnum. III. History, botany and pharmacognosy of *Viburnum opulus L. var. americanum* (Miller) Ait' *J Am Pharm Assoc*. 22: pp 444–62. **Emmenagogues:** Hoffmann, D, 1991. *Thorson's Guide to Medical Herbalism*. Thorson's, UK. p 146. **Mugwort:** Mills, SY, 1988. *The Dictionary of Modern Herbalism*. Lothian Publishing Company Pty Ltd, Melbourne. p 11. **Ladies mantle:** McIntyre, A, 1995. *The Complete Woman's Herbal*. Hodder Headline Australia Pty Ltd, Rydalmere, NSW. p 110; Kielczynski, W, 1997. personal communication. **Shepherd's purse:** Mills, S, 1991. *Out of the Earth*. Penguin, UK. p 316. **Vitex agnus castus—for PMS:** Amman, W, 1979. '[Premenstrual water retention. Favourable effect of *Agnus castus* (Agnolyt, Reg. trademark).]' *Z Allg Med*. 55(1). pp 48–51. **Breast soreness:** Opitz, G, Liebl, A, 1980. '[The conservative treatment of mastopathy with Mastodynon (Reg. trademark).]' *Therapie der Gegenw*. 119(7): pp 804–9; Wuttke, W, Jarry, H, Leonhardt, S, 1994. '[*Agnus castus* as dopaminergic activity principle in premenstrual mastodynia.]' *Ars Medici*. 84(13): pp 850, 853–4, 856. **Stopped periods:** Amann, W, 1982. [Amenorrhea. 'Favourable effect of *Agnus castus* (Agnolyt, Reg. trademark) on amenorrhea.]' *Z Allg Med*. 58(4): pp 228–31. **Menstrual irregularities:** Peters-Welte, C, Albrecht, M, 1994. ['Menstrual cycle disorders and PMS. Study on the use of *Vitex agnus castus*'] *TW Gynakologie*. 7(1): pp 49–52 (Germ.). **Latent hyperprolactinaemia:** Roeder, D, 1994. ['Therapy of cyclical disorders with *Vitex agnus-castus*'] *Z Phytother*. 15(3): pp 157–63. **Liquorice and Peony Combination:** Takahashi, K, Kitao, M, 1994. 'Effect of TJ-68 (shakuyaku-kanzo-to) on polycystic ovarian disease' *Int J Fertil Menopausal Stud*. 39(2): pp 69–76; Takahashi, K, Yoshino, K, Shirai, T, et al, 1988. 'Effect of a traditional herbal medicine (shakuyaku-kanzo-to) on testosterone secretion in patients with polycystic ovarian syndrome detected by ultrasound' *Nippon Sanka Fujinka Gakkai Zasshi*. 40(60): pp 789–92. and adenomyosis, endometriosis: Mori, T, Sakamoto, S, Singtripop, T, et al, 1993. 'Suppression of spontaneous development of uterine adenomyosis by a Chinese herbal medicine, Keishi-bukuryo-gan, in mice' *Planta Med*. 59: pp 308–11. **and fibroids:** Sakamoto, S, Yoshino, H, Shirahata, Y, et al, 1992. 'Pharmacotherapeutic effects of Kue-chih-fu-ling-wan (Keishi-bukuryo-gan) on human uterine myomas' *Am J Chin Med*. 20(3–4): pp 313–17. **and breast soreness:** Inoue, M, 1988. 'The treatment of benign mastopathies with traditional Sino-Japanese medicine (Kanpo)' *Kanpo Igaku*. 12(5): p 127. **Black**

cohosh, and menopause: Duker, EM, et al, 1991. 'Effects of extracts from *Cimicifuga racemosa* on gonadotrophin release in menopausal women and ovariectomised rats' *Planta Med.* 57: pp 420–4. **and hormonal imbalance:** Harnischfeger, G, Stolze, H, 1980. 'Proven active substances from natural materials. Black snake root' *Notabene Medici.* 10(5): pp 76–83. **Effective as synthetic oestrogen:** Duker, E, Lothar, K, Hubertus, J, et al, 1991. 'Effects of extracts from *Cimicifuga racemosa* on gonadotrophin release in menopausal women and ovariectomised rats' *Planta Med.* 57(5): pp 420–4. **Ginger:** Suekawa, M, Ishige, A, Yuasa, K, et al, 1984. 'Pharmacological studies on ginger. I. Pharmacological actions of pungent constituents, (6)-gingerol and (6)-shogaol' *J Pharmacobiodyn.* 7(11): pp 836–48. **Cinnamon:** Willard, T, 1991. *The Wild Rose Scientific Herbal.* Wild Rose College of Natural Healing, Calgary, Canada. pp 85–7. **Jamaican dogwood:** The BHMA Scientific Committee, PR Bradley, ed, 1992. *British Herbal Compendium.* British Herbal Medicine Association, Dorset. pp 139–40. **Feverfew:** McIntyre, A, 1994. *The Complete Woman's Herbal.* Hodder Headline, Rydalmere, NSW. p 131. **Said to cause mouth ulcers:** Mitchell, JC, Geissman, TA, Dupuis, G, et al, 1971. 'Allergic contact dermatitis caused by *Artemesia* and *Chrysanthemum* species. Role of sesquiterpene lactones' *J Invest Dermatol.* 56(2): pp 98–101. **St John's wort for depression:** Linde, K, Ramirez, G, Mulrow, C, et al, 1996. 'St John's wort for depression—an overview and meta-analysis of randomised clinical trials' *British Medical Journal.* 313: pp 253–8. **In menopause:** Mills, SY, 1991. *Out of the Earth.* Penguin, UK. p 513. **Motherwort:** Culpeper, N, (Reprint) *Culpeper's Complete Herbal.* W Foulsham & Co Ltd, New York. p 239; Yeung, HW, Kong, YC, Lay, WP, et al, 1977. 'The structure and biological effect of leonurine' *Planta Med.* 31: pp 51–6. **Social use:** Leung, A, Foster, S, 1996. *Encyclopedia of Common Natural Ingredients Used in Food, Drugs and Cosmetics.* John Wiley, New York. pp 330–1. **Abuse:** Mathews, JD, Riley, MD, Fejo, L, et al, 1988. 'Effects of the heavy use of kava on physical health: summary of a pilot study in an Aboriginal community' *Med J Aust.* 148(11): pp 548–55. **Kava kava:** Warneke, G, 1991. '[Psychosomatic dysfunctions in the female climacteric. Clinical effectiveness and tolerance of kava Extract WS 1490]' *Fortschr Med.* 109(4): pp 119–22. **Dandelion root:** Madaus, G, 1976. *Lehrbuch der Biologischen Heilmittel.* Georg Olms Verlag, Hildesheim. p 2675. **Juniper berries:** Agrawal, OP, Bharadwaj, S, Mathur, R, 1980. 'Antifertility effects of the fruits of *Juniperus communis*' *Planta Med.* (Suppl): pp 98–101. **Calendula:** *British Herbal Pharmacopoeia*, part 1, 1976. British Herbal Medicine Association, West Yorks. pp 38–9.

Chapter 9 Self care

Top 20 diet hints—triglycerides and health risks: Erasmus, U, 1993. *Fats That Heal, Fats That Kill.* Alive Books, Burnaby, BC, Canada. p 57. **Oily fish and allergies:** Linscheer, WG, Vergroesen, AJ, 1994. 'Lipids' *Modern Nutrition in Health and Disease*, eds ME Shils, JA Olsen, M Shike, Lea &

Febiger, Philadelphia. pp 47–88. **Seed oils and PMS:** Horrobin, DF, 1983. 'The role of essential fatty acids and prostaglandins in the premenstrual syndrome' *J Reprod Med*. 28(7): pp 465–8; Puolakka, J, Makarainen, L, Viinikka, L, et al, 1985. 'Biochemical and clinical effects of treating the premenstrual syndrome with prostaglandins synthesis precursors' *J Reprod Med*. 30(3): pp 149–53. **Yoghurt and oestrogen-dependent cancer risks:** van't Veer, P, Dekker, JM, Lamers, JWJ, et al, 1989. 'Consumption of fermented milk products and breast cancer: a case-control study in the Netherlands' *Cancer Res*. 49: pp 4020–3. **RDA of protein for women over 20:** Crim, MC, Munro, HN, 1994. 'Proteins and amino acids' *Modern Nutrition in Health and Disease*, eds ME Shils, JA Olson, M Shike, Lea & Febiger, Philadelphia. p 27. **Caffeine and fertility:** Wilcox, A, Weinberg, C, Baird, D, 1988. 'Caffeinated beverages and decreased fertility' *Lancet*. 2: pp 1453–6. **RDA of alcohol for women:** Pols, R, Hawks, D, 1991. 'Is there a safe level of daily consumption of alcohol for men and women. Recommendations regarding responsible drinking behaviour' *NH&MRC* pamphlet, Canberra. **Plant oestrogens—clover and infertile sheep:** Bennets, HW, Underwood, EJ, Shier, FLA, 1946. 'A specific breeding problem of sheep on subterranean clover pastures in Western Australia' *Aust Vet J*. 22: pp 2–12. **Plant components and oestrogenic effect:** Setchell, KDR, Adlercreutz, H, 1988. 'Mammalian lignans and phyto-oestrogens. Recent studies on their formation, metabolism and biological role in health and disease' *Role of Gut Flora in Toxicity and Cancer*. Academic Press, London. pp 315–45. **Foods with plant oestrogens:** Setchell, KDR, 1985. 'Naturally occurring non-steroidal estrogens of dietary origin' *Estrogens in the Environment II*, ed John A McLachlan, Elsevier, New York. p 69; Beckham, N, 1995. 'Phyto-oestrogens and compounds that affect oestrogen metabolism—Part 1' *Aust J Med Herbalism*. 7(1): pp 11–16. **Phyto-oestrogens and lighter, less frequent periods:** Phipps, WR, Martini, MC, Lampe, JW, et al, 1993. 'Effect of flax seed ingestion on the menstrual cycle' *J Clin Endocrinol Metab*. 77(5): pp 1215–19; Cassidy, A, Bingham, S, Setchell, KDR, 1994. 'Biological effects of a diet of soy protein rich in isoflavones on the menstrual cycle of premenopausal women' *Am J Clin Nutr*. 60: pp 333–40. **and oestrogen-dependent cancer risk:** Adlercreutz, H, 1990. 'Western diet and Western diseases: some hormonal and biochemical mechanisms and associations' *Scand J Clin Lab Invest*. 50(S201): pp 3–23. **and menopausal symptoms:** Wilcox, G, Wahlqvist, ML, Burger, H, et al, 1990. 'Oestrogenic effects of foods in postmenopausal women' *BMJ*. 301: pp 905–6. **and breast cancer in Asian countries:** Goldin, BR, Adlercreutz, H, Gorbach, SL, 1986. 'The relationship between estrogen levels and diets of Caucasian American and Oriental immigrant women' *Am J Clin Nutr*. 44: pp 945–53. **Soya products in Asian diets:** Adlercreutz, H, Hamalainen, E, Gorbach, S, et al, 1992. 'Dietary phyto-oestrogens and the menopause in Japan' *Lancet*. 339: p 1233. **Oestrogenic effects of phyto-oestrogens weaker than body-made oestrogens:** Price, KR, Fenwick, GR, 1985. 'Naturally occurring oestrogens in foods—A review' *Food Additives and Contaminants*. 2(2): pp 73–106. **Competitive inhibition with phyto-oestrogens:** Shemesh, M, Lindner, HR, Ayalon, N, 1972. 'Affinity of rabbit uterine oestradiol receptor for phyto-oestrogens and its use in competitive protein binding radioassay for plasma coumesterol' *J Reprod Fertil*. 29: pp 1–9. **Reducing the risk of oestrogen-dependent cancers with competitive inhibition:** Adlercreutz, H, Mousav, Y, Clark, J, et al, 1992. 'Dietary phytoestrogens and cancer: in vitro and in vivo studies' *J Steroid Biochem Molec Biol*. 41(3–8): pp 331–7; Adlercreutz, H, 1988. 'Lignans and phyto-oestrogens: possible preventive role in cancer' *Progress in Diet and Nutrition*. eds C Horwitz, P Rozen, Karger, Basel; Setchell, KDR, Borriello, SP, Hulme, P, et al, 1984. 'Nonsteroidal estrogens of dietary origin: possible roles in hormone dependent disease' *Am J Clin Nutr*. 40: 569–78; Messina, M, Barnes, S, 1991. 'The role of soy products in reducing risk of cancer' *J Nat Cancer Inst*. 83(8): pp 541–6. **Tamoxifen and phyto-oestrogens:** Messina, M, Barnes, S, 1991. 'The role of soy products in reducing risk of cancer' *J Nat Cancer Inst*. 83(8): pp 541–6. **Slowing down aromatisation in fat tissues:** Adlercreutz, H, Bannwart, C, Wahala, K, et al, 1993. 'Inhibition of human aromatase by mammalian lignans and isoflavonoid phytoestrogens' *J Steroid Biochem Mol Biol*. Feb, 44(2): pp 147–53. **Isoflavonoids and lignans stimulate liver production of SHBG:** Setchell, KDR, Adlercreutz, H, 1988. 'Mammalian lignans and phyto-oestrogens. Recent studies on their formation, metabolism and biological role in health and disease' *Role of the Gut Flora in Toxicity and Cancer*. ed I Rowland, Academic Press Limited, London. pp 315–45; Rose, DP, 1993. 'Diet, hormones, and cancer' *Ann Rev Publ Health*. 14: pp 1–17; Adlercreutz, H, Hockerstedt, K, Bannwart, C, et al, 1987. 'Effect of dietary components, including lignans and phytoestrogens, on enterohepatic circulation and liver metabolism of estrogens and on sex hormone binding globulin (SHBG)' *J Steroid Biochem*. 27(4–6): pp 1135–44. **Hormones bound to SHBG may be how phyto-oestrogens lower incidence of hormone-related diseases:** Adlercreutz, H, Mousavi, Y, Clark, J, et al, 1992. 'Dietary phytoestrogens and cancer: in vitro and in vivo studies' *J Steroid Biochem Mol Biol*. Mar, 41(3–8): pp 331–7. **Bone density:** Arjmandi, BH, Alekel, L, Hollis, BW, 1996. 'Dietary soya protein prevents bone loss in an oviarectomised rat model of oesteoporosis' *J Nutr*. 126(1), pp 161–7; Tsutsumi, N, 1995. 'Effect of coumestrol on bone metabolism in organ culture' *Biol Pharm Bull*. 18(7): pp 1012–5. **Hot flushes:** Murkies, AL, Lombard, C, Strauss, BJG, et al, 1995. 'Dietary flour supplement decreases post-menopausal hot flushes: Effect of soy and wheat' *Maturitas*. 21: pp 189–95. **Vaginal dryness:** Wilcox, G, Wahlqvist, ML, Burger, HG, 1990. 'Oestrogenic effects of plant foods in menopausal women' *Br Med J*. 310: pp 905–6.

INDEX

OTHER RECENT BOOKS FROM ALLEN & UNWIN

WOMEN, HORMONES AND THE MENSTRUAL CYCLE
Herbal and medical solutions from adolescence to menopause

Ruth Trickey

There is a plethora of books on the subject of women's health and natural medicine, but few critically review the available research or give an in-depth indication of the application of these remedies. *Women, Hormones and the Menstrual Cycle* outlines the orthodox management of conditions and attempts to indicate when medicine or surgery or natural medicine might be more appropriate. The book emphasises dietary and other lifestyle interventions for prevention of disease and puts women's health, particularly the natural therapist's management, into a historical context. Sharing her extensive practical experience in this area, author Ruth Trickey provides readers with a range of treatment options so that they have greater control over their decision-making.

ISBN 1 86448 525 6

REAL GORGEOUS
The truth about body and beauty

Kaz Cooke

This bestseller has already brought confidence and fun to thousands of girls and women around the world in need of an image boost. *Real Gorgeous* delivers no-nonsense information about size, shape, self esteem and the cellulite scam. Beauty tips will never be the same after this! Packed with jokes, cartoons and up-to-date resources for nationwide services, it will make you laugh and help you make friends with your body.

ISBN 1 86448 226 5

IF NOT DIETING, THEN WHAT?

Dr Rick Kausman

If Not Dieting, Then What? is a straightforward, no-nonsense guide to weight management which addresses the substantial evidence that weight-loss treatments may worsen rather than improve long-term physical and psychological health.

So how do you manage your weight? There is a solution—and it's all about attitude. *If Not Dieting, Then What?* shows you how to look at food in a more positive way and move away from the 'no pain, no gain ethos', as well as explaining how to fine-tune fat content without sacrificing food enjoyment. Author Dr Rick Kausman has two weight management and eating behaviour clinics. In *If Not Dieting, Then What?* he shares his, and his clients', experiences with the reader.

ISBN 1 86448 682 1